ACROSS
THE
UNIVERSE

ACROSS 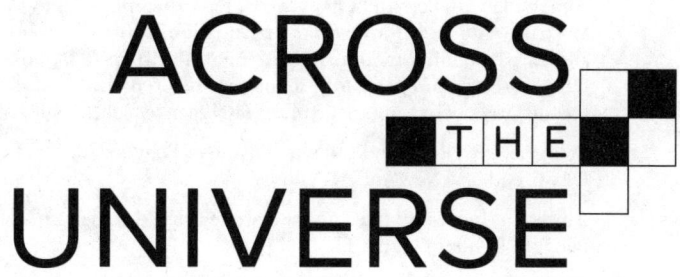 UNIVERSE

The Past, Present, and Future of the Crossword Puzzle

Natan Last

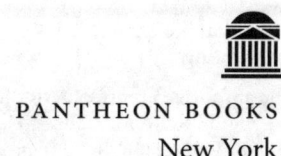

PANTHEON BOOKS
New York

FIRST HARDCOVER EDITION PUBLISHED
BY PANTHEON BOOKS 2025

Published by Pantheon Books, a division of Penguin Random House LLC, 1745 Broadway, New York, NY 10019.

Pantheon Books and the colophon are registered trademarks of Penguin Random House LLC.

Grateful acknowledgment is made to the following for permission to reprint previously published text and song lyrics:

Janani Jha: for permission to reprint lyrics from "Sunday Crossword"; *Will Wegner:* for permission to reprint lyrics from "Word Nerd," music by Charlie Romano, lyrics by Will Wegner, and book by Will Wegner, Simon Rabinowitz and Charlie Romano; and *Wisława Szymborska Foundation:* for permission to reprint text from "The Three Oddest Words" by Wisława Szymborksa.

Portions of this work originally appeared in slightly different form in the following publications: chapter 4 in *The New York Times,* chapter 6 in *The New Yorker,* portions of chapter 5 in *The Juggernaut* and *The Atlantic,* and passages on the *Times*'s diversity efforts in *The Henry Ford Magazine.*

Library of Congress Cataloging-in-Publication Data
Names: Last, Natan, author.
Title: Across the universe : the past, present, and future of the crossword puzzle / Natan Last.
Other titles: Past, present, and future of the crossword puzzle
Description: First hardcover edition. | New York : Pantheon Books, 2025. | Includes bibliographical references and index.
Identifiers: LCCN 2025016067 (print) | LCCN 2025016068 (ebook) | ISBN 9780553387704 (hardcover) | ISBN 9780553387711 (ebook)
Subjects: LCSH: Crossword puzzles—History.
Classification: LCC GV1507.C7 L28 2025 (print) | LCC GV1507.C7 (ebook) | DDC 793.73/209—dc23/eng/20250428
LC record available at https://lccn.loc.gov/2025016067
LC ebook record available at https://lccn.loc.gov/2025016068

penguinrandomhouse.com | pantheonbooks.com

Printed in the United States of America
1st Printing

The authorized representative in the EU for product safety and compliance is Penguin Random House Ireland, Morrison Chambers, 32 Nassau Street, Dublin D02 YH68, Ireland, https://eu-contact.penguin.ie.

For Hannah,
my fellow palindrome,
to the moon and back

The cross word solver becomes a collector, a connoisseur of words. They lose, to him, their mundane purpose of a suitable medium for the exchange of thoughts, and take on an esoteric significance. . . . He and Hamlet are one. "Words, words, words"—except that he has the advantage of the melancholy one. Hamlet's words ran in decorous file, one after the other; the solver's twine and intertwine, each leading to others, resulting in a harmonious whole unapproached by any except the masterpieces of classic literature.

—F. GREGORY HARTSWICK, introduction to 1924's
The Cross Word Puzzle Book

Anger, ire, temper, rage!
Era, epoc, eon, age!
Do, re mi and fa, sol, la!
Egyptian Sun God—Ra! Ra!! Ra!!!

—JOSEPH B. ROBISON,
"Crossword Puzzlers' Cheer,"
in a 1964 *New York Times* letter to the editor

Contents

Author's Note

Crossword entries appear in this book in all capitals, ensuring they stand out from the mortal words around them; I have kept any spaces between words for ease of reading. When incomplete entries are discussed, I will note unknown letters with question marks, as in, [Black Halloween animal] for the three-letter word ?AT. Equally common but potentially newer to the casual solver is the placement of clues within brackets, not quotation marks. I use this notation not least because, in a book that profiles many of the crossword world's leading lights, the reader might otherwise become overwhelmed by quotation marks, and in a book so obsessed with letters, I would hate for punctuation to get in the way.

In general, I have opted to introduce crossword jargon when it becomes relevant to the discussion at hand, rather than including a full glossary here, in fear it might overwhelm more than illuminate. Still, it's worth noting this book is mostly concerned with American-style crosswords, which enforce certain conventions, to which I frequently refer: the grid is rotationally symmetric (so if you spun it 180 degrees, the black square arrangement would look identical), there are no "unchecked" white squares (that is, every letter appears in both an Across and a Down answer; this is also called "double-checking"), and every word in the grid is at least three letters long. The grids are usually odd-by-odd in dimension, frequently 15-by-15. Many puzzles have themes, in which multiple answers relate in some way; the other main puzzle type is thus called "themeless." One tricky theme type, rebuses, involves squeezing multiple letters into a single square, which I represent with brackets: thus, in a puzzle punning on the phrase "Boxed Set," you might find the entry BA[SE T]EN, with SET appearing in just one box, and so BA[SE T]EN requires only five squares in the grid, not seven. Finally, as above, words in the grid may be called "entries" absent their clues, and "answers" when their clue appears alongside them, though these terms are often used interchangeably.

This book also discusses the interplay between crossword writers and their editors. To deflate an assumption I've often heard, that editors of puzzle sections write every puzzle, I try to always attribute a puzzle's assets—an interesting word, a zany theme, or a cute clue—to its author. In some cases, though, it is impossible to know if a clue is the puzzle writer's original, or the editor's substitution, or if indeed that brilliant pun comes from the puzzle writer's best friend, while the two word-associated on a Zoom call. All great writers steal, whether their lines run merely horizontal or not.

Introduction:
It Turns into a Different Story

[Launching pad?], 11 letters[*]
—ANDREW J. RIES, *Aries Rows Garden,* 2019

Will Shortz, editor of the *New York Times* crossword puzzle since 1993, has a favorite clue. From the August 11, 1995, puzzle, not two years into Shortz's tenure, the clue is [It turns into a different story], and the answer—a grid-stretching fifteen letters, and a twice-dastardly misdirection; I can't stall for time any longer—is SPIRAL STAIRCASE. In the *Times,* only on Friday or Saturday is such lateral-thinking wordplay fair game, with "turn" and "story" all of a sudden made literal. It turns out it was Shortz who, among other renovations, sharpened the incline of the daily puzzle's difficulty, in which solvers climb precipitously from anyone-can-do-it Mondays to multiple-day-affair Saturdays. And it was Shortz who, so the story goes, let the normally black-and-white grid overflow with color—the very first *Times* puzzle he edited, on Sunday, November 21, 1993, featured rebuses: single squares representing full words, in this case colors of the rainbow, hidden within longer words or phrases, as in SH[RED] or AL [GREEN]. It was also Shortz, like the mustachioed postmodernist he resembles, who opened the grid to new types of crossword entries: more proper names, slang terms, even brands—not just dictionary definitions and arcana—furnishing the puzzle's rec room with vowel-heavy stalwarts like IKEA, LEGO, and OREO. Before his tenure, this last entry was normally clued as [Mountain: comb. form], indicating the Greek prefix όρεο-, or oreo-, which means mountain, but you knew that.

Now, three decades into Shortz's editorship, and more than a century after its invention, the crossword is turning into a different story. A new generation of *cruciverbalists,* raised on Shortz's *Times* puzzles as the gold standard of the grid, is remodeling it. From its humble beginnings as a hand-inked diversion in the 1913 Christmas issue of the *New York World*—the publication ran a weekly supplement winkingly titled FUN, where Arthur Wynne's "Word-Cross" was born—the crossword is being spirited into the twenty-first century, emerging from the vintage stateliness of a spiral staircase into, depending on your architectural taste (and which modern crossword constructors you survey), a neon virtual world; an overstuffed loft heaving with salon walls and étagères; a chattering campaign headquarters, all capital letters and exclamation points; or a spotlit black box theater.

This remodeling is happening because the crossword has never been more popular, or more democratic. The *Times* mobile app alone boasts over a million digital-only subscribers, and as blogs, newsletters, and accessible crossword software proliferated, so too did indie crossword puzzle sites. It's also happening, as this book will argue, because the crossword is a uniquely capacious artifact, ready to absorb and recast any group's predilections and passions into the puzzle form. Since Shortz took over, sects of crossword fiends have crammed their frames of reference into the black-and-white grid, as though it were a display case, hoping to remake the puzzle in the image of their intellectual and social cliques. Largely younger, less upper-class and white, more tech-savvy and solidaristic—not as beholden to Shortz's modus operandi, but undeniably propelled by its more progressive elements—this vanguard of cruciverbalists has fallen in love with puzzle-making and solving. In the process, they've found themselves changing, and being changed by, the crossword puzzle's story.

This is also a moment when the crossword has never been more controversial. The puzzle has become big business: the *Times* Games app, part of a suite of digital products that brought in some $1.1 billion in 2022 revenue, effectively cross-subsidizes the rest of the paper. As one *Times* staffer put it in a 2023 interview: "The half joke . . . repeated internally is that *The New York Times* is now a gaming company that also happens to offer news." That financial success has spawned a crop of competitive products. In 2023, Apple launched a native crossword app, and the release of a project called Puzzmo was touted as Hearst "challenging [the *Times*'s] gaming dominance," though the Gray Lady's market position seems anything but imperiled.

Among legacy outlets, one of the *Times*'s primary challengers is *The New Yorker*'s Puzzle & Games Department. The magazine added a digital-only weekly crossword in 2018, an offering so successful that editor David Remnick did something relatively unprecedented—he added the feature to the weekly print edition—then asked its editor, Liz Maynes-Aminzade, how quickly she might expand, to keep up with the *Times,* from one to five puzzles a week. When, in January 2022, the *Times* spent at least $1 million to purchase the viral daily word game Wordle, in which players have six chances to guess a five-letter word, the *Times* announcement stressed that "the [paper] remains focused on becoming the essential subscription for every English-speaking person seeking to understand and engage with the world. . . . *New York Times* Games are a key part of that strategy." Will Shortz majored in Enigmatology at Indiana University (a course of study he designed), not journalism, or business either—but suddenly, the three were beginning to blur.

Meanwhile, as the crossword drew more eyes to it, and as those eyes spun slot-machine-like, threatening to resolve into dollar signs, the puzzle went in for more criticism. Seen by many as apolitical—no different from some moldering, colorless reference book, clue and answer fused in encyclopedic one-to-one relation—the crossword revealed itself to be a force of cultural arbitration. People (constructors, editors, solvers, a budding set of crossword critics) in all their flaws, with all their biases, decided what was crossword-worthy and what wasn't. More private eyes turned into public scrutiny, and the *Times* stumbled in that gaze. Why—and to whom—was eighteenth-century opera fair game but BIGGIE SMALLS or the Destiny's Child song BOOTYLICIOUS obscure? Why, argued a rising chorus, was [Husband's spouse] so often a default clue for WIFE, never mind the parade of women's names clued by reference to their husbands: ELSA, now almost always the *Frozen* queen, spent decades in cluedom as [Albert Einstein's second wife]. Why was GAY EROTICA flagged by an editor as a potentially offensive entry, when EROTICA had appeared dozens of times? In one puzzle, the entry MEN, originally clued unremarkably by the constructor, had been edited by the *Times* puzzle staff, in a misshapen bid at progressivism, to read [Exasperated comment from a feminist]. In 2019, the *Times* allowed the racial slur BEANER as an answer (clued as [Pitch to the head, informally], as in baseball) and an actually exasperated solver uproar ensued. After well-known constructors threatened to withhold their submissions from the paper, Shortz issued a non-apology. An open letter to the *Times,* which I helped write and organize and which was signed by nearly six hundred subscribers and puzzle lovers, wondered if the *Times* was due for an editorial shake-up.

◼

If it looks as if the stoic crossword is being dragged into the twenty-first century, its many heirs apparent are engaged in a cultural game of tug-of-war. Who gets to decide what the crossword, shorn of its tweedy image and replaced with something a bit more neon, might become? In the wake of inclusivity issues at the *Times* and the paper's occasionally ham-fisted attempts to resolve them; in light of the wildfire-like proliferation of crossword offerings in *The New Yorker, New York* magazine, *USA Today,* and an expanding galaxy of puzzle blogs, battle lines over the crossword's future have been drawn, then crossed and crossed again.

Will Shortz brought progress and new renown to the crossword—but to him it remained a game, something we do to escape the world. This book is about the people who want the crossword not only to progress past Shortz's immense and salutary legacy—innovating the form with new themes, new types of words, new grid designs—but who earnestly ask if the crossword itself might be a tool of progress: by introducing solvers to a more modern lexicon, by scrubbing the puzzle of harmful language, by highlighting culture and cultural workers not normally canonized in the grid, and by embracing new models of collaboration, revenue generation, and payment. These puzzlers ask not just whether the crossword can be more, but whether it can do more, too: not only help us escape the world, but help us reshape it.

Among the warring parties are techies more likely to say they "build" or "construct" puzzles, rather than write them. They wield software to unearth quirks of language, rank entries quantitatively in a "wordlist" (though most constructors nowadays do), and assess puzzles with metrics like Freshness Factor Percentile (did the puzzle introduce as-yet-unpublished words?) and Scrabble Value (a proxy for the number of J's, X's, Q's, and Z's in the puzzle's entries). To them, crosswords are poised to become the next chess or Go—a vaunted intellectual pastime that might, when run through the silicon gauntlet of machine learning, unleash sleek universal truths about the human mind.

Then there are activists intent on injecting the crossword with the same sensitivity to language's power they've come to demand in other contexts. At a minimum, this project involves peppering the crossword grid with never-before-seen answers, words and phrases often coded as Too Obscure by editors reviewing submissions when what's meant is Too Black, Too Foreign, Too Political, Too Feminist. But the maximalist vision is procedural and economic: changing the way crosswords are submitted, selected, edited, and compensated at mainstream publications like the *Times;* remaking the personnel at these institutions and, in parallel, building alternative venues, audiences, and revenue models online. "Puzzles are like poetry," the *Times*'s inaugural crossword editor, Margaret Farrar, once quipped: "low paying." These constructors refuse to accept existing payment mechanisms as a given.

There are also a set of tastemakers, less taken with the techies' product management appeals to an imagined avatar of the "average solver," and more likely to view the crossword as a mixtape. In these hands, the crossword becomes a love letter to the solver who under-stands GWENDOLYN BROOKS, COLSON WHITEHEAD, BODAK YELLOW as crossword-worthy, solver and constructor alike delighted when their pop culture pops up in the puzzle, especially references deemed too "niche" by editors at mainstream publications. The cross-word might become less a game than a gallery, an exercise in cura-tion. And if you don't recognize everything in the grid, that's okay, you might look it up after and learn something. Solving streaks are for the biohackers, the perspiring quantified life enthusiasts, not us true con-noisseurs of the form. The crossword is more than just a game, it's art: not only a robust medium in itself, but a form whose history and pres-ent practice dovetails with that of modernist literature, avant-garde visual art, and performance.

This typology is meant as neither mutually exclusive nor collec-tively exhaustive. Part of the intrigue of putting into boxes the very people who put things into boxes is how cross-pollination and tension is the norm; impeccable taste in poetry and just as impeccable solv-ing streaks need not be contradictory. But the crossover goes deeper. Take the technologists: this book will feature the efforts of hobbyist coders who use software to automate "wordlists" wiped of offensive language or weigh words differently depending on the constructor's target outlet. It'll feature the mathematically minded slinging statistics to flag, automatically add, and highly rank neologisms or loanwords like CHEUGY, RIZZ, HYGGE, and COWORKING, or interestingly spelled snippets of culture (like PYNK, the Janelle Monáe song, or JYN ERSO, Felicity Jones's *Star Wars* character) so that crossword software more frequently suggests them as entries. And it'll feature software developers hosting free webinars or Twitch streams on how computers can improve puzzle-making or distributing free tools for developing crossword themes on their website—attempts to democratize the tools of the trade, to say nothing of demystifying crossword construction across generational divides.

This book takes seriously the people who see the puzzle as a tool of progressivism, just as it takes seriously those whose rejoinder is "This is just a game"—whether that refrain is meant as a refusal of politics, or as a politics of refusal in itself. It's no coincidence that the crossword exploded in popularity during the lockdowns of the COVID-19 pandemic, when so much was sacrificed at the altar of productivity, and when the crossword was a refuge just as much as it was a trackable, quantifiable daily task. The puzzle's origins, as we'll see, orbit the two world wars: a "crossword craze" in the 1920s was spurred by Jazz Age leisure and socioeconomic makeover in the wake of World War I; the *Times* resisted adding a crossword puzzle until Farrar thought it might distract the home front during World War II. I ask, alongside the groups in this book, whether today's second crossword craze is a haven from the craziness of the world or, darkly, a kind of spiral staircase: something clever, something indeed distracting, which nevertheless leaves us in the same rickety building where we've been the entire time.

"Constructing a puzzle," wrote Shortz's predecessor at the *Times*, Eugene T. Maleska, "is like building a house." The answers in the grid "are its bricks and mortar. But the clues provide the interior decoration." Boring, unadorned clues ("dry as dust") produce a "dull or shabby atmosphere"; a good clue—like a corner-table lamp, a cross-generational plate set—should "sparkle," show deliberateness of selection, and stimulate interest, "result[ing] in delight for the solvers as they travel from room to room."

Maleska, in his book-length reflection *Across and Down*, charges the old guard of clue writers with a decorative ethic of "laziness and timidity." For decades, the average crossword clue was a one-trick appliance, a machine of simple definition. In Arthur Wynne's inaugural "Word-Cross" of 1913, DOVE is clued as [A bird]. No arguments here. Maleska cites [Stinging insect] as the sort of clue that turned solvers themselves into automatons, calling this sterility a "stimulus-response practice"—the solver entered BEE if the answer was 3 letters and WASP if it was 4, thinking not required. The "timidity" Maleska cites is a desire for orderly unobtrusiveness, for the neighbors to come

over, see everything in its place, and nod sagely, sheathing their sting-
ers: this is a house; the dictionary says so. To stray from sourceable
definition would be to invite first a mountain range of raised eyebrows
appearing there above the picket, then a mailbox crammed with complaints, strongly worded letters about strongly lettered words.

In the late 1930s, as the craze of the mid-1920s entered a more tran-
quil phase, a new set of clue writers rejected spartan definition in favor
of gaudier wallpaper. BEE was no longer [Stinging insect] but, in a Jack
Luzzatto clue Maleska called a "breakthrough," [Nectar inspector]. A
clue could be a music box, tinkling with playful rhyme or alliteration:

Morsel a horse'll eat	OAT
His chief has a fief	ESNE
Foiler of forty felons	ALI BABA
Feed feasters for a fee	CATER

And then there were puns. The pun! Of all a crossword's gimmicks,
the pun has always felt to me like the fundament, the house's cement.
A solver may cry foul when a crossword devilishly insists she enter
words backward, dredge up long-forgotten or never-committed trivia,
squish multiple letters in a single cell, or write outside the borders of
the grid. But a groan is not the body implicating fairness, only taste;
"I see what you did there" is a registering of annoyance just as much
as literal acknowledgment. A punny crossword clue participates in
what scholar Jonathan Culler, joking, calls "a world of yoking"—
"allowing signifiers to affect meaning by generating new connections,"
but also hitching those affected connections to the quotidian act of
clear definition: the clue, like the joke setup, resolves into an answer. A
punny clue—and Maleska was to divide these into *Clues to Amuse* and
Clues to Confuse—can be, in the kitchen of the crossword, a toaster:
the heat of brainpower warming our day-old language, the solver's
satisfying ding of solution. Each chapter of this book takes as its epi-
graph a particularly fiendish pun clue, stretchy wordplay sometimes
signaled by a question mark; Maleska's favorites, at the dawn of this
style, included:

Item stolen while thousands cheer .... BASE

Article appearing daily in English newspapers .... THE

They made a star trek... MAGI

Nutcracker's suite... NEST

It was also in this era that clues began to show personality. Delinked from dictionary overtness, the constructor was now free, essentially, to free-associate; having done so, she was also free not to repeat herself, to rearrange the furniture each time she was forced once again to clue IKEA, SETTEE, or SOFA. "The cruciverbalist will make it a point of honor," wrote the French novelist—and crossword constructor—Georges Perec, "to find for each of these a clue that no one has used before." By "each of these" Perec was referring to *crosswordese:* a term to which we will frequently return, but for Perec words that "when all is said and done only exist in crosswords." Perec challenged himself to define the digraph IO—variously the letters I and O, the moon of Jupiter, the priestess of Greek myth that Hera transformed into a cow, and so on—one hundred different ways; in the introduction to his 1979 book *Les mots croisés,* he was only up to twenty-eight. To give you an idea:

The last we heard from MacDonald's farm

Cowgirl

Lionheart

Coming back from Boise

Drops of iodine

The ultimate in audio

Regional center

Opening of *Iolanthe*

Idaho's borders

Eastern Ohio

Was she cowed by Zeus?

The vast majority of these are clues for the letters I and O (which are the literal "center" of the word "regional," for instance) and wouldn't fly in a *Times* puzzle, especially under Maleska. (The more Greek mythology the merrier, though. Maleska was a former Latin and English teacher and liked his references highbrow. He once wrote to the constructor of a 1979 puzzle, before the entry was clued exclusively this way and decades after the relevant book was published: "Please give me proof of ORC as a Tolkien creature.") Maleska, known for his cantankerousness, typed his solvers as I've typed constructors: instead of Techies, Activists, and Tastemakers, Maleska's Sleepers accepted the puzzle without complaint; Squawkers and Quibblers took it personally if they couldn't finish; Leapers thought they'd caught Maleska in an error, but thought wrong; and Gotchas, who indeed got him, were the "elite" alighting on a rare mistake and so earned a certificate of membership in Maleska's Gotcha Club.

In 2020, half a century after Perec's run of IO clues, the comedian Ada Nicolle ran The OREO Cluing Project, in which she crowdsourced more than two hundred clues for the cookie, written by some fifty constructors. No spirals and no staircases, just twists and black-and-white sleevefuls: OREO was [One demolished by a twister?]; it was, in a reference to a 1970s commercial and an echo of Maleska's beloved OAT clue above, [What a "kid'll eat the middle of" first]; it was, in the talky, editorializing style you couldn't get away with in the *Times* [Brand that collabed with Owl City for the INCREDIBLE "Wonder-filled Anthem"]; it was, now with a giggly smirk, ["No m____ _xen!," cry heard during the Industrial Revolution, perhaps]. If clues and answers could come from the back of Maleska's Latin textbook, they would also come from clowns in the back of the classroom, developing their own brand of wordplay, snickering as they folded the crossword to make a paper airplane.

Before I solved in the back of a New York City classroom, before I constructed my first *Times* crossword at sixteen, I was pulled out of class. I was born deaf in my left ear, and in elementary school was assigned an audiologist, who taught me the basics of lip-reading and

American Sign Language. I have been lucky to experience partial deaf-
ness less as disabling and more as a forced reorienting of my attention: if I want to hear you, I have to look at you, attending to the way
language is bodily—words as columns of air shaped by lips. At the
same time, I was very young when I first realized I'd say "What?" on
missing a word or three in a sentence, only to find, before my inter-
locutor clarified, that my brain had filled in the blanks with the likeliest candidates—words as an abstract probabilistic system, a linked
semantic net. In some sense, I love language because I have to; I love
crosswords because they combine these two incarnations of the word,
the physical grid and the floating clue.

In high school, we got the *Times* delivered as fodder for discussion
in AP U.S. History. I did solve in the back of class, though mostly my
friends and I did the puzzle together during our free period, collec-
tivizing our knowledge just to get past Tuesday. After my freshman
year, I had a summer job as a docent at the Brooklyn aquarium, in
Coney Island; our laminated badges got us free rides on the Cyclone,
the boardwalk's rickety wooden roller coaster that feels, clamoring
by the water, like a reassembled shipwreck, and my coworkers and I
must've ridden it a hundred times by summer's end. All the guides-in-
training had to pick a marine animal to specialize in. I chose the sea-
horse; almost everyone else chose the walrus. Bored in Seahorses 101,
I started doodling on graph paper—scratch paper was always graph
paper in my home; my dad was a middle school math teacher—and
the doodles began to take the form of rudimentary crosswords. No
clues yet, just getting words to intersect: drawing with letters.

I was hooked. I graduated from graph paper to software and
mailed my first submissions to the *Times* along with a squeaky cover
letter, composed with help from my dad. Shortz took the first Sunday puzzle I submitted, which was themed around every high school
kid's great love: trigonometry (children of teachers are often class
clowns and teacher's pets both). It had [COS]MO KRAMER crossing
DIS[CO S]TU at a rebus square for cosine, COS. Crosswords began
to seem like the kitschy version of unraveling life's great code, and I
started to install wordplay everywhere: I became obsessed with ana-

grams, naming the jazz-funk band I was in after an anagram of the legendary bassist CHARLES MINGUS, drafting surrealist vignettes centered on absurd rearrangements of other musicians' names, letting the letters dictate meaning: ERIC CLAPTON became NARCOLEPTIC, so that was a sleepy, bluesy Western; MILES DAVIS was DEVIL AMISS, a Dantean romp through a bebop underworld. I went to my first American Crossword Puzzle Tournament and met my heroes: the person who handed me my laminated name tag was Elizabeth C. Gorski, whose "grid art" puzzles boasted both visual and verbal fireworks. Her best-known is also one of my favorites: themed around the Guggenheim Museum, it features nine artists with work in the Guggenheim's collection, and its black squares mimic the building's iconic spiral shape. When it ran, staffers reported visitors strolling the spiral ramp of the museum, Gorski's puzzle in hand.

In college I fell a little out of love with crosswords, developing other academic interests: neuroscience, economic and immigration policy, poetry. Though I continued to construct through and after undergrad, though I teach classes on how to make crossword puzzles to people younger and older than I, it wasn't until researching this book that I fell back in love with puzzles—so infectious is the zeal of today's constructors, so determined are they to make the puzzle anew, and so thorough my vicarious re-enchantment. I've come to love crosswords less as a condensed version of Everything Language Can Do and more as a word game deceptively flexible enough to adapt to these new constructors' visions. The art critic Rosalind Krauss, in *The Originality of the Avant-Garde and Other Modernist Myths,* analyzes how the grid in visual art has come to stand, in an apparent contradiction, for both mysticism and materialism. Its practitioners, however, knew only the transcendental story: Piet Mondrian or Kazimir Malevich, two of the grid's pioneers, weren't discussing canvas, pigment, or graphite in their treatises: "They are talking about Being or Mind or Spirit. From their point of view, the grid is a staircase to the Universal, and they are not interested in what happens below in the Concrete." I'd like to tell both stories, the Universal and the Concrete, spiraling around each other.

The Crossword Should Be Data

Hello, World

[Faux pas?], 6 letters[*]
—JOON PAHK, *Outside the Box,* 2020

T he story begins with a baby, or at least the idea of one—it was 1989, summer in suburban Auburndale, Massachusetts, at the west end of leafy Newton along the Charles, most of the vinyl-sided homes keen to resurrect the analog witchiness of old New England by opting for gas lamps instead of streetlights, candles on the sill instead of electric overheads. Eric Albert and Peg Primak had decided to start a family. Peg, a manager at Bolt, Beranek and Newman (BBN, the R&D behemoth and precursor to Raytheon, the missile and defense technology outfit) was gifted at navigating the ecru nooks and crannies of corporate bureaucracy, and didn't want to quit. Eric, who'd worked as a computer programmer for a decade and jonesed for something more independent ("I'm no good at being an employee," he told me, "I think like an owner"), thought he'd try being a stay-at-home dad. In the meantime, he needed a new job—something he could do remotely, something more entrepreneurial—since New England homes and New England babies weren't cheap.

In 1989, there were barely a million American stay-at-home dads (that number has since doubled), and about as many suburbanite workers who didn't commute by car to an office park; the overlap may as well have been the null set. Eric was an outlier. As it happened, he was spending a few days that summer with a merry band of outliers, the members of the National Puzzlers' League. Launched in New York in 1883, the League, which issues a riddle-riddled monthly newsletter named *The Enigma,* was founded "to provide a pastime of mental relaxation for lovers of word puzzles, to raise the standard of puzzling to a higher intellectual level, and to establish and foster friendships among its widely scattered members." At the 1989 convention, in the lobby of a Cleveland hotel, Eric had an idea: he could become a professional crossword puzzle writer. He pictured sitting in his den, baby balanced on his lap, tax-deductible reference books fluttering open like manta rays, as he dashed off grids to editors he already knew from the League.

Eric canvassed his fellow conventiongoers. Collectively, as if referencing how their technicolor "recreational linguistics" might be for the mind what a Mardi Gras second line is for ear and eye, NPL members are known as the Krewe. Individually, members of the Krewe are known by "noms," cryptic pen names inflected with festive wordplay or personal accents. Eric sought advice from *Hex* (the puzzle power couple Henry Rathvon and Emily Cox, colleagues at BBN), *Double-H* (Henry Hook, a surly, quick-witted Brooklynite known as "the Marquis de Sade of the puzzle world"), and *WILLz* (Will Shortz, a play on Will + "short" Z, then the editor of *Games* magazine; he would take over the *Times* puzzle editorship four years later). Photo captions from that year's convention read like a yearbook from a Wookiee magnet school: "Back row: [. . .] Hudu, Ai, Grams, Qaqaq, Smaug, Faro, Blade, Alf, Sluggo, Ulk (behind Sluggo)."

So spoke the G(r)eek chorus: "Don't do it." To many of them, puzzling was a hobby, only that, and besides, everyone wanted their byline in the *New York Times* Arts & Leisure section, willing to suffer the slings and arrows of a freelancer's pittance in pursuit of nerdcore bragging rights. The flood of submissions was one reason rates were so low: $15 to $75 for a 15-by-15-square crossword, the standard for dailies; $50 to $250 for a Sunday-sized 21-by-21. "Few people could grind them out quickly enough," Eric wrote at the time, "to be able to afford both food and shelter."

But maybe a computer could. Back then, crosswords were made entirely by hand. Graph paper, pencils, erasers; a miscreant's penchant for puns; a mystic's delight at serendipity—these were the tools of the trade. One constructor ordered specialized scratch pads stamped with 15-by-15 grids from a company in Maine. And when they needed a 7-letter word whose third letter was X, constructors might haul out a reference like *The Crossword Answer Book*, a doorstopping dictionary facsimile whose section headings were semi-filled-in strings, like neon signs with letters selectively dimmed and flickering: ?N?B??, ?N??B?, ??NB?? Form and function, as in any genre, followed material constraints. The prolific constructor Brendan Emmett Quigley— puzzledom's punkest rocker, whose shock of red hair and warlock beard make him part Velvet Revolver frontman and part retirement-era David Letterman—has said he built countless grids in the 1990s centered around flashy 7-letter words, packed like sardines in a crossword's corners; the reference book he owned didn't go up to 8s.

When Eric returned to Newton from Cleveland, he cast around for existing crossword construction software, but there wasn't much to speak of. Mary Virginia Orna, a chemistry professor at the College of New Rochelle, used her lab's x-y plotter to print professional-looking grids, but it didn't help construct them. The few commercially available programs produced only "criss-cross" lattice grids from user-supplied dictionaries, waffle-like puzzles where the words rarely crossed and that often lacked the canonical 180-degree symmetry of modern grids. Mel Rosen, a well-known puzzle-maker, editor, and member of the Krewe (nom: *Quip*), sold Eric a copy of *The Crossword Puzzler*, a program he'd written for the IBM PC that helped enter, store, and retrieve clues; autoformatted numbered grids and clues for printing; and even boasted a nascent search mechanism, fetching words that matched a

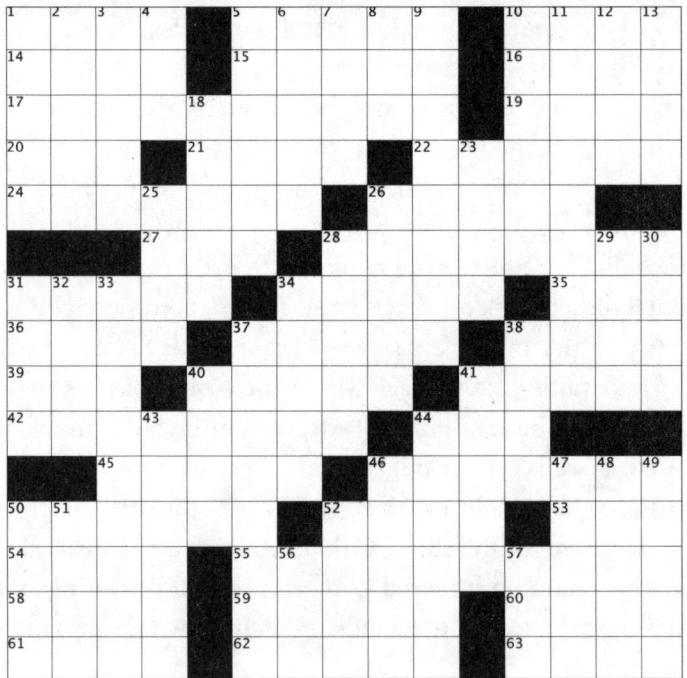

specific pattern of letters. It certainly softened the constructor's burden. "But I didn't want to make the job easier," Eric wrote. "I wanted to make the job go away."

◼

Eric was born in Boston in 1957. His mother was a biology professor with a PhD from Brown, an accomplished woman of science at a time when graduate programs still rarely admitted women. His father, a computer scientist, exposed Eric to math from a young age. By the time he was eight, Eric had memorized solutions to puzzles by the legendary Sam Loyd, a prodigal chess player turned "recreational mathematician"—that is, a practitioner of "mathematics uncontaminated by utility," in the words of writer and mathematician Martin Gardner. Loyd's "Famous Trick Donkeys" puzzle was used as a promotional item for (and later sold to) P. T. Barnum and his circus. (When Loyd died, in a kind of oedipal rearrangement, his son Walther

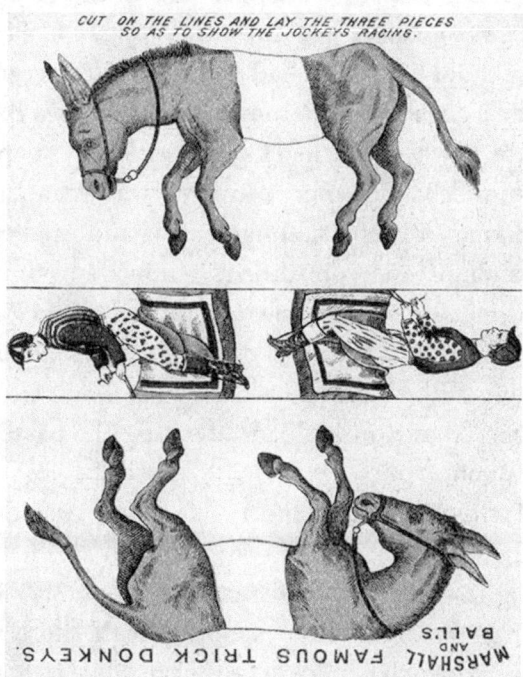

changed his name to Sam, and continued his father's work of producing puzzle books and toys.) Eric and his father would solve the *Times* crossword as a pair, announcing a clue number when one of them knew its answer, giving his co-solver a chance before writing it in.

In high school, Eric landed his first coding job. He did research for Edmund C. Berkeley, a computing pioneer whose 1949 book *Giant Brains, or Machines That Think* all but predicted internet search ("Suppose that you go into the library of the future and wish to look up ways for making biscuits. You will be able to dial into the catalogue machine 'making biscuits'") and email (before "going to South America for a year, we [will] see our address book as a spool of magnetic tape. When we wish to send out announcements, we put a stack of blank envelopes into the machine"). Eric would fiddle with the refrigerator-sized instruments after school, fussy and expensive enough that Berkeley kept them behind locked doors. Then on to Brown University, where he was an early beneficiary of the school's Open Curriculum, which abolished core requirements and allowed students to take any number of classes Pass/Fail. Eric, who attended Brown at the same time that Talking Heads was forming just down the slope of College Hill at the Rhode Island School of Design, had a very 1970s undergraduate experience. Already a capable programmer, he opted for a BA rather than BS degree in the newly christened Computer Science department, just as the field—more abstract, more creative—was extracting itself from the blockier diktats of Electrical Engineering and Applied Mathematics. He made an impression on Andries "Andy" van Dam, the graphics pioneer whose mentorship, at Brown, of several future Pixar filmmakers is believed to be the origin of the *Toy Story* protagonist's name. He ended up taking all his nonmajor classes Pass/Fail. He was the only man in a survey course on Lesbian Literature (he passed, he says, in more ways than one).

Outside of schoolwork, Eric and a close friend, Alan Frank, cowrote perhaps the first-ever distributed computer game. Eric had devoured one of the earliest teletype "interactive fictions," in which players read preprogrammed text and responded with short commands, a limited number of which would move the narrative forward. The game was William Crowther's 1976 *Colossal Cave Adventure,* a cross between *Dungeons & Dragons* and Crowther's experiences exploring and mapping Kentucky's Mammoth Cave, the longest cave system in the world. That story begins:

> You are standing at the end of a road before a small brick building. Around you is a forest. A small stream flows out of the building and down a gully.

What's next?

Alan and Eric built new functionality on an IBM 360 mainframe—"That was no joke," he says, "that was real computer science"—so others could design their own levels in the game. Years later, after overhearing Eric's name at a Brown reunion, a faculty brat turned game designer thanked Eric for his service; playing it, the man said, was the reason he'd gone into game design in the first place. Eric and Alan were also members of the university's Scrabble club. A friend who owed Eric a favor unearthed a digital copy of *The Official Scrabble Players Dictionary,* and together he and Alan programmed a set of tools to give themselves a competitive edge. Their software spit out a list of the 7-letter words (bingoes, in Scrabble lingo) that, given the overall distribution of tiles and the existing board, were likeliest to appear on a rack.

After graduation, Eric and Alan decided to live together in Medford. Eric wended his way through a glossy hedge maze of software jobs, gigs that, come the full moon, revealed some Halloween-ish underside. He liked the technical work at BBN (he'd worked there too, as did Crowther; everyone did, they "basically invented the internet," says Eric) but felt stifled under the fluorescent spotlight of management. He worked for a start-up run by three MIT professors that buckled under the founders' corruption; one of the professors was John Donovan, a management guru whose high-priced, high-theatrical seminars earned him the nickname "the Johnny Carson of the training circuit," and whose litany of misdeeds includes forged documents, a decades-long legal battle over one of his son's fortunes, and falsely claiming another son hired Russian hit men to assassinate him. (He was saved by his belt buckle, he said, which had magically deflected the bullets, leaving just a flesh wound in his stomach.)

After all that software mishegas, computer programming for pay came to remind Eric of the Sherlock Holmes story "The Red-Headed League." In it, a pawnbroker with red hair is handsomely paid to copy out the *Encylopaedia Britannica*—numbing, fruitless clerical work, meant to distract while criminals pilfer a bank nearby. It was not the income-generating but the recreational tinkering that lit up Eric's circuits, and soon he would train his algorithmic gaze on a problem that served as a precursor to computer-generating crosswords: word squares.

■

Word squares are crossword fossils, grids of letters arranged so the same words can be read horizontally or vertically. Chisel swapped for pencil, an answer key in search of clues, they have the eerie, extraterrestrial heft of Stonehenge or crop circles. The best-known specimen is the Sator Square, a 5-by-5 Latin creation first discovered in 1936, carved into a stucco column in the ruins of Pompeii's Palestra Grande, dateable to before 62 CE:

```
S A T O R
A R E P O
T E N E T
O P E R A
R O T A S
```

Read row by row or column by column, the square offers the same palindromic message: SATOR AREPO TENET OPERA ROTAS, "The sower Arepo holds the plow." In the centuries to come, the sentence became a kind of counterspell; one imagines flapping black robes, slits of etched letters brimming with orange light. In the fourteenth century, it is said, the square could quench wildfire; in the fifteenth, it cured the insane. To many, the crossed palindrome at its center, TENET ("he holds") represented Christ; the sower might have been a reference to the parable of the sower, in Matthew 13. The square has been inscribed on the walls of abbeys and chapels, scratched into amulets and books, a lexical mandala tattooed the world over by mystics and paranoids. Around 1830, a Dutch doctor in Pennsylvania included the inscription in a medical manual, the block-letter engraving of Pompeii traded for inked manuscript cursive as florid and witchy as the flick of a wand. Patients were instructed to write the square on a piece of buttered bread, then consume it, as a cure for rabies.

Late in the twentieth century, Eric and his friend Alan were methodically furnishing word squares of increasing scale, tracking their progress like rock climbers advancing from V2s to V5s. They'd worked their way up from 3-by-3s you could fill off the top of your head to 7-by-7s requiring a dog-eared *Oxford English Dictionary* nearby. Everest, to them, was the 9-by-9. As far as they knew, the first 9-by-9 square in history had appeared on December 28, 1897. Constructed by Arthur F. Holt ("the master formist of his time," beamed Eric), the square ran in the Chicago *Inter Ocean* "back when newspapers were enlightened enough to carry that sort of thing."

Nearly a century later, in the November 1980 pages of a recreational linguistics magazine called *Word Ways,* a 9-by-9 square produced by Wayne Goodman of Chicago was touted as "probably the finest" construction to date. It had its blemishes—chief among them its bottom row, SLESTERED. Resembling a past tense verb from Lewis Carroll's "Jabberwocky" or a Britishism synonymous with "drunk," the word, like "moist" or "bulbous," wears its meaning on its phonological sleeve, and is Scots for "engaged in dirty or sloppy work." When, in the pre-internet era, word squares circulated, their entries' sources followed like throat-clearing functionaries, vouching for them. In *Word Ways,* Dmitri Borgmann, author of the seminal *Language on Vacation,* appraised the full 9-by-9 that contains SLESTERED thus:

FRATERIES are refectories (dining halls) in monasteries; REGI-
MENAL is of the nature of a regimen, such as a systematic diet;

AGITATIVE is tending to agitate, disturb, or excite; TITANITES
are brown or black monoclinic calcium silicotitanates; an EMA-
NATIST is a believer in creation by effluxes from the Absolute; to
RETITRATE (found only in the Century Dictionary Supplement,
1909–14) is to redetermine the concentration of a solute; an INI-
TIATOR is an explosive initiating the explosion of a main charge;
EAVESTONE is a township in West Riding, Yorkshire, England (see
various British atlases and gazetteers, such as the Survey Gazetteer
of the British Isles, published in Edinburgh by John Bartholomew
in 1943); and SLESTERED means engaged in dirty or sloppy work.
Because this last word is Scottish instead of English, it disqualifies
the square from a first-class ranking. All words not identified as
to source can be found in Webster's Second Edition and in other
dictionaries.

```
F  R  A  T  E  R  I  E  S
R  E  G  I  M  E  N  A  L
A  G  I  T  A  T  I  V  E
T  I  T  A  N  I  T  E  S
E  M  A  N  A  T  I  S  T
R  E  T  I  T  R  A  T  E
I  N  I  T  I  A  T  O  R
E  A  V  E  S  T  O  N  E
S  L  E  S  T  E  R  E  D
```

This list of justifications could just as easily read as an anaphoric poem;
some of its lines have, to me, a matter-of-fact attractiveness ("an EMA-
NATIST is a believer in creation by effluxes from the Absolute" may
as well be a line by William Blake). And if the entries are so gathered because their letters form happy di- and trigraphs with the words
above and below—this consonant sleeping snugly head to toe with that
vowel—then they generate, inevitably, associations with their struc-
turalist bedfellows, the way song lyrics might be chosen first for syl-
labic fit, only to evoke or weave a narrative. "The pattern of the thing,"
Vladimir Nabokov told an interviewer at *The Paris Review,* "precedes

the thing. I fill in the gaps of the crossword at any spot I happen to choose."

What was the pattern of Goodman's thing? FRATERIES sets a monastic, collaborative tone; TITANITES and RETITRATE wear the ammoniac white coat of science; EAVESTONE has a Dickensian depth; and everyone finishes with ink on their fingers, totally SLESTERED. Present in the word square is the crossword writer's great pleasure: words plucked from their contexts and joined with vocabulary that, but for the crossword's curatorial arithmetic, they'd otherwise have nothing to do with.

Eric thought a computer could best Goodman's SLESTERED 9-by-9. In 1988, during a phone conversation with his friend Murray Pearce, the latter suggested Eric first attempt a computer-generated 8-by-8, as a proof of concept. The two of them did some back-of-the-envelope calculations and discovered it would take the fastest supercomputer in the world (it was the 1980s, so that machine would be more of a hulking Olympian than a slim, iPad discus) one hundred quintillion years (100,000,000,000,000,000,000,000) to check for every valid 8-by-8 using Eric's database. The solution space had to be pruned, and Eric worked up a few shearing techniques.

For one thing, he could start the search at the bottom row of the square, not the top. Since English orthography is "ending-poor"—there are far more letter combinations that begin words than end them—this would quickly discard unworkable combos. For another, he could employ a principle in algorithmic design called "forward propagation." If, say, the program chose the word FLAPJACK for the bottom row, it could, even before considering the row above, ensure there existed 8-letter entries that ended with F, L, A, P, J, C, and K. If it discovered there were no 8s ending in J, for example, then it moved on to another candidate.

The program took Eric four days to write. Alongside the 1,000-line algorithm was a database of about fifty thousand 8-letter entries, cobbled together from far-flung corpora (medical and legal dictionaries; geographical compendia called gazetteers; and the digital Scrabble list he and Alan handled in college) and sporting such flash as two-word phrases like COOL JAZZ (again, it was the late 1980s). Then there were the hardware constraints: Eric's personal computer, an 8-megahertz IBM PC/AT clone, had only 640 kilobytes of memory and a measly 20-megabyte hard disk. The evening he finished the program, he unleashed it on the full fifty-thousand-entry database, then turned in for the night. After a few hours of tossing and turning, dreaming no doubt of word cubes and hypercubes, he woke for a post-witching-hour check-in. The program, having muscled through forty potential bottom-row words, hadn't found a square. Disappointed, he went back to bed.

By morning, the program had danced its way through the first sixty words, but still no square. At that rate, it'd take almost a year to work the whole database—an obvious improvement on a hundred quintillion, but still an immense commitment. Eric couldn't see himself devoting his machine's meager processing power night after night to this logological quest, and considered packing it in. But that very evening, the program discovered its first 8-by-8. Seeing it neat and glistening in phosphorous green terminal letters, Eric was hooked. A phone call to Alan resulted in additional algorithmic boosts, and within a few months Eric was off to the races, expanding to 8-by-8s with unusual bottom-row entries (more FLAPJACK than ASSESSED) and 7-by-7s seeded with particular words. "My friends with 7-letter names," Eric wrote, "started getting unique presents."

Still, the 9-by-9 shimmered beyond his reach. It wasn't until Eric switched jobs that he felt up to the task; now his desk sparkled with a 20-megahertz IBM 386 clone with a nimble 90-megabyte hard disk. He could run the program on his personal device at home, and every night and weekend at work. Like a machine-age Dorian Gray, his work computer hummed along comfortably as his personal one flecked and crashed and darkened, a portrait of technological decline. That device, Eric wrote, soon went "to the great hardware museum in the sky." But on June 27, 1989, it was the personal machine, not the company one, that had a viable 9-by-9 waiting when Eric returned home from work, like an old dog with slippers in its mouth:

```
N E C E S S I S M
E X I S T E N C E
C I R C U M F E R
E S C A R P I N G
S T U R N I D A E
S E M P I T E R N
I N F I D E L I C
S C E N A R I Z E
M E R G E N C E S
```

Because every entry can be found in *Webster's Second Edition,* the square was one of a kind. On seeing it, a passage by physicist Richard Feynman occurred to Eric: "I went on and checked some other things, which fit, and new things fit, and I was very excited. It was the first time, and the only time, in my career that I knew a law of nature that nobody else knew." (That night he called Murray Pearce and they talked, giddy, for hours.)

What things were gathered here, what patterns emerged? If the Sator Square and Wayne Goodman's 9-by-9 happened, by divine providence, to sing the gospel of sowers, monks, and emanation, Eric's seemed to speak in the close-fisted metaphysics of determinism. It was as if this square, these particular words, awaited Eric at the end of his journey, and always had. There was the NECESSISM (a hard-line anti-free-will philosophy) of EXISTENCE, the seemingly *e*-less MERGENCES, the seemingly *ence*-less CIRCUMFER, the last of which had a mathematical cast. There was the countable infinity of SEMPITERN: "eternal" means "outside time and thus lacking temporal duration altogether," but "sempiternal" means "having infinite temporal duration," like the runtime of a program that hums on into nothingness. ("All the eternal questions," writes Meghan O'Gieblyn in *God, Human, Animal, Machine,* "have become engineering problems.") All these words were INFIDELIC next to the devoutness of Goodman's FRATERIES or EMANATIST, or to the nominally godly work to which the Sator Square had been put. Ted Clarke, a frequent contributor to *Word Ways* from Newquay, Cornwall, England, put the John Henry–esque tale in verse, gesturing to the 10-by-10 that awaited a new generation of the faithful:

> *It's known that for one hundred years*
> *Puzzlists strove for what appears*
> *Could not be done within the span*
> *The Good Lord had alloted man. [. . .]*
>
> *The ten-square seems so convolute,*
> *With certain facts not in dispute,*
> *The best computers of the world,*
> *At this problem bravely hurled,*
>
> *May need a full quadrillion years*
> *To run through all successive tiers*
> *Of permutations from the list*
> *Of valid words which now exist. [. . .]*
>
> *Such Sisyphean effort goes*
> *To swell esteem for all of those*
> *Who've almost formed a perfect square*
> *And yet had no computer there.*
>
> *The late Dmitri Borgmann's name*
> *Already's in the Hall of Fame;*
> *Although he only managed seven,*
> *He earned his place in wordplay's Heaven.*

It's as if the word square were a two-dimensional Babel, bricked with pixels instead of mortar. When Eric was building his program, there was more than a bit of this purism going around, the notion that heaven might be first and foremost for those who'd sweated it out on paper. He ignored it; if anything, "logology by computer" (as it was called in the pages of *Word Ways* by none other than Alan Frank) had only deepened his attunement to the structure of language. Those very insights, after all, scaffolded his algorithm. "It must be emphasized," reads a history of the Sator Square, "that the early Christians . . . were much more attuned to symbols and arcane meanings than people of the 21st century." Maybe, and not unironically, computers could return us to that state of attunement: an Eden potted with binary trees, the palindromic Eve learning to code in Python.

The word square journey emboldened Eric, but computer-generating crosswords was a different ball game. In a word square, the entries needed a dictionary's imprimatur, nothing more, since the square was meant to be stared at. In a crossword, the entries had better be gettable, and preferably good, since a puzzle was meant to be savored, then solved.

Once he and Peg decided to have a child, Eric gave himself a year to see if he could develop a satisfactory program to kick-start his new career. Craving an academic edge, he took a stack of quarters to MIT's Barker Engineering Library, housed in the Pantheon-inspired Building 10 beneath the campus's iconic Great Dome. The library admitted nonstudents; in the capacious oculus, natural light streaming in from above, Corinthian columns lining the Dome like dendrites, Eric photocopied scientific papers. It made for tedious reading. By and large, researchers focused on whether a computer could furnish a crossword at all, ignoring the caliber of the resultant grid. In a paper entitled "Search Lessons Learned from Crossword Puzzles"—written by Stanford computer scientists Matt Ginsberg, Michael Frank, Michael Halpin, and Mark Torrance, the first of whom would go on to develop the AI crossword *solver* Dr.Fill—Eric encountered the following sentence: "Why use a word with a Q when one with an S can be used instead?" Database search problems are often attacked by casting a maximally wide probabilistic net, but words with a Q are interesting precisely because of their rarity; the scientists wanted to minimize what Eric wanted to maximize. "I was going to get no help from my academic colleagues," Eric wrote. "I would have to go it alone."

One August Saturday, he locked himself in his air-conditioned office at work and spent thirteen hours assembling a rudimentary crossword program. To test it, he seeded a 3-by-4 grid with two constraints: the initials of Peg's first, middle, and last names in the top row (MKP, M for Margaret and P for Primak) and his (ERA) in the bottom. A few nerve-wracking minutes later, a valid fill materialized on-screen, and Eric let out a victory whoop. Relieved, he left the program alone, hoping to return on Monday morning with new prospects for the 3-by-4 array.

```
M  K  P
E  E  L
T  R  E
E  R  A
```

Come Monday, the program hadn't found a single additional fill. Eric's "spirits sank to my sneakers. Crossword constructors had nothing to fear from a competitor that failed to exhaust the possibilities for 12 letters in 36 hours. I put the program out of its misery." Again, Eric mined Alan Frank and others for algorithmic grease, and again, their wisdom dialed up the program's speed; in a matter of weeks, it could exhaust the possibilities for a 12-letter 3-by-4 box in less than twenty minutes.

Up to that moment, the program churned through *every* valid fill for a given section—without discernment. But there were thousands of possibilities for a mere 3-by-4 swatch. How many would pass muster as a corner in a *New York Times* Monday? "The program," wrote Eric, "had to acquire some taste." He and Peg together began a regimen of aesthetic arbitration, devoting days to rating every 3- and 4-letter word in Eric's database—thousands of entries—on a crude scale: 0 meant great, 1 meant average, 2 meant "bleah." When the program sprang back to life, newly armed with quantitative judgment, Eric couldn't believe the results. The grids it generated were, in crossword parlance, *clean:* fewer abbreviations, shabby archaicisms, or unheard-of names. The program had learned to privilege "good" words over "bad," something no other crossword software, Eric believed, had ever done before.

In March 1991, baby Gus was born, and Eric quit his day job. He strollered around Newton, wheeling under maples and into "mothers' groups" for coffee and gossip before asking, in this liberal bastion, if they might change that phrase to "parents' group." (They did not.) Then he came home and ranked words.

The rubric had mutated since he and Peg finished the 3s and 4s. Now, the rating system boasted thirteen categories, scored from 0 ("Fabulous") to 12 ("Very yucky"); like in golf, the game was minimization. Much of the labor was demotional, sending undesirable words further down the batting order, to better position the heavy hitters. He marked down words with prefixes or suffixes (DE-, RE-, -ENCE, -ATION). He marked down crosswordese (OLEO, ARIA, EPEE). Worried it might reek of corporate boosterism, he marked down trade names like NIKON. If he thought an entry had insufficient prospects for an interesting clue (pronouns or prepositions; fill-in-the-blanks like OF LA as in ["Man ___ Mancha"]), he marked it down too.

What scored highly? Writing for *Games* magazine on "what a word's worth," Eric indicated traits then prized by constructors and solvers alike: full names, multiple-word phrases, entries with rare, high-Scrabble-value letters like J, Q, X, or Z. But another criterion, inevitably, was just gut aesthetic judgment—words Eric associated with flighty signifiers like "hipness" or "vividness." His final category names, with examples, follow, each an index of Eric's sensibility. For the most part, he could fill grids using only entries with a score of 9 or lower.

0—*FABULOUS* (KUMQUAT, QUICK FIX, FORT KNOX)
1—*GREAT* (NEW YORK, AL HIRT, GAME PLAN)
2—*VERY GOOD* (AMAZON, JAWBONE, CLAPTRAP)
3—*COLORFUL* (TULIP, BABOON, MOONLIT)
4—*ABOVE AVERAGE* (ASPARAGUS, MACAO, QUALITY)
5—*AVERAGE* (INN, ECONOMY, ROUTINE)
6—*BELOW AVERAGE* (TIPS, KNOCKED, DARED)
7—*BORING* (LATERALLY, ELLS, FEEBLEST)
8—*FLAWED* (YOU'LL, OCT., FRERE)
9—*STRETCHING* (COWY, BITERS, I'M NO)
10—*YUCKY* (COWIER, ANOA, LOYS)
11—*SPECIALIZED* (UCALEGON, NOSARIAN, <obscene>)
12—*VERY YUCKY* (BERT L., SHILFA, TRABEAE)

Starting in March, Eric ranked a thousand words a day, come hell or high water. Two years in, he finished the 9-letter entries. "Word-ranking," he wrote, "is a hobby I can recommend only to those who get overstimulated watching paint dry." After his word square odyssey, Eric's database now teemed with some 750,000 entries. It was a cauldron bubbling over with computer-readable corpora of every predilection: unabridged English dictionaries, phrase books, thesauri, proper noun lists culled from primitive digital quiz games that Eric had had to decrypt. Then there were the crossword-specific baubles, some dull and some shinier, which he'd added himself, one by one by one. "Whenever some wise guy says doing crosswords by computer isn't 'really' work," Eric mused, "I think to myself, 'You've obviously never spent a day typing in 4,000 Roman numerals.'"

It paid off. Eric sold every single puzzle his proprietary program generated, to outlets like *Games* magazine, *The Washington Post*, *Dell Champion Crosswords*, and *The New York Times*. The puzzles were a far cry from the lifeless pap the automation naysayers feared; if anything, fueled by a database comprised of thousands of instinctive micro-decisions about a word's "goodness," the resulting grids inherited Eric's voice more clearly than those he'd fashioned by hand.

Still, Eric dreaded losing his competitive edge, and feared that computer-generated grids would be held to a higher standard. For a time, he kept his methods a secret. Years later, on learning many of Eric's early submissions featured computer-generated grids, *Times* puzzle editor Will Shortz shrugged. The puzzles were good, he said. He couldn't tell the difference.

"Crosswords," Eric told me, three decades after he'd written his program, "were a mistake."

"Like the Dow Jones Industrial Average," he added. Both failed every conceivable test of what you'd want in a word puzzle, or a stock index, but stuck around through sheer American exceptionalism, or the smudged inertia of the news business, or bribes from Big Graph Paper.

Eric came to believe crosswords were too constrained, too limiting. Time and again, the conventions of American-style puzzles to which we will frequently return—rotational symmetry and double-checked entries, to name two—conspired to have him clue the word AREA for the thousandth time. Abroad, word games were linguistically libertine: Eric pointed to non-English crosswords (in which symmetry is usually dropped) and British-style cryptics (which discard double-checking in favor of lattice-shaped grids) as offshoots he wished had more purchase in the United States, since their grids tend to be much easier to produce.

And yet Eric's innovations powered a revolution in crosswords. Technology of the kind he pioneered today underlies not just the manufacture of *fill* (the interlocking words in the grid) but also the other three tasks (placement of *black squares, theme* development, and even writing *clues*) that a crossword constructor undertakes.

I say *constructor,* but a cruciverbalist—the Latinate term whose glasses I can hear falling down its nose—has a surprisingly wide set of nouns to choose from: *constructor, maker, creator, writer, setter.* Each, I have found, corresponds more or less to a different compositional stage, and even, in extremis, to a distinct puzzling ethic. Brainstorming a theme feels like *creating*: noticing a relationship among phrases, panning for additional examples, and plotting a two-dimensional scavenger hunt for your solver. Building a grid feels like *constructing*: trafficking in the mathematics of letter distributions, establishing the good bones of a pleasing black square placement, then adding striking balustrades and turrets of phrases, neologisms, interesting names—all of it cemented, when needed, by the "glue" of crosswordese. And composing clues, unsurprisingly, feels like *writing*—part poetry and part prose, half trivia night and two-thirds dad joke. There are many constructors, like myself, who prize the context-switching of these radically dissimilar demands. And there are just as many specialists, for whom one stage produces the greatest pleasure; the rest may as well be contracted out, to a willing collaborator, or to a machine. Georges Perec, the French writer of the constraint-based Oulipo school who also wrote a weekly crossword for the newspaper *Le Point,* mused that filling a grid is

> a tedious, meticulous, maniacal task, a sort of letter-based arithmetic where all that matters is that words have this or that length, and that their juxtapositions reveal groupings that are compatible with the perpendicular construction of other words; it is a system of primary constraints where the letter is omnipresent, but where language is absent.

On the other hand, writing clues, for Perec, "is fluid, intangible work, a stroll in the land of words, intended to uncover, in the imprecise neighborhood that constitutes the definition of a word, the fragile and unique location where it will be simultaneously revealed and hidden." Perec, like Eric, worked from home; unlike Eric, his process was entirely analog. Building grids (the "diagram," to French constructors) was kitchen-table finagling, done "with obstinacy and tenacity, groping, counting, erasing"; writing clues could happen anytime and anywhere, "at any hour of day or night, without thinking about it, strolling, letting one's attention float freely in the wake of the thousand and one associations evoked by this or that word." For Perec, there would always be room to clue AREA in a decorous, evocative way.

Perec's puzzles rarely featured themes, but most American puzzles do. In the documentary *Wordplay,* Merl Reagle, the beloved late constructor of Sunday-sized, joke-ridden puzzles for the *San Francisco Chronicle* and *The Washington Post,* shows viewers the American version of Perec's strolling: he drives around Florida's strip malls, sifting for puns in the all-caps capitalist letter bank of billboards, awnings, roadside signage. "DUNKIN' DONUTS—put the 'D' at the end, you get 'Unkind Donuts,' which I've had a few of in my day," he says. Many of Reagle's themes emerged thus: after noticing a quirk of language in the suburban wild, he'd generate as many examples as he could. Like a stack of IHOP pancakes, Reagle's puzzles teetered with carbohydrate-loaded groaners, some of them misshapen, but each one avuncular, maximalist, and delicious. The *Times* grid he created in concert with his and Will Shortz's appearance on *The Simpsons* (a Sunday puzzle titled "Sounds Like Somebody I Used to Know") boasts NIKITA CRUISE CHEF clued as [Moscow V.I.P. who liked to cook on a ship?] directly above LINDSAY LOW HAND ["I have no face cards" actress?]. To fit these answers one atop the other, the stack oozes with some sticky crosswordese going down: the high-fructose SEHR [Ilse's "very"], "partial" phrases severed from their wholes like stray pieces of burnt batter (JOHN OF clued as [English duke ___ Gaunt] or IN A as [Hell ___ handbasket]). But Reagle's syrupy glee is, ultimately, infectious.

Would Eric's software change anything? It might in the first case (instantly producing pairs like DUNKIN -> UNKIND) but struggle to in the second (where the puns are sound-based, and stretchy; though digital phonological databases exist, I know of no corpus that'd easily unearth KHRUSHCHEV -> CRUISE CHEF). Brainstorming by cortex might offer insights about English spelling (moving the D to a word's end is likelier to work if the word already ends with an N, like UNKIND -> DUNKIN, or a vowel, like DANTE -> ANTED). But brainstorming by corpus will ensure you don't miss any gems (DRUG

FREE becoming RUG FREED, what happens when someone's toupee falls off).

Today, software doesn't just help constructors come up with theme answers, it expands the horizon of what's possible. Joel Fagliano, a digital editor at the *Times* and creator of the 5-by-5 mini crossword, had noticed that as he spelled certain phrases, every letter would appear twice except one: in COMMON SENSE, there are two O's, two M's, two N's, two S's, and two E's; C is the only nonrepeating letter. But when he tried to produce other examples, he floundered, "generating insane-looking pages in my notebook of scribbled out words," many of which were insufficiently exciting to him (e.g., INSUFFICIENCIES, which repeats everything—including four I's—except the U). Fagliano enlisted a coding-savvy colleague to dig through his digital wordlist. Not only were the resulting phrases lively and diverse (HIPPO-CRATIC OATH, SHE'S ALL THAT, LOS ALAMOS, BAR MEMBER, PRIDE PARADE, UNDER DURESS, SETS A DATE, MIAMI DADE, PRETTY PENNY, and GOES UNDERGROUND) but Fagliano was able to add a final flourish. Their nondoubled letters spell, in order, REMAINDERS.

Some constructors remain skeptical of crosswords by computer. This might be out of an aestheticized Luddism ("A computer looks really stupid tucked behind your ear," winks Henry Hook), but over-reliance on software is possible too. When I teach classes on crossword construction, I often, after slotting in the theme answers and placing the black squares, activate autofill, just to show students that a valid crossword can be generated from the humble beginning of a few inputs. I see their eyes flash with a sense of deception—was it really this easy all along? Was there no wizard behind the curtain, only a man brandishing grids with the press of a button, assenting to whatever language happened to appear?

In reality, autofilled grids are usually as easy to spot as AI-generated text: the words feel haphazardly picked, the long nontheme answers are valid but dull (think READDRESSING or BRINGING UP TO), the proper nouns don't look like they mean much to the constructor. The best constructors are curators: they'll have spent countless hours manicuring their wordlists, forming, just as Eric did, strong opinions about the "goodness" of certain words. They remove the offensive or uninteresting, they prioritize the desirable. When filling a grid, they don't click autofill and call it a day, they go slot by slot by slot, sizing up each potential word, aiming for a wide frame of reference across the entire puzzle—a full meal, as film critic and constructor Kameron Austin Collins likes to say. Like a word square, a lovingly filled crossword corner has a found poetry to it. I remember solving, in high school, a 2007 Gilbert H. Ludwig *Times* puzzle, whose lower-right section had the Down answers CHIGNON [Hair bun] next to AMPHORA [Antique jar] next to NOSTRUM [Quack remedy]. I didn't know these words at the time, and they looked, lined up in column, impossibly stately and meticulously picked, like mannequins donning the latest fashions from abroad.

In fact, computer assistance has become so ubiquitous that constructors now take pride in doing what a computer cannot. Adam Wagner and Brooke Husic published a *Times* Thursday in March 2023 with the theme answers RIB ROAST, CRAPSHOOT, DROPKICK, and GOT CAUGHT. Each unit in these answers can be clued by the same synonym: CRAPSHOOT can be ["Drat!" / "Drat!"], since both CRAP! and SHOOT! mean "Drat!" RIB ROAST is [Tease / Tease], DROP-KICK is [Quit / Quit], and GOT CAUGHT is [Heard / Heard]. Wagner pointed out that computers are great at letter-based search, bad at sound-based search, and awful at clocking meaning. "[My] favorite thing about this puzzle is how human the theme is. No code . . . just two friends texting each other messages like 'what are words that have . . . synonyms?'" It's worth noting the two friends in this case have, between them, some four degrees in math and computer-related fields; theirs is not the counsel of Luddites. Likewise, Ricky Cruz, who fell in love with crosswords relatively recently, during the COVID-19 pandemic, will often take a break from his construction software and fill, say, a 5-by-4 corner by hand. Relying on his mind's dictionary and not the computer's ensures he actively likes everything in the fill, as opposed to passively approving his wordlist's suggestions; it also allows him to come up with fill the software's wordlist may lack.

Clue-writing, in the main, remains a human-led pursuit. There are databases of previously published clues for a given word, but reusing an old clue is lazy at best, and at worst verboten. Trawling for inspiration is okay, though. Today's constructors might explore how a word has been previously clued in the *Times* to get the creative juices flowing: seeing deceptive clues for ART that tend to pun on words like "oil," "drawing," and "work" might help you generate [Drawing room?] for ART STUDIO. Eric did a version of this. At one National Puzzlers' League convention, he wrote a program to spit out all the three-letter strings he didn't have clues for. ART will have been clued dozens of times, but was QJJ or CAC or EWR anything? In tiny font, he printed out the words, gathered a dozen or so Krewe members in a hotel room, passed around copies, and told them to shout out any associations. It was like a group therapy session, Eric scribbling furiously on a sofa: *Now I'm going to show you a list of three-letter strings, and I want you to say whatever comes to mind.* RLS—those are the initials of Robert Louis Stevenson, add that to the database. EVO Morales of Bolivia was just then forming the Asamblea por la Sobernía de los Pueblos—ASP, if you need another clue for that. Didn't people shout OPA at weddings? Didn't you read about such and such leap forward with IVF? And so on, ETC, until everything and everyone had a meaning.

It's fitting Eric would use three-letter strings as a kind of linguistic Rorschach with the Krewe because after crossword puzzles he'd switch careers again, and become a therapist. Before Gus was born, as Eric's programming jobs wearied him, he'd spent time measuring out his next move, "talking with my cat" and paging through a then-popular self-help book called *Wishcraft*, which chronicled drastic career changes: "Cindy Fox was a waitress. Now she's a pilot. Peter Johnson was a truck driver. Now he's a dairy farmer." Eric was a computer scientist, a game designer, a crossword constructor, a father; he'd volunteered on a suicide hotline and taught sign language. Now he'd be a therapist, but not just any kind: a couples therapist for lesbians.

Wishcraft's directives were not so detail-oriented; this three-word compound came after much reflection. The *couples* part was clearest: "Relationships have always been compelling to me," Eric says, cheery but resigned, "partially because I've butchered so many of them." *Therapist* on realizing that his whole life he'd privileged product over process, that the job was done when the program worked, when the puzzle was solved or constructed, and so efficiently delivering the product was what distinguished you from the crowd. What he wanted was a task impossible to perfect as you performed it, where the minutes ticked away whether you said something or not, and so you'd better get talking, see what you had to say in the act of gaining the courage to say it.

Lesbian, then, out of a sense of justice. Eric identifies as a man, if "a somewhat peculiar guy"; he doesn't love any of the descriptors on offer for his orientation in the world, but sometimes uses "queer" in the newer, catholic sense of the word. But since his youth, he's had strong feelings of identification for "people finding ways to be who they are in a universe that is not necessarily supporting them"—for anyone who, fittingly for a crossword lover, "makes a life that requires being outside of the box."

In his contributions to *Word Ways,* you can see Eric shifting, when the moment permits, from recreational to political linguistics. Here he is, over the moon with his discovery of a 76-letter pangrammatic window (a stretch of text featuring all 26 English letters) in Book One of Milton's *Paradise Lost,* or brainstorming "Old MacDonald words" (i.e., featuring the vowels EIEIO in order, like PREDIGESTION), or composing "Tom Swifties," quotations linked to punny adverbs (e.g., "*I got the first three wrong,* he said forthrightly"—that is, getting the fourth one right). Here he is again, twinkle in his eye, trying to sex up logology wherever possible, noting that in the song "Sodomy" from the 1960s rock musical *Hair,* the word "sodomy" is sung to the melody notes So, Do, Mi. And here he is, sitting up straighter, removing his glasses with professorial resolve, explaining that the term "homophobia" "was originally coined and used as a political/analytical device whose major point was relabelling: instead of homosexuality being a . . . perversion, the negative attitudes toward homosexuals were to be considered [perverse]," or arguing a reader-submitted story denigrating "skin-tight denims or other queer dress," and featuring a joke at the expense of gay men who died in the AIDS epidemic, has no place in *Word Ways*.

Even the outlet's title had a double meaning: *Word Ways* was about play, sure, but Eric was keenly aware of how words are one way we make a life; how language, playful or otherwise, shapes our world. Eric strove for linguistic openness in his new profession, both in the consulting room (discussing sex directly decades before it was commonplace; ever the engineer, his blog includes posts like "Making Your Vibrator Really Hum") and in his community of practice (a member of PCFINE, not a tech support group but the Psychodynamic Couple and Family Institute of New England, he'd been lobbying for years to change "Couple" to "Relationship," as he began seeing more non-monogamous clients).

He'd done the same for his previous career in crosswords. In 1996, Faith Eckler, who with her husband, Ross, went by *Faro* in the National Puzzlers' League, circulated a round-robin letter airing her frustrations with the *Times* puzzle, now under the direction of Will Shortz. Eckler cited slang ("The sense of 'get down, so to speak' = boogie escapes me") and "the frequent use of clues which depend on a knowledge of pop culture. I see a clue like 'record producer Brian' and haven't the faintest idea who he is (or was)." Not having heard of (or heard) Brian Eno is confusing, though perhaps no major sin; longing for the era when ENO was clued instead as [Wine: Comb. form; var.] strikes a darker chord. Shortz replied ("There's a generation gap the other way, too. Just this week I got a letter from a young reader [who] keeps seeing references in crosswords to Dogpatch, and he wants to know who or what Dogpatch is!") and Eric backed him up. "I'm firmly on the side of Will Shortz in this matter," he wrote:

> Crosswords have always been full of pop culture. The peculiar thing is that the pop culture in crosswords has remained the same while decades have passed. I remember vividly solving puzzles when I was ten or so, and I quickly learned that "apple cider girl" was "Ida."

I had no idea what it meant, and it was a real thrill twenty years later when I was playing through a collection of early 20th century sheet music and came across "Ida, Sweet as Apple Cider."

When I was ten, that clue was referring to the pop culture of my grandparents! Now I'm an adult, and there's yet another adult generation after me, and it's about time that my and their culture began being reflected in puzzles.

If anything, Eric had for years been trying to make the puzzle racier. "Why are crossword puzzles so damn dull?" he wondered in a 1993 issue of *Crossword Magazine*. Margaret Farrar, the architect of modern crossword conventions and the *Times*'s inaugural puzzle editor, devised what's called the "Sunday Morning Breakfast Test"—the notion that crosswords should avoid cross words, ought to chew with minimal noise, activate only the mind and politely elide the body. No "death, disease, war and taxes," Farrar wrote; the *Times*'s early puzzles nevertheless, as we will see, almost compulsively reference the destruction of World War II. To Eric, this was family-friendliness with an outdated sense of the family; it belittled the crossword as a medium by pretending to know what its solvership could handle. (It wasn't strictly the fault of editors after Farrar, either; "I'm friends with most of them," wrote Eric, "and these folks are as kinky as they come.") The therapist in Eric thought sex wasn't so weighty that it couldn't appear in a crossword: "The things that make us sweat, the things that make us hot, the things that make us uncomfortable, are precisely the things that make us feel most alive." The crossword lover in Eric wanted others to invest the puzzle, as he did, with the cultural heft of movies or books: "Most people in the business, including publishers, editors, and even constructors themselves, just don't take crossword puzzles seriously as a form."

■

The first time I speak with Eric, he asks if my name comes from the Hebrew word for "gift." His childhood best friend was named Nat

Hellerstein, and he remembers learning that Nathaniel (literally, "God has given") and Jonathan (the "Jo" is cognate to Jehovah or Jah) were essentially identical names. The same, he discovered, is true of the Greek-derived Theodore and Dorothy. It astonished him, this biblical connective tissue lurking behind all these common names, linking their histories like a letter-based predestination.

When Eric joined the National Puzzlers' League, he selected the nom *Eric*. It's rare for a Krewe member to use their real name, rarer still to offer the tongue-in-cheek origin stories Eric did. On the League's website, Eric explains *Eric* was the most common male name given in Sweden in 1973, which he happened to know "as a longtime fan of all things related to Stockholm." Also, *Eric* is the solution to the cryptic clue [Wild rice], since "Eric" and "rice" are anagrams. Also, *Eric* is a reversal of the French word *ciré*, a fabric with a brilliant finish. *Et voilà*, Eric.

At the time he was trying to be witty, but "speaking now as a therapist," Eric thinks the nom represents "a deep psychological thing that runs throughout my life." Eric likes being one of the crowd, but he's drawn to crowds where he can distinguish himself in ways he is sometimes oblivious to, where it's comfortable to be different among the different. The only man in his Lesbian Literature course at Brown; the only man in his Group Work course during his Counseling Psychology master's. He liked playing avant-garde German board games with his friends but didn't (as the rest of them did) learn the language, in order to read, like a Marxist study group, the instructions in the original. He would join the NPL, but rather than take a pseudonym he would produce numerous "pseudo-derivations" of *Eric*; after all, he'd always, like all of us, been a fiction, a phrase that meant different things depending on context, a word whose etymological roots dove deep and logarithmic in many directions at once.

The more I talked to Eric, the more I felt connected not only to the various stories of his life, but to the fact that the stories of his life were various. There were cosmetic resonances: we were sons of math-loving fathers; we'd both gone to Brown, bonding over how the signage in Providence, Rhode Island, could, for the length of a street, dictate your behavior: on POWER you'd drop to the concrete for push-ups, on BENEVOLENT you'd give anyone the clothes off your back, on HOPE you'd believe it was all going to be okay. And there were aspirational resonances: Eric seemed genuinely happy, having converted his diverse interests into three distinct careers, all of them fastened and fascinated by language. (Eric has a folder on his computer called "Résumés," with three files laying out three histories, each of them buffed and polished to look as though "I was made to do this job my whole life.") But I felt Eric's story extending not only backward but forward, that the kind of motley crossword lover he was—mathematical yet literary, playful yet politically engaged, highbrow yet raunchy—was precisely the profile of many of the figures I describe in this book, and precisely the kind of contradictory predilection the crossword quilts together.

On December 11, 2022, Eric suffered a hemorrhagic stroke of his cerebellum. He's lucky to be alive; around 50 percent of patients die in a month, half of those within the first two days. When we first spoke in April 2023, I immediately asked if his language had been affected, then regretted it. But he was fine, he said, just some residual vertigo. The neurologists don't know why the stroke happened, or how he recovered his cognition so quickly. He says he repeated the French he was learning to himself in the ICU. I imagined him, was almost ashamed to imagine him, saying *ciré ciré ciré, épée épée épée*—as if the accent marks were stray neurons in need of repair—or an item from James Joyce's *Finnegans Wake* I'd just seen in *Word Ways* because it's the only "word" with five or more Q's: *Quoiquoiquoiquoiquoiquoiquoiq!* In Joyce's *Wake,* it's preceded by the line: "He lifts the lifewand and the dumb speak." I remembered analyses of Broca's aphasia I'd read studying neuroscience in college, how stroke patients whose language had abandoned them could sometimes recruit the right-hemispheric circuitry devoted to music instead—could sing even if they could not speak. I imagined Eric's new partner, a professional musician he calls his "sweetie," getting him to belt "Ida, Sweet as Apple Cider" or "Sodomy" from *Hair.*

In the hospital, besides checking his French, Eric thought about his clients. "I could do couples therapy right now, if I could only sit up," he remembers thinking. I ask him if crosswords inform his therapy; the famed French psychoanalyst Jacques Lacan, after all, advised his analysts-in-training: *"Faîtes des mots croisés."* ("Do crossword puzzles.") But he says no. He has more of an engineering mindset as a therapist. His sessions run less on *Get what you want* than *Want what you get*. He says reframing can fix anything: a broken heart, a failing partnership, a flagging mind. "If I had to say it," he says, "in one sentence: What is the best story we can find that's gonna work for you?"

CHAPTER 2

Crosswords for Fun and Profit

[Who's there, in a joke], 9 letters*

—REBECCA GOLDSTEIN AND CLAIRE L. RIMKUS,
 "out and outstanding," 2022

In 2009, the year I turned eighteen, I was Will Shortz's summer intern. Mornings, I'd wake up at my childhood home in Midwood, Brooklyn, take the Q to the 4 to Grand Central, then Metro-North to Westchester, an almost two-hour pilgrimage to Shortz's home in a tidy hamlet called Pleasantville. The stations, once you're out of the Bronx, oscillate between wrought-iron names and marshmallow ones: Valhalla, then Mount Pleasant, then Hawthorne, then Pleasantville. I was an outer-borough kid, son of a public school teacher and a waitress; I smirked at the fact that Mount Pleasant, not Valhalla, was a suburban cemetery, a cul-de-sac in extremis; up here, words could only mean so much.

If it was raining or fiercely cold, Shortz would pick me up, but usually I'd walk from the Pleasantville station to Great Oak Lane, in the middle of which sat Shortz's heaving Tudor-style home. Outside, the structure's black half-timbered detailing and light-gray stucco looked like a cozy, agreeable crossword: bowed by suburban breeze, gracefully aged. Inside, his house is part museum, part Elks lodge, all wood panels and rafters and leaning towers of Sudoku books. Glass cases teem with puzzle knickknacks from centuries past. Shortz once let me hold an original Sam Loyd puzzle, a Trick Donkeys more than a hundred years old. There are crossword cuff links from the craze of the 1920s. There's an oddly beautiful bracelet made up of enamel 5-by-5 crosswords connected by sterling silver links. The clock in the second-floor office is a crossword; the hour and minute hands, you might have guessed, are pencils.

Shortz was the first adult I met who worked from home. He'd greet me at the front door donning crossword print sweatpants, confirming in two visual languages that my workday would be gimmicky, but relaxed. I typed up email correspondence dictated by Shortz, getting faster and faster at keying the dreamed of "Crosswords—Yes!" subject line to lucky submitters. I prodded about maybe swapping AOL for Gmail. I typeset and formatted puzzles in the *Times*'s proprietary system, thrilled I could, pinky finger on the Backspace key, disappear a lavishly serifed letter in that iconic font, a fairy-tale ogre lugging a magic eraser.

One week, I descended a flight of indisputably haunted stairs to the cellar, where I was to delicately comb through a shelved archive of the *New York Herald Tribune,* printed during the crossword craze of the 1920s. If an advertisement, article, or cartoon referenced crosswords, I recorded its issue, page, and title. Shortz, a history buff and the only person to have majored in Enigmatology, was at work on some kind of authoritative compendium. Mostly, I took pictures of Jazz Age flappers on the Society page, and porkpie-hatted Dapper Dans who, when interviewed, said things like "Most of the time I smoke a pipe, but a pipe won't do for all occasions." That seemed true. I said, in the basement of the home of the crossword editor of *The New York Times,* "Take a letter!," over and over in a mock 1920s accent, thinking it was the funniest thing; I have no idea if he heard me, thinking in turn it was a kind of displaced rebellion, since I had to take dictation myself. I mooned over a 1925 broadside called "A Philosophical Discussion of Radio," which emerged around these reverent, thin-lined sketches of transistor circuits; they struck me as beautiful the way schematic drawings then always struck me, desperate in their imagined perfection, as beautiful; alongside the sketches leaned breathless, italic testimony illuminating technology's brave new world. After the summer, I made a Facebook album of these sepia slivers of interwar life and tagged some college friends in them, titling the album, embarrassingly I think, "In my younger and more vulnerable years . . ."

Whatever my youth, Shortz trusted me with editorial work. Every Friday, before proceeding to the study, he'd test his NPR *Weekend Edition* quiz on me in the living room, toughening it up for on-air contestants if I got the answers too readily. (There was a radio setup in a back room off the parlor that resembled, in my memory at least, an antique cockpit.) Upstairs, clipboard and pencil in hand, he'd let me suggest new clues for publication, for pop culture entries in particular; I once ventured, successfully, a new clue for LEIA: [Film character known for her buns]. When, that June, a woman with a voice identical to my grandma Emma's left a boiling voicemail on Shortz's phone—she'd taken offense to the entry JEWFRO in a Joel Fagliano Monday puzzle, offering a thicket of unreason I've forgotten the specific thorns of—I, a nice Jewish boy just like Joel, advised there was no need to respond; the entry, I assured Shortz, was fine, unnoteworthy. I didn't really have a strong opinion one way or the other, but it made no sense to me, at the time, to make such a ruckus over a game.

Occasionally we had visitors. Ellen Ripstein, a celebrated speed-solver and 2001 American Crossword Puzzle Tournament champion, would deliver a crate of paper submissions—a hundred or so manila envelopes mailed to the *Times*'s office in midtown—to Shortz's home every week. Organizers of local crossword tournaments—there was an annual one held in Bryant Park, another in a church in Jackson Heights, Queens—drove to Westchester to fit their vans with the easel-like stands, gridded dry-erase boards, and fist-sized adhesive squares that speed-solvers competed on in the championship rounds, and which Shortz kept in the garage. Paula Gamache, a constructor who lived in nearby Rye, came by here and there to help with correspondence. Gamache was legendary in puzzle circles for stamping SKINNY BITCH—[Saucily titled best-selling diet book]—at 1-Across in a 2008 *Times* Saturday, eliciting whispers of *You can do that?* from constructors, and no doubt a mixtape's worth of miffed voicemails on Shortz's machine. Gamache always wore heels and a leather jacket, never said a word to me and barely one or two to Shortz before vanishing with gum-popping nonchalance into the study, where her heel-tapping, the chatter of an early 2000s Mac keyboard, and more snapping gum mixed in industrial syncopation, like a click language for dominatrices. A no-nonsense derivatives trader in her fifties, she seemed to relish sending the dreaded "Sorry, but this theme didn't excite Will" rejection emails, and her nonexcitement at Shortz's nonexcitement excited me. This was Shortz's stock rejection line, sharpened to initialism (TDEME—theme didn't excite me enough); once, a constructor on the receiving end of one too many TDEMEs grumbled she ought to include a few pills of Viagra in the envelope with her next submission.

Mostly, Shortz and I worked alone. If we needed to verify the spelling of a song title, Shortz would heft a *Billboard Encyclopedia of Music* from the shelf, while I, much more quickly, would google it. "Hmf," Shortz would say, the folksy, equine sound he made while thinking, "Hmf hmf." If we needed a new puzzle to edit, Shortz padded to the study's closet, unlatched a creaking door, and pawed through shelves marked by day of week, sheafs of accepted puzzles piled high on each (acceptance and publication could be years apart, and Shortz was always balancing theme variety with submission date). It was a charmingly disorganized, disarmingly small operation; sometimes he'd take a puzzle off the shelf seemingly at random, ignoring the one on top. An angel shouting UNFAIR! and a devil grinning WHIMSICAL! capped my shoulders. I thought I might take advantage of it.

I mentioned how many young constructors now attended Brown University, where I ran a Puzzle Club; Zoe Wheeler, Jonah Kagan, and I, who'd all published puzzles in the *Times*, had begun teaching our friends the basics of construction. The *Times* had run a special week of puzzles the previous year, and had one ready for the coming September—in 2008, "Teen Puzzlemaker Week," and soon in 2009,

"Half-Century Puzzle Week," in which every constructor had been contributing puzzles to the *Times* for fifty years or more—so I proposed "Brown University Puzzlemaker Week." It had less pomp and circumstance than a string of wunderkinder or accomplished veterans, but Shortz liked the idea. In 2010, when it ran, I couldn't believe my suggestion in the second-floor study kicked it all off. Our club was profiled on NPR, in the *Times* and *The Chronicle of Higher Education,* but more importantly, we were invited to an episode of *The Martha Stewart Show* focused on puzzles. During a commercial break, we asked Stewart if she was a solver. "Well, I did a lot of crosswords when I was in prison," Stewart said, winking.

Throughout the summer, Shortz flickered between an avuncular image and a brotherly one. I wasn't, I find myself hasty to assert, easily intimidated by larger-than-life figures, and Shortz's sturdy, midwestern folksiness discouraged it. Anyway, working-class city kids tend to flinch at demanded genuflection. The environment offered, or we projected, a sense that survival required a leery competence, one correlated with age, responsibility: riding the subway alone, knowing which strangers to talk to, and so on. But fluency with highbrow media—of which the *Times* puzzle was exemplum—could act like a cultural fake ID. I knew Shakespeare quotes because of the crossword, I knew words like INURE and ARIA and TOILE because of the crossword, I knew who ASTA was, what an EPEE did, which colors resembled ECRU or OCHER. Solving the crossword meant I knew, or knew of, what my friends' fancy Manhattan parents knew; *writing* the crossword only raised my index of precociousness—every metropolitan parent, part bouncer and part admissions officer, keeps a mental list of impressive kids and their odd hobbies. It was, though I couldn't have articulated this at the time, the cheapest method I saw for tapping into the glamour of the adult world, a faux-worldliness that gave me a world; a rite, however wobbly or elitist, of passing.

We were a study in contrasts in that way, Shortz and I—the outerborough kid stepping quickly, as if out of necessity, into adulthood; the adult who'd crafted a job—a life!—centered on a slice of childlike play. There were hints of a willed arrested development: he ate like a latchkey kid; lunches were a can of Campbell's soup and packaged chicken patties. (I'd grown up with an immigrant mom who cooked ornate, multi-course Mediterranean dinners and a dad with an adventurous palate, and devoured Shortz's fallout shelter meals with something like reverse exoticism.) As we ate, he'd put on vinyls of his favorite bands, with his most beloved being, of course, Green Day. He liked all the 1990s and 2000s alt rock mohawked rebels; I remember a week where we blasted the Vines's *Highly Evolved* every single afternoon. One day, I twiddled my thumbs as Shortz took phone calls with accountants, real estate agents, and other men who wore suits in daylight; as far as I could tell, Shortz was all but liquidating his puzzle fortune—the millions amassed through crossword, KenKen, and Sudoku books, his winsome caricature on their covers—to purchase a warehouse in Pleasantville, and turn it into a local table tennis club. (Shortz, a devoted and talented player, drove to nearby towns like Tarrytown every night after editing to get in a few hours of competition.) Double the play—spend down your game-gotten riches so you can more easily play another game: it sounded like the fever dream of a five-year-old, by turns earnestly utopian and head-scratching, and by summer's end, I couldn't tell if that was a good or bad thing.

▮

Huddled like gargoyles made of terra-cotta and limestone, reliefs and colonettes like ears leaning to ingest the scuttlebutt from City Hall over on Broadway, the buildings on lower Manhattan's Park Row—"Newspaper Row" in late-nineteenth-century parlance—housed the *New York Tribune,* the New York *Sun,* and *The New York Times.* None of these enormous structures, at the turn of the twentieth century, featured a crossword editor scribbling inside.

The seeds of what would be called the crossword craze were tilled a few buildings over, at 99 Park Row, where the sixteen-story *New York World* headquarters rose like an overgrown state fair pumpkin to solemnly scrape the sky. At 309 feet, the building was for a time the world's tallest, outdoing Trinity Church on Broadway (284 feet)—"physical

ratification," write historians Edwin Burrows and Mike Wallace in *Gotham*, "of the passage of metropolitan power from sacred to secular." That was at the behest of Joseph Pulitzer, who'd bought the *World* in 1883, magicked it through swaggery self-advertising and gonzo gimmickry into a seven-figure daily circulation—the most popular in the city—and asked his architect, George Post, to design with his paper's supremacy in mind. Construction was completed in 1890. Pulitzer had an office in the glittering golden dome that topped the building like a papal miter, with frescoed ceilings and walls of embossed leather. He could look down his nose and pooh-pooh a full six stories above the *Tribune*'s puny campanile; his editors on the eleventh floor joked they could open a window and "spit on the *Sun*"; once, so the story goes, someone emerged onto Pulitzer's top floor and barked, "Is God in?"

Behind that bombast slinked a weekly color supplement called FUN, whose riddles, ads, comics, and one-liners were a tabloidist's kitsch, the Park Row newsies tittering by a French Renaissance column as in the golden dome above Pulitzer cleared his throat, swizzled a whiskey. FUN launched in 1911 and by 1913 was the charge of the Liverpool-born Arthur Wynne. Plagued by writer's block, empty print inches, and a Christmastime deadline, Wynne, in December 1913, came up with a diamond-shaped interlocking set of squares, alongside which he'd written clues; rather than Across and Down, Wynne indicated the clues by their beginning and ending squares, 4-26 instead of 4-Down. Above the grid, he instructed readers, "Fill in the small squares with words which agree with the following definitions." He called his creation a "Word-Cross Puzzle."

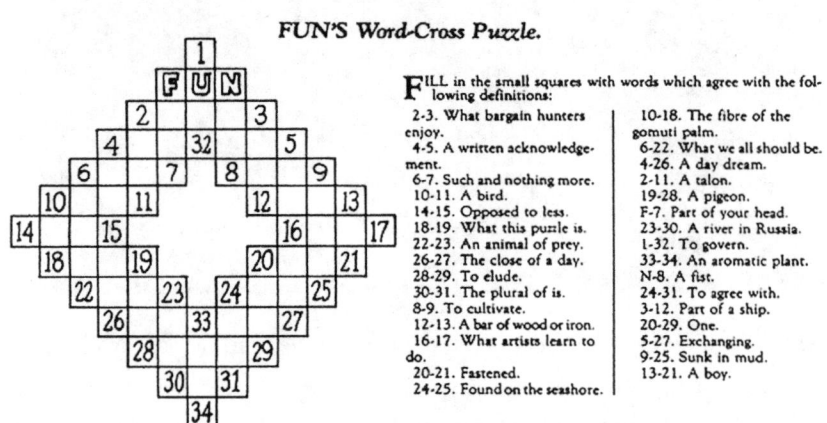

FUN'S *Word-Cross Puzzle.*

FILL in the small squares with words which agree with the following definitions:

2-3. What bargain hunters enjoy.
4-5. A written acknowledgement.
6-7. Such and nothing more.
10-11. A bird.
14-15. Opposed to less.
18-19. What this puzzle is.
22-23. An animal of prey.
26-27. The close of a day.
28-29. To elude.
30-31. The plural of is.
8-9. To cultivate.
12-13. A bar of wood or iron.
16-17. What artists learn to do.
20-21. Fastened.
24-25. Found on the seashore.

10-18. The fibre of the gomuti palm.
6-22. What we all should be.
4-26. A day dream.
2-11. A talon.
19-28. A pigeon.
F-7. Part of your head.
23-30. A river in Russia.
1-32. To govern.
33-34. An aromatic plant.
N-8. A fist.
24-31. To agree with.
3-12. Part of a ship.
20-29. One.
5-27. Exchanging.
9-25. Sunk in mud.
13-21. A boy.

Wynne, in retrospect, can seem more tech entrepreneur than inventor. The Word-Cross resembled the "cross-word enigma" found in the popular British children's magazine *St. Nicholas,* which asked for a word gestured at by rhymed cryptic clues, and which the Liverpudlian Wynne would likely have encountered as a kid. Instead, his great innovation was packaging: where newspaper games often stopped at instructions, leaving any grid-drawing to the solver, Wynne, deploying the latest in printing capability, stamped the blank puzzle grid directly on the pages of FUN. He'd created, as *Times* writer Deb Amlen puckishly put it, the "first mobile game."

And a viral one at that. Nearly overnight, the puzzle became a sensation, wrenching readerly attention away from other sections and foreshadowing the viability of a subscriber model: "The only thing I give a hang about," wrote one solver, "on your page or in your Sunday magazine is the crossword." Two weeks in, a typesetting error spun the *World*'s puzzle around the axis of its hyphen, and the Word-Cross became the Cross-Word. Seven weeks in, Wynne, who'd so far written every crossword himself, included a note atop the February 1 puzzle, which had the breeziness of a seven-*year* retrospective:

> FUN's cross-word puzzles apparently are getting more popular than ever. The puzzle editor has received from readers many interesting new cross-word puzzles, which he will be glad to use from time to time. It is more difficult to make up a cross-word puzzle than it is to solve one. If you doubt this, try to make one yourself.

The dare worked. Maybe too well: a year later, a more frantic headnote introduced the March 7, 1915, puzzle:

> Everywhere your eyes rest on boxes, barrels and crates, each one filled with cross-word puzzles patiently awaiting publication. However, the editor of FUN hopes to use them all in time. The puzzle editor has kindly figured out that the present supply will last until the second week in December, 2100.

This was Wynne's second innovation, and it was a prescient one: molding amateurs into freelancers. Wynne, writes Ian Bogost, Simon Ferrari, and Bobby Schweizer in *Newsgames: Journalism at Play,* had ginned up "a nearly endless supply of puzzles, had at very low cost: an early example of what Web 2.0 proponents call *user-generated content.*" It was an economic model of unpaid or precarious labor that would spread like wildfire as worker power declined in the late twentieth century, and which the monetization demands of the social media era would exacerbate; all of it started with the crossword.

By the time I was working for Shortz, the *Times* puzzle was the gold standard of the grid, but initially that paper would resist adding a puzzle. Meanwhile, everyone else got in on the action: *The Pittsburgh Press* began publishing one in 1916, *The Boston Globe* in 1917. In January 1925,

Time listed twenty-three papers nationwide that carried crosswords, including *The Washington Post, The Kansas City Star,* the *Chicago Tribune,* and the *San Francisco Chronicle.* The nascent craze seemed concentrated in New York, where it'd begun: nine of the twenty-three were Manhattan dailies. That *Time* article pitted a New Yorker against a Wisconsinite on the question of longevity:

> Said one Rudolph E. Vogel of Milwaukee, antagonist: "This cross-word craze will positively end by June!"

> Said one Alfred Coster Schermerhorn of Manhattan, protagonist: "The crossword puzzle is here to stay!"

Schermerhorn, like any Manhattan protagonist, was right. (After all, *Time* had asked a Schermerhorn—a descendant of the early Dutch settlers of New York whose ship-chandler family name still adorns a subway stop, a Brooklyn street, and a row of South Street seaport counting houses—about longevity.) By 1924, the *World* had upped its puzzle frequency from weekly to daily. Also in 1924, the *Herald* and *Tribune* merged to form the *New York Herald Tribune* (the archives of which I flipped through in Shortz's basement) and not only added a daily crossword column, but began hosting an annual solving tournament: the National All Comers Cross-Word Tournament. The inaugural competition's winner, Ruth von Phul of Manhattan, was so fast that newspapers began including her solving time next to that day's puzzle as a kind of red toreador's flag, a preview of the rage-inducing digital game leaderboards almost a century to come.

The very first issue of *The New Yorker,* published on February 21, 1925, featured a column by the fictional "Busybody" called "Jottings About Town," with wry, self-evident one-liners about city life. "Many people may be interested to know that the real name of Edna Ferber, the writer, is Edna Ferber"—it was that sort of languid deadpan. Something else, here, from Busybody: "Judging from the number of solvers in the subway and 'L' trains, the crossword puzzle bids fair to become a fad with New Yorkers."

It would, after some resistance, bid fair to become a fad with one New Yorker in particular: Margaret Farrar. She was born Margaret Petherbridge in 1897 in Brooklyn, where her father was an executive at the National Licorice Company, the inventors of Twizzlers. She studied at the genteel Berkeley Institute in Park Slope, then on to Smith College in Northampton, Massachusetts. After graduating in 1919, she returned to New York, where a roommate helped her land a position as secretary to the executive editor of the *New York World,* John O'Hara Cosgrave. Hoping to shift into journalism, Farrar was crushed when Cosgrave assigned her to assist Wynne with the crossword. At that point, in 1921, she hadn't solved a single one. The puzzle was "a sort of necessary nuisance in the obscurest corner of the paper" and hers was a "ridiculous" job. Like a black-and-white Bartleby, she preferred selecting each week's grid solely on aesthetic appeal, forwarding it to typesetters never having uncapped her pen; when readers shook their fists about errors or misprintings, she dismissed their complaints as "the work of cranks."

In 1922, a new writer moved into the office next door to Farrar's. The *World* had hired legendary columnist Franklin Pierce Adams—F.P.A., as he signed his work; born Franklin Leopold Adams but changed on the occasion of his bar mitzvah to sound more presidential—away from the rival *Tribune,* Pulitzer no doubt grinning wickedly in his golden dome. F.P.A. was a versatile wordsmith. His column, "The Conning Tower," helped launch the writerly careers of Dorothy Parker, Moss Hart, George S. Kaufman, and Edna St. Vincent Millay. One afternoon back in 1910, so the story goes, hoping to duck out early to see the New York Giants at the Polo Grounds, F.P.A. was held up by the foreman at the *Evening Mail*'s newsroom. Like Arthur Wynne before him, the foreman needed eight more lines to fill out column space. F.P.A. quickly produced "Baseball's Sad Lexicon," a poem about the natty and well-oiled 6-4-3 double plays turned by Chicago Cubs shortstop Joe Tinker, second baseman Johnny Evers, and first baseman Frank Chance, all of whose polysemic surnames, like the vowelly ALOU family's after them, had the makings of a crossword entry. The poem goes:

> *These are the saddest of possible words:*
> *"Tinker to Evers to Chance."*
> *Trio of bear cubs, and fleeter than birds,*
> *Tinker and Evers and Chance.*
> *Ruthlessly pricking our gonfalon bubble,*
> *Making a Giant hit into a double—*
> *Words that are heavy with nothing but trouble:*
> *"Tinker to Evers to Chance."*

Gonfalon! An old word for "pennant"—put that in a crossword. (Someone would, in a 1963 Sunday; FPA, as it happens, is an answer in the inaugural *New York Times* crossword, written by Charles Erlenkotter and edited in 1942 by Margaret Farrar, who would become the paper's first puzzle editor; EVERS has dutifully been clued as [Diamond middleman?] and [Tinker's target?].)

F.P.A. reserved a few "sad" and "heavy" words for Farrar. He, it turned out, was a crossword fanatic, and wouldn't stand for the *World*'s sinking standards. Every Monday, a little too glum, he'd march into her office to air his grievances about the weekend's puzzle. Still, when she finally solved the fruits of her Bartlebyesque shirking, she was appalled to feel

> the throes of acute agony that come to all solvers of puzzles on discovering definitions left out, numbers wrong, hideously warped definitions, words not to be found inside of any known dictionary, foreign words—very foreign words—and words that had no right to be dragged out of their native obscurity. Then and there, with my left hand reposing on a dictionary and my right raised in air, I took an oath to edit the crosswords to the essence of perfection.

Now, there would be rules; now, there would be systems. The puzzle would be set a week in advance, not at the eleventh hour, so Farrar could examine and when necessary amend the clues, grid designs, or typography. Entries would be mostly dictionary words, and sourceable; out with the arcane, in with the interesting. Grids should avoid "unchecked" letters: each square should appear in both a horizontal and a vertical answer. Clues, unlike in Wynne's confusing start-to-finish convention, would be numbered only by starting square, and indicate whether they went across or down: 3-Horizontal instead of 3-7. Grids should be rotationally symmetric, and sparse with black squares, to allow for all-over interlock. Wynne noted in 1914 that "cross-word puzzles for FUN continue to arrive in all shapes in sizes"; Farrar would go on to insist on uniform shape (square) and predictable size (odd-numbered by odd-numbered grids, usually 23-by-23 for the Sunday puzzle). She paid more attention to solver response. She conferred with constructors, incorporated their advice. She'd run the puzzle as smoothly as a 6-4-3 double play, Tinker to Evers to Chance. She'd begun, in other words, to manage the crossword like a product.

◼

You could write the biography of the crossword as a recital of late-nineteenth- and early-twentieth-century changes in technology and business, which is to say you could write it as a series of double plays: smooth movements of hands that belied, even deliberately hid, the painstaking labor and hard-won skill behind them.

In the beginning was the *World,* its five-floor gilded dome gleaming like the cortex of a king. When Pulitzer bought the *World* from financier Jay Gould in 1883, the paper had a daily circulation of 22,000. A year later that number was nearly 100,000, by 1898 it would be half a million, and soon the *World,* under Pulitzer's direction, would be the first nationwide paper to reach a million daily subscribers. When Pulitzer contracted George Post to build him his skyscraper, he'd envisioned a dome that symbolized "the highest ideals of journalism: liberty, justice, democracy and 'true Americanism'"—never mind that it was his tabloidist's knack for gossip, gonzo stunts, and melodrama that made the *World* so popular. And when Post—or more accurately the army of skilled workers behind him—completed construction in 1890, the intricate red sandstone façade, Renaissance ornamentation, and figurative sculpture "gave the tower an Old World character and made

BROADWAY CABLE CAR POSSIBILITIES.

it look to be made of masonry" rather than the advanced metal-cage construction—the crossword grid of steel bones—that Post had used in the walls. In the metal was the secular skeleton of progress; in the sandstone, according to the *World*'s own booklet printed for the building's debut, "there is a sermon."

In 1893, Pulitzer became the second newspaperman to purchase a high-speed rotary color press (those early adopters at the Chicago *Inter Ocean* beat him to it). Again the sacred and the profane, the high and the low, were subject to a business-led switcheroo: Pulitzer planned to use the press's bright reds and blues to reprint masterpieces of Western art, but was convinced by his Sunday editor, Morrill Goddard, to launch the first-ever color comic supplement, which would morph into Arthur Wynne's FUN. The inaugural issue ran on May 21, 1893, and, in a bid for market share, cost a nickel—half the price of the "fancy weeklies."

And Wynne, often credited with "inventing" the crossword, would later admit "all I did was take an old idea as old as language and modernize it," in this case by capitalizing on the era's high-speed presses and printing the blank grid directly on the page. Or, at least, by asking it be printed that way: formatting the crossword was so labor-intensive and unforgiving a task that Wynne's typesetters frequently rebelled at the tedium, omitting clue numbers, decapitating definitions; Wynne seemed not to care about their carelessness.

Inventor or not, Wynne was business-minded, and tried to patent the crossword. At the time, it would've cost some $35 to file and issue a patent, and a typical patent lawyer's fee would have been around $70—in total, well over a thousand of today's dollars. Wynne didn't have it, and asked the *World* to cough it up. Business manager F. D. White and assistant manager F. D. Carruthers—their twinned initials apparently predestining the men for money management—informed Wynne it was too risky an investment for so fleeting a phenomenon; the crossword "was just one of those puzzle fads that people would get tired of within six months." The crossword, thanks to their forecast, remained open to all.

Why did people have so much time for puzzle fads? By the late nineteenth century, large-scale industrial production and craft deskilling—a process by which skilled workers are replaced by introducing technologies operated by lower-paid nonspecialists—had led, writes cultural historian Ian Gordon, "to work becoming something one did for a living rather than the way one lived." Middle- and working-class Americans emerged from gunmetal boxes labeled OFFICE or FACTORY into a newly clarified sphere of life: LEISURE. Into this glassy orb rushed spectator sports, circuses, minstrel shows, vaudeville, amusement parks, dime novels, humor magazines, and so on. In the prosperous aftermath of World War I—with Americans "bathed in money" and reveling in military success—the fads took on a competitive cast, as though recapturing the spirit of armed conflict, but aiming it, with much lower stakes, at lavish frivolity: flagpole sitting, yo-yoing contests, beauty pageants, Mah Jongg. *Leisure,* after all, is forever in a double play with its etymological second baseman, *license,* from the Latin *licere,* "to be allowed." There was a sense in this period, not just that Americans wanted to play, but that finally, they were allowed to.

One winter evening in 1924 Mr. Richard L. Simon came home from dinner at his aunt Wixie's house with an idea.

He was a man of letters, now, and that's why Wixie had invited him over. After Columbia and a tour in World War I, Simon had gone to work for a friend of his father's—a sugar importer who liked the way Simon, born to a musical family, played the organ. Next he had a stint as a piano salesman. On a house call, he tried selling one to Max Lincoln Schuster, then an editor of an automotive magazine, who wasn't buying. Spotting a copy of Romain Rolland's *Jean-Christophe,* a novel about a German composer, Simon switched the conversation to books, and the two men bonded over mutual literary and musical tastes.

Simon stopped selling pianos and started selling books at Boni & Liveright ("BONE-eye," "LIVE-right," like a Pynchonesque law firm) and within a year, a promotion to sales manager at his back, he had amassed some $8,000 in savings and pledges from relatives and friends. It was the dawn of modernism; Horace Liveright had just then come back from Paris, where he'd offered T. S. Eliot a $150 advance to publish his book-length poem, *The Waste Land,* which one critic would later claim "*may* be a great poem; on the other hand it may be just a rather pompous cross-word puzzle." Simon announced he was leaving Boni & Liveright to establish a publishing house with Max Schuster.

("It's a terrible time to walk out on me," Liveright moaned. "Can you suggest anyone to replace you?" Simon called up his high school and college buddy, Bennett Cerf, who'd edited Columbia's humor magazine, *The Jester,* and was then disentangling himself from a job at a Wall Street brokerage, where he'd gamely lost a good deal of money shorting the stock of Piggly Wiggly grocery stores. Cerf had always wanted to work in publishing and resented Simon's meteoric rise in the industry, later grumbling "Dick Simon never read ten books through in his entire life." After a strange courtship ritual—in which, as a favor to Liveright, Cerf accompanied the writer Theodore Dreiser to an afternoon baseball game that the latter man, bored, sulky, whisked them from around the sixth inning—Cerf took the job. Later, once Boni & Liveright went bankrupt and Cerf purchased the majority of their assets, he'd go on to found Random House. As smooth as an old-boy handshake: Liveright to Simon to Cerf.)

Simon and Schuster had a business license, an office on 37 West 57th Street, and a telephone operator. But they lacked a debut manuscript. At dinner that chilly January night, Aunt Wixie asked her nephew if he knew where she might buy a book of crossword puzzles; accounts vary as to whether she was asking for herself or for her niece. Either way, Simon was intrigued—there was no such book; maybe there ought to be—and soon he and Schuster were on their way from midtown to Newspaper Row, to consult the crossword experts of the *World*. Before meeting with Margaret Farrar (then Petherbridge) and her new editorial colleagues Prosper Buranelli and Gregory Hartswick ("surely a formidable trio of proper nouns," Petherbridge to Buranelli to Hartswick), the pair looked in on their old pal, F.P.A.

"There are two friends of mine out here," F.P.A. informed Farrar, "with an idea for a book. They're nice guys but discourage them." F.P.A. was certain his colleagues would "lose their shirts." The *World*, on hearing that sobering notion of a *book* of *crosswords,* pronounced it "the worst idea since Prohibition." Sellers advised Simon and Schuster that the public wasn't interested in puzzle books. Undeterred, the two men made an offer: Farrar, Buranelli, and Hartswick would be paid the "then-munificent advance" of $25 each to sift through the *World*'s "drawerful of unpublished puzzles" and prepare fifty for the book; the authors of those puzzles would be paid nothing.

As publication drew nearer, Simon and Schuster began to have second thoughts. They might have seen galleys of their book-to-be, which lacked a traditional cover and instead nakedly displayed the collection's first crossword, like a courtly fool stripped of his garments. The very first Down clue (called Vertical 1) came with a kind of talky preface from Farrar, Buranelli, and Hartswick, but it seemed almost designed to mock Simon and Schuster: "Now, VERTICAL 1—let's see, an exclamation in two letters, beginning with H. Ha! Ha!" They worried they'd be pigeonholed, "typed as game-book publishers at the start" and "hooted out of the publishing business." They spiraled, succumbing to "intimations of early bankruptcy," felt they were courting "the disgrace of their good name," these serious men of letters pumping the words SIMON and SCHUSTER with trivial hot air, until the letters were fat illegible balloons pricked into oblivion by a skyscraper's spire. If the puzzle book was to enter the world stark-naked, the two men would duck beneath a cloak of pseudonymity. They set up a dummy imprint, Plaza Publishing, taken from the exchange of their telephone number: Plaza 6409.

When *The Cross Word Puzzle Book* was published on April 10, 1924, each edition included a Venus pencil. "One does not merely read The Cross Word Puzzle Book," went a Simon & Schuster ad, "*one writes in it*. More than that *one lives in it*." The book cost $1.35, steep for those days, perhaps anticipating a more affluent following, and was acquired primarily by mail order. Days later, Simon and Schuster couldn't get into their office. A pile of orders, just under the mail slot, was blocking the door.

It's hard to overstate the instant success of *The Cross Word Puzzle Book*. That first run of 3,600 copies sold briskly, the crossword grid transported by booksellers across and beyond the urban grid of New York; ten more printings quickly followed. Before the year was up, three more puzzle books were issued, available now at bookstores. On a single day before Christmas 1924, 150,000 copies left the shops for the fire-warmed, expectant hands of solvers. That year, three Simon & Schuster collections (they'd long since discarded the Thalia mask of Plaza Publishing) took the top three slots of the nonfiction bestseller list. For the second edition, priced more modestly at 25 cents, one eager distributor placed an order for 250,000—then the largest single purchase in publishing history. Simon & Schuster has never, in the century since its founding, not had a crossword puzzle book in print. One hundred thirty-three of them were edited by Margaret Farrar; she was compiling her 134th at the time of her death.

The economic impact is equally hard to overstate. For the house, of course, which always wins; Simon & Schuster netted some $600,000 in revenue by the close of 1924, around $10 million today. But also for the landscape of the publishing world. Given the gargantuan orders, Simon & Schuster agreed, in case of low sales, to take back unsold copies from bookstores—the first instance of a publisher allowing returns. The practice was designed to protect bookstores, back then much tinier mom-and-pop entities compared to the huge houses. But by the end of the twentieth century, after a consolidation spree, the sinewy megachains now held all the power, and could bully the atrophied publishing industry with the risk of returning huge orders to the houses.

The literary landscape would shift yet again after Margaret Petherbridge married John C. Farrar in 1926, swapping her formidable name for his. Her father had taken her substantial royalties from *The Cross Word Puzzle Book* and invested them in U.S. Steel and Standard Oil. Years later, she would use this money to underwrite her husband's publishing business. In this manner, the crossword puzzle launched three of the most prominent houses in American letters: Simon & Schuster, directly, through bestselling compendia of crosswords; Random House, indirectly, since Dick Simon handpicked Bennett Cerf as his replacement when the former went into business with Schuster; and Farrar, Straus and Giroux, financed by crossword money augmented by stocks in the age's oil and steel behemoths. A city of words on a bedrock of black-and-white.

Among the totems, knickknacks, and ephemera in Will Shortz's home-cum-museum, and one of his favorite items, is a copy of the 1924 book inscribed by Dick Simon and Max Schuster, sent to its source of inspiration. "To Aunt Wixie," the inscription reads,

> whose idea, announced on January 3, has finally taken material
> form in this first copy of the first edition of the first publication of
>> Simon and Schuster Inc.
>> Alias The Plaza Publishing Co.
>
> With many thanks
Dick
Max

⬛

"STUMPED?" asks a full-page *Times* ad on August 5, 1990. "Get on the phone. And get the answers that'll help you get through the cross-word puzzle. [. . .] Call 1-900-884-CLUE for the crossword answer you need."

It was the dawning of the age of audiotex. Callers paid a fee or sat through ads in order to leave voicemails or engage with preset, recorded programming. Media companies loved it; so did advertis-ers. At first, the systems were at best incidental to the companies' pri-mary content. ABC (known then as Capital Cities) used a 900 line to sign up 1.6 million subscribers to *Episodes,* a magazine about its soap operas, charging the subscription price to phone bills and saving mil-lions in mailing costs. *USA Today* provided ski conditions on a 900 line, drawing caller fees and ad buys from Miller Lite. *Entertainment Weekly* started one enabling readers to hear selections from records reviewed in the magazine. The *Atlanta Journal and Constitution* ran ads by churches and synagogues offering free previews of sermons by phone—the first commandment is on the house, subscribe to hear the other nine.

Media companies soon let their audiences interact with the main event. In 1991, *Newsweek* instituted a letters-to-the-editor 900 line, charging readers $1.95-plus to call in their diatribes; one paid for the pleasure of airing displeasure. NYC weekly *The Village Voice* sup-planted its personal ads with a system that let anyone place print ads without cost, but charged them $25 for a voice mailbox, and callers $1.49 a minute to respond. On learning their "clue hotline" was profit-able, the *Times* added one for its restaurant reviews, bestseller lists, and sports coverage.

Solvers used a touch-tone telephone to punch in month and day of the puzzle puzzling them. Press 1 for Across, 2 for Down, punch in the clue number. Listen to the voice spelling out the answer, so methodi-cal and slow as to flirt with chastisement. 75 cents for the first minute, 50 cents for each additional.

1-900-884-CLUE was one of three more attempts to integrate crosswords, business, and technology in the late twentieth and early twenty-first centuries: one failure, one tepid victory, one revolutionary success. Writing in *Crossword Magazine,* longtime constructor Henry Hook figured the hotline appealed to the "immediate gratification generation," those twitchy kids who couldn't wait until tomorrow's paper for answers to be revealed or corroborated. This, of course, is the time-honored, even good-natured tradition of intergenerational whingeing, an ahistorical blindfold over the elder's eyes as he pins some grave new sin on his inheritors. It ignores the fact that, despite the century-old convention of printing today's solution in tomorrow's (or next week's) paper, library dictionaries were so thoroughly mangled during the craze of the 1920s that puzzle solvers were often barred from using them; that the crossword craze led to a boom business in thesauruses, another aid for solving; that among the novelty items the craze would generate were wristbands with miniature dictionaries attached to them—"ür-FitBits," as Adrienne Raphel calls them—delivering immediacy on the very hand one wielded to fill the grid. And the generation after audiotex could, if they chose, check or reveal their grid in digital puzzle apps, or, when stumped, simply google. As long as there have been crosswords, there have been determined solvers, duty-bound reference books, and technologies for connecting the two; the puzzle, I'm afraid, must be completed today.

But where technology might connect the solver to some inanimate oracle, it could also mediate the solver's connections with other people. That's the fantasy of audiotex, which mimics the intimacy of a phone call. And the fantasy extends beyond the technology: Hook, in his piece on the clue hotline, tells the story of a seventeen-year-old boy who spent opulently on 1-900-884-CLUE to impress his parents with a finished puzzle, as a stand-in for his erudition, his adultness. ("They were impressed," jokes Hook, "until they got the phone bill!") This too is a time-honored tradition. During the craze of the 1920s, the crossword was a tool for dissolving social barriers; ephemera depict young men and women cozying up to one another, a puzzle between them, the woman free to ask, "You naughty boy—it couldn't be that word!" The same way solvers rifled through dictionaries, they called up zoos ("What is a word in three letters meaning a female swan?") and pestered passersby for an Egyptian sun god in 2. The absorption of the crossword meant people sometimes didn't do their jobs; the specialized knowledge the crossword required meant they'd call up the people who did and shake them down for a word or two. This can feel invasive, as when someone with a violin case leans over your shoulder on the subway to tell you 32-Across is AMATI, not STRAD; it can also feel validating, a display of collective knowledge, as when a tourist asks you and your seatmates on your otherwise silent commute how to get to Carnegie Hall.

Perhaps it's no surprise that attempts to tech up the crossword that lacked a social, knowledge-sharing aspect never took off. In 1994, the toy company Herbko International, Inc., released the New York Times Crossword Companion Roll-a-Puzzle System. The System was "something between a Palm Pilot and a player piano." Solvers loaded a cartridge of fresh crosswords into the Luminator, a plastic box that backlit the puzzle (four AA batteries required). Wynne's mobile word game had gone electric. Like 1924's *Cross Word Puzzle Book,* the Crossword Companion came with an attached pencil. Solve a puzzle, scroll forward to the next, replace that cartridge with a fresh one. The gimmick, like all gimmicks, was simultaneously ahead of its time and behind it, innovative and retrograde at once. Between the confusing design—was that light necessary?—and hitching legal battles about which crosswords could actually appear on those cartridges, the Crossword Companion was relatively companionless.

In 2017, the artist Camille Henrot presented *Days Are Dogs,* an installation in Paris's Palais de Tokyo museum in which representations of each day of the week unfolded in cavernous rooms. "Sunday night" contains a shabby mound of obsolescence, shoved into a corner as though under a childhood bed: rotary phones with tangled cords like the limbs of the dying, Fortran 77 displays, old schoolbooks, newspaper bundles, pain relievers for menstrual cramps. Among the junk: a heap of shrink-wrapped New York Times Crossword Companion Roll-a-Puzzle Systems. If the crossword must be done today, what better icon of jaundiced gadgetry than the room's putative hoarder, holding on to an unsolved crossword on an obsolete machine.

■

"Why are they murdering us?" said Dunn Miller, a sixty-four-year-old librarian from Oakland. "We're losing one of our stars." "I feel as if you've told me an old friend has a few months to live," said Kurtis Scaletta, a forty-year-old writer of children's and young adult novels. On learning the news, Sam Szurek, sixty-three, a copywriter from the Upper West Side, said his wife, Karen, a psychotherapist, would be "heartbroken."

It was July 2009, and crossword puzzles were dropping like flies. *The Atlantic's* monthly cryptic, called The Puzzler and constructed by Henry Cox and Emily Rathvon (basically "Brangelina to hard-core puzzle enthusiasts") was shuttering. *The Washington Post* had decided the year before to axe its Saturday acrostic. The crossword in the New York *Sun* went kaput, as did the rest of the paper.

In the aftermath of the 2008 financial crash, magazines and newspapers were cutting pages. Crossword puzzles, acrostics, and Sudokus were being left on the production-room floor. *The New York Times Magazine* had recently started publishing in a smaller format and, as a result, had shifted some puzzles online. Its editor, Gerald Marzorati, had been playing typesetting Tetris for months, trying to squeeze the regular crossword, a second word puzzle, and a numbers puzzle like Sudoku or KenKen, all on a single page. But shrinking the puzzles, his team decided, was impractical. Instead they'd swap puzzles between print and the website week to week, depending on how much ad revenue came in. Similarly, web traffic on The Puzzler, said James Bennet, editor of *The Atlantic,* couldn't justify the expense. "We've had to focus on the core of our journalistic mission," he said.

At that moment, the newspaper as a cohesive unit was decomposing, and the marriage of convenience between puzzles and journalism was yellowing. Clay Shirky, a writer on the internet's effects on news media, noted in a 2009 speech at Harvard: "The idea that someone who is doing a crossword puzzle may also want news about the coup in Honduras or how the Lakers are doing—it doesn't make any sense." Shirky was delivering an early sermon about that holiest and most profitable of prophecies, which could double as the title of a Victorian novel: *The Unbundling of Content.* "It's *never* made any sense," Shirky went on, "in terms of what the user wants."

This was, it turns out, the exact opposite of Margaret Farrar's brief when she began editing the *Times* puzzle, which from the beginning was to contain "a flavor of current events and general information"—coups, sports, warts, and all—"a blatant attempt," writes Lynn Feigenbaum in "Crosswords at a Crossroad," "to give puzzling sufficient gravity and pedagogical status for a newspaper with the motto 'All the news that's fit to print.'"

In any case, what the user wanted was her Puzzler back; it would reemerge, its ink dried into pixels. Two thousand twelve would be the first year the *New York Times*'s daily digital circulation exceeded its print circulation. In June, the ratings agency Moody's declared the U.S. newspaper industry's outlook "negative," citing "relentless" declines in revenue. In July, Shirky's prophecy came true: the *Times* started charging home-delivery subscribers an additional fee ($39.95 a year—same for nonsubscribers) to get its online daily and Sunday puzzles. (The puzzle still appeared in print.) The branding was Gilded Age, luxurious: they called it "Premium Puzzles."

As with audiotex, the crossword was the tip of the spear. Just as 1-900-884-CLUE gave way to 900 lines with the *Times*'s restaurant reviews, in 2014, after the success of the crossword's unbundling, the *Times* launched its Cooking product. Initially a digital repository for some eighteen thousand recipes, it introduced subscriptions in 2017. Originally published in the *Times* in 1994, Molly O'Neill's recipe for Old Fashioned Beef Stew (stewing meat, onion, carrots, potatoes; like a Sunday puzzle, "the ideal project for a chilly weekend") was viewed almost six million times in 2021. That same year, both Puzzles and Cooking hit a milestone: one million digital subscriptions. The *Times* leads the pack among English language publishers, and as of 2022 reported some 8.8 million digital-only subscriptions (with *The Wall Street Journal* a distant second at 3.2 million), engagement numbers that helped it weather an otherwise stormy transition from an ad-based revenue model to one built on paid content.

That kind of success has led other outlets to up their game. *New York* magazine's stand-alone entertainment site, *Vulture*, added a daily 10-by-10 puzzle alternately written by Stella Zawistowski and Malaika Handa, in 2022. *The New Yorker*, whose Puzzles & Games offerings are led by Liz Maynes-Aminzade, launched a 15-by-15 crossword on its website in 2018. The feature was so popular—the magazine could draw a straight line from solvers to renewers—it quickly multiplied from a weekly to a daily feature. It was also a born-digital crossword: both unencumbered by space constraints (if still bound by that outlet's cheeky, endearing style guide) and able to use the puzzle as a portal (featuring an answer each day that, when solved, linked to a relevant piece in the magazine). Outlets like *Vox*, *The Atlantic*, *Defector*, *Atlas Obscura*, CNN, *Slate*, and *Hyperallergic* have all added or expanded crossword offerings since 2019. In 2023, to compete with the *Times*, Apple added crosswords edited by Ross Trudeau to its native News+ app. Also in 2023, the release of a project called Puzzmo, which offers "reimagined mainstays like the crossword," was framed as Hearst "challenging [the *Times*'s] gaming dominance." When, in 2022, the *Times* acquired the word game Wordle "for a low-seven-figure sum," the company's press release showed just how much difference a decade can make. Where in 2009 *The Altantic*'s James Bennet had justified cuts to games offerings as a high-minded return to "the core of our journalistic mission," in 2022 the *Times* saw games and its journalistic mission as fundamentally intertwined:

> The *Times* remains focused on becoming the essential subscription for every English-speaking person seeking to understand and engage with the world. *New York Times Games* are a key part of that strategy. Our games already provide original, high-quality content and experiences every single day. Wordle will now play a

part in that daily experience, giving millions more people around the world another reason to turn to The Times to meet their daily news and life needs.

Success, and the technology powering it, also radically altered how the crossword is edited. In 2014, the *Times* brought its app in-house. What was once a small and largely analog outfit centered at Shortz's home on Great Oak Lane has expanded to a start-up-like operation housed in the *Times*'s skyscraper at 620 Eighth Avenue. As Farrar shaped the puzzle into a product, its edges, in the twenty-first century, would be rounded into a digital brand. That meant more people power: the Games department now employs a small army of dozens of software engineers, product managers, user experience designers, marketing analysts, and so on. In 2020, the *Times* brought on Jonathan Knight as a general manager, a games industry veteran and former executive at Zynga and Electronic Arts, where he helped develop megahits like *Words with Friends, Farmville,* and *The Sims.* The ranks of the editorial team have swelled in turn: Shortz is now flanked by Joel Fagliano, who edits the 5-by-5 Mini crossword; Sam Ezersky, responsible for the honeycombed word search Spelling Bee; Tracy Bennett, who oversees Wordle; Wyna Liu, the editor behind the *Times*'s next big hit, the associative Connections; and Christina Iverson, who writes the Easy mode clues for the Friday puzzles. Behind them is an editorial director, Everdeen Mason, and writers like Deb Amlen, Sam Corbin, and Caitlin Lovinger interfacing, as Farrar did at the *World,* with their audience, cranks and noncranks alike. They solicit solver stories. They write up primers on crosswordese. They treat them like honored patrons ("*Times* crossword solvers are customers and we're the business; we wanna make our business better for customers," Ezersky has said) even if the customer is not always right (GABAGOOL is not a word, Ezersky, who delimits Spelling Bee's dictionary, has also said). And as Arthur Wynne's FUN supplement did a century ago, they bring a little color and a lot of change—the kind that jangles in a pocket, the kind that makes things new—to the newspaper. When the Crossword app was renamed Games, the icon switched from a black-and-white

a Sunday; 134 other clues await their attention. But just then Wyna finds a fun quote: "Can't act, can't sing. Balding. Can dance a little," a judgment issued by a studio talent scout at Astaire's first screen test, says Quote Investigator. They do the fact-checking dance—this quote's also in *Britannica,* great; who said it, exactly, an executive or some low-level flunky? and was it said or written?—but it stays. When the puzzle runs, the normally rancorous Rex Parker, who reviews the *Times* puzzle every day, will say: "ASTAIRE isn't that exciting on its own, but the clue is a fantastic bit of trivia." All that googling is worth it.

The analog process Shortz and I plodded through is gone, and the life cycle of a *Times* crossword is now almost entirely digital. Submitted PDFs—empty puzzle grid, solution grid, then two columns with clues on the left and answers on the right—show up in the customer care software Zendesk, which the *Times* has repurposed as a virtual inbox. Everything in the digital slush pile is combed through and sorted with tags for Maybes (anointed by the full team) and Second Opinions (in which one editor leans no and wants another set of eyes). If a puzzle is accepted, it gets sent to an Airtable inventory broken out by day of the week (a replacement for the paper piles in Shortz's closet) and is color-coded by stage: yellow for "in production"; green for "first edit" (Shortz still does the final edit on every puzzle); and purple for "unassigned." Joel makes a point to tell me the *Times* has a tool to scan the submitted PDFs, so that no one has to type up the already typed-up clues, and I nod in gruff acknowledgment of the fact that he had to do what I had to do, as if both of us had been apprentices to a great and meticulous watchmaker with a penchant for superfluous cranking.

And the one-on-one editing Shortz and I did has been ceded to committee. (That includes those not on this particular call, like Sam Ezersky and Everdeen Mason, and changes the submissions process too; Mason once tweeted about "graphically explaining how diva cups work to Will Shortz during a Maybes review.") Joel, the youngest on this call, is nevertheless the old salt, having edited alongside Shortz since graduating college in 2014. As a result, he's developed a hyper-tuned radar for the *Times*'s difficulty levels: "These clues are coming in a hair easy," he says, as the group continues editing. "Closer to Tuesday than Wednesday." (*Times* Sunday puzzles aim for a Thursday-level difficulty.) As the clues pile up, Wyna, Tracy, and Christina keep adding Wikipedia tabs until their browsers swell with incommensurate bits of trivia. Wyna tracks down the various spellings of the African PIRI PIRI sauce ("These are all just hot sauce sites!" she laments, trying to verify the name derives from the Swahili. "I don't trust those for etymology"). Christina suggests a reference to Harry & David gift baskets when they need a new clue for BOSC pears; they toy with [Bartlett alternative] and settle on [Anjou alternative]; the alliteration strikes them as poetic. The original clue for EVIDENCE was [Best case scenario?], but Joel lingers, unsure the wordplay works; when Tracy says "What about [Case study?]?" Joel smiles, says, "Perfect," and keys it in.

It's hard to believe that after all the Wikipedia tabs and fine-tuning of puns, this puzzle will be solved, in a matter of months, by some millions of people. (In 2023, if you include games beyond the crossword, *Times* Games were played more than a whopping eight *billion* times.) The business implications would be flabbergasting to a previous generation of constructors. To help pay for business school at Wharton in 1974, the constructor Ed Julius signed a contract with Bantam Books to write a series of six crossword books, which earned him a fan letter from an undergrad at Indiana University, one Will Shortz. In addition to classes on Financial Accounting, Julius would go on to teach a one-unit course at California Lutheran University called "Crossword Construction for Fun and Profit." Four decades later, the profit from puzzling fun would be so central to the *Times* brand that politics would get mixed in, though of course politics was there all along. The power of the *Times*'s puzzle meant the rest of the paper was better-fed. It also meant the union representing *Times* workers could, in 2022, capitalize on the image to make their righteous demands look appropriately black and white: in a crossword facsimile posted by the union's Twitter account, 1-Down was [Company whose workers are asking for a fair contract] for NYTIMES, 1-Across was [Journalists, designers, security guards, news assistants and more make this] for UNION, and 2-Across was [What 1A does if 1D doesn't settle the contract by December 8]. Rhyming slogans are for protest signs; to hit the *Times* where it hurt, the Guild invoked the part of the paper that both lists facts and makes money.

The new editors at the *Times* are conscious of this pressure. When they get to 25-Across, OD ON, they hitch. Many constructors don't like using that entry anymore, Joel notes, since its usual clues, like [Take too much of], seem to callously make light of overdosing. Wyna voices her distaste for the entry. Joel wants to avoid it. It crosses BAO. Well, could that be BAU crossing UDON? It turns out the constructors had had BAU / UDON in their submission, with BAU clued as the initialism for "Business as usual," but Shortz wasn't a fan of that entry, and changed it to BAO / OD ON. The group goes back and forth. They toy with different clues for BAU—it's how you say "building" in German, after all. Together, they make a decision. They put BAU back in the grid, and move on to another clue.

CHAPTER 3

The Science of Letters

[Second derivative function?], 15 letters[*]
—BROOKE HUSIC, *xwords by a ladee*, 2021

D eb Amlen, humorist and senior editor for the *New York Times* puzzle column "Wordplay," posted a story to her Facebook page on December 11, 2022. Deb has a gift for gab and, as longtime ambassador to the *Times*'s online solvership, is quick with a quip on Twitter (now called X). When the *Times* puzzle page is down, and petulance spirals like an at sign drawn in blood, she's never far behind with a tweet of "I didn't do it."

But this story had a more fabulist slant. It began:

> Once upon a time, there was a person named Alice who loved doing crossword puzzles. She enjoyed the challenge of fitting the right words into the right spaces and loved the feeling of accomplishment when she successfully completed a puzzle.

> One day, Alice tackles a particularly tricky puzzle. She jots down the answers that come right away, but soon, alas, she's blinking at an incomplete grid. *She looked at the clues over and over again, but no mat-*

ter how hard she tried, she just couldn't seem to figure out the answers. Determined—*she refused to let the puzzle defeat her*—she spends a few more hours chewing over the crossword. When that doesn't work, she takes a walk.

Alice next experiences something familiar to stumped solvers and blocked artists alike: the buzz of the neurological back burner, invisibly simmering on a problem even when, perhaps especially when, we've aimed the heat of our attention elsewhere. The first time I finished a Saturday *Times* crossword, notoriously the paper's most grueling, I was at the beach with a high school girlfriend and her family, staring at the Arts section for hours. I remember the puzzle to this day, a tour de force by the themeless maestra Karen M. Tracey; I'd never seen a James Bond movie—I was fifteen, your honor—wasn't much into cars, and needed the adults' help getting the clue [Ride for 007] for ASTON MARTIN. After going for a swim, I returned to the puzzle, all of a sudden armed with answers that hours ago had mystified me. It's the earliest memory I have of my crossword subconscious, with all the foggy, mischievous omniscience of the Cheshire Cat, deducing something under the hum of my perception, slyly apprising me of its progress like letters materializing on a cake. I did the rest of the crossword, but it felt like I didn't do it.

Alice finishes her puzzle too; what kind of story would it be if she didn't? And like any fable, there's a tidy moral at the close: Alice *learned that persistence and a clear mind were key to solving even the most difficult of crossword puzzles.*

Still, Alice's solving woes form a taut, bloodless narrative, in more ways than one: Deb didn't do it. She'd fed ChatGPT, the language-generating artificial intelligence, a prompt: "Write a short story about a person who is having trouble solving a crossword puzzle." Through the looking glass of a laptop screen, the AI had invented Alice.

□■□

AI is all over the news today. Machines can diagnose illnesses, trade stocks, and drive cars (kind of). Even if you welcome our robot over-lords, AI's accelerating encroachment on seemingly humanist pursuits might trouble you. Many of those recent inroads implicate one of our species' most cherished faculties: language. Could an AI ever be as funny as Deb? (Not anytime soon, she tells me, winking.) Could it tell a good story? (Sure, it invented Alice, but could it invent *Alice in Wonderland*?) Could it, as AI Alice did, solve a crossword?

"As long as there have been computers," Oliver Roeder writes in *Seven Games: A Human History,* "their programmers have harnessed human games." In 1956, at the Dartmouth Summer Research Project on Artificial Intelligence, today considered the field's curtain-raising event, the academics gathered didn't mince words: "We think of machines performing the most advanced human thought activities—proving theorems, writing music, or playing chess."

Out of this midcentury loftiness emerged two camps. One thought games were model homes, abstract blueprints in which to hone the AI techniques they'd then apply to messier, more pressing issues. Another thought games already were the world, or at least the best version of it, crystalline cities lining a high-minded Utopia. AI players, on this view, uncover not just new gameplay, but new truths about humankind. The philosopher Bernard Suits once dreamed of a Utopia in which "advanced technology has solved all the problems of scarcity" and, rather than "pastimes," games were seen as "clues to the future. And their serious cultivation . . . is perhaps our only salvation."

But chess is one thing—the rules are finite, every move is communicable by math. How would an AI deal with a crossword's cognitive cacophony: linguistic ambiguity, devious themes, musty esoterica, visual puns? AI Alice used *persistence and a clear mind* to solve her crossword, I slacked off and collected the wisdom of a crowd for mine—what would an AI use? And what would an AI that could solve crosswords reveal about us?

❑■❑

Down the rabbit hole, then, past the puffing Caterpillar and the Cheshire Cat's vaporous grin to a table beneath a binary tree at which are massed a mad tea party of game-playing AIs.

I'll introduce you. There's the gruff and graying patriarch, BKG 9.8, which in 1979 beat Luigi Villa in backgammon, 7–1, becoming the first computer program to defeat a world champion at a board game. (Its creator, Hans Berliner, acknowledges the machine caught some lucky dice rolls.) There's Chinook, named for somber westerly winds native to its creator's coastal Canada, whistling a little guiltily over the circumstances of besting Marion Tinsley at checkers, in 1994. (Tinsley, a minister and mathematician who wore a Jesus pin to the match, resigned, too ill to keep playing. Two days later, he was diagnosed with pancreatic cancer; a reporter for a Christian newspaper asked Chinook's programmer, Jonathan Schaeffer, "Are you the Devil?") There's Deep Blue (chess, 1997), brash and ironic in its custom black turtleneck; Quackle (Scrabble, 2006), open-source and unpretentious; AlphaGo (Go, 2016), with its air of superiority and preference for Earl Grey; and DeepStack (Texas hold 'em, 2017), nursing a hot toddy while its algorithm toggles between exclamations of "All in!" and "Off with their heads!"

Into this scene waltzes Dr.Fill, an AI that solves crosswords. Its creator, Matt Ginsberg, removed the space between the period and "Fill" to stop autocorrect—a kind of tutting AI little brother—from changing it to "Dr. Phil." Dr.Fill was Ginsberg's second choice for a name. His first, on polling other cruciverbalists, was Deep Clue, but IBM said it was too similar to Deep Blue.

In 2021, after a decade of decent showings at the annual American Crossword Puzzle Tournament, Dr.Fill finally came in first. Or rather, it would have; the AI solves every tournament puzzle, appears in the official standings, but cannot, per ACPT organizer Will Shortz, register as a competitor, or vie for the $5,000 top prize. "The tournament," Shortz said, "is for humans."

Crosswords have occupied Ginsberg's mind three times in his life. The first was in 1976, when he was studying at Wesleyan University, where he had an "archenemy."

There was another undergrad who did everything Ginsberg did (abstract mathematics, programming, astrophysics), "just not quite as well," he says. "It was important to me that that situation be maintained. And it was important to him that that situation not be maintained." If the teenaged Ginsberg showed an early talent for imagined battle, he was precocious in other ways too: he'd go on to get his doctorate in math from Oxford at the age of twenty-four, then found and run a string of successful companies, all of them powered by AI. Perhaps as a result, he speaks with a kind of twinkly compression, like a jester delivering a PowerPoint. At Wesleyan, his undergraduate rival attempted a computer program that produced crossword puzzles. And he failed. "I figured, well, this is perfect," says Ginsberg, who swooped in and built his own crossword generator, the first instance, he believes, of such a program ever existing.

The second time was in the early 2000s, when Ginsberg was the CEO of a small software company based in Eugene, Oregon, called On Time Systems. (One imagines the White Rabbit was a seed investor.) The company drew on the bag of constraint satisfaction tricks Ginsberg had developed in graduate school—finding solutions that satisfy multiple conditions; think scheduling a meeting given a set of time slots—to solve industrial optimization problems. One client, the U.S. Air Force, used the company's Worldwide Aeronautical Route Planner (WARP) to efficiently route cargo planes around bad weather while still obeying air traffic rules, saving an estimated twenty million gallons of jet fuel annually.

One year, the team hired someone for an executive-level position who, Ginsberg told me, "was terrible. He never did anything, he always had an excuse, the excuse was always long, and he believed his excuses." Eventually, Ginsberg delegated a task with a clear due date; if he didn't complete it by then, the employee would be fired. He didn't do it. Ginsberg was so stressed by the whole thing he fired the man by email, then took a month off to decompress.

Casting around for a hobby, Ginsberg talked to a friend, Pete Muller, who was busy publishing crosswords in *The New York Times*. Muller is another mathy dabbler, a quantitative hedge fund manager and successful singer-songwriter who, with his quick smile, inconspicuous glasses, and placid eyes, looks like if Bill Gates had loved Joni Mitchell more than computers. One year, Muller's techie trading firm PDT Partners netted $150 million. The next, he released his fourth studio album, *Dissolve*—as though the music were a crossword-solving release valve—with charting singles "God and Democracy" and "San Diego (When You Coming Home)."

Ginsberg thought, *I can do that*. He made a handful of crosswords and mailed them all to Will Shortz, who rejected every last one. "Some of those were not rejection-worthy," Ginsberg told me. "Some of those he should have taken. But I was hooked."

In 2007, after constructing for a couple years, he began getting acceptances. His early puzzles displayed what'd become Ginsberg's trademark range. Sometimes literally: his Sunday, February 3, 2008, puzzle, titled "Just Follow Directions"—as though Ginsberg were shaking his fist at a bug-ridden piece of code—featured answers that ranged outside their origin rows and columns. The answer to 11-Across, clued as [Pineapple desserts], was UPSIDE DOWN CAKES; solvers entered UPSIDE going across, then followed directions by entering CAKES going *down*.

Having published a few puzzles, Ginsberg attended his first ACPT in 2008. There, he discovered something: he was a lousy solver. Ginsberg already had an inkling of this: he told me when his own puzzles run in the *Times*—a year or so after acceptance, sometimes two-plus after submission—he is wholly unable to solve them. But seeing the speedsters live is another matter entirely. Tyler Hinman, the champion in 2008—and who, as a twenty-year-old, became the youngest-ever ACPT champ in 2005—can solve an easy Monday *Times* puzzle in a superhuman sub-two minutes. (It might take even an experienced solver fifteen to twenty minutes.) When wunderkinder in one field meet wunderkinder in another, dark clouds form. Ginsberg must've thought, *I can't do that*.

For the third time in his life, then, Ginsberg found himself occupied by crosswords, wondering if he could build an AI to outrace Hinman. The goal wasn't to rig up some automated training module, a linguistic pitching machine lobbing him clues so Ginsberg himself could improve. Nor was it, at first, easily typed by the twin traditions of game AI: it was no expedition into new computational frontiers, or a quest for crosswordesque illuminations of the human condition. Dr.Fill, as Ginsberg was to christen his monster, was born of spite. "It was my revenge on all the people who were so much better at solving crosswords than I was," Dr. Ginsberg says, smiling.

◻◼◻

Mary Shelley's *Frankenstein* is a revenge plot. Victor—Dr. Frankenstein, Dr. F before Dr.Fill was Dr. F—seeks revenge on the world for his mother's untimely death; she dies of scarlet fever just weeks before he leaves for the University of Ingolstadt. Grief-stricken over this unnatural "evil," he buries himself in natural philosophy experiments, bent on controlling the uncontrollable: "infusing life into an inanimate body." And Frankenstein's monster ("the creature"), ridiculed and attacked for his "hideousness," in turn swears revenge on mankind. He kills Victor's brother William and frames Justine Moritz, William's nanny, for the crime; later, when Victor refuses to construct a "female companion" for him, he strangles Victor's newlywed, Elizabeth.

Frankenstein is also a drama of artificial intelligence. Midway through the novel, confronting his creator at Mont Blanc's Mer de Glace, the creature articulates the "original era of my being," when he could produce only "uncouth and inarticulate sounds." By the time of his reminiscence, he has read and reflected on Goethe's *The Sorrows of Young Werther* (to him an alienating text), Plutarch's *Lives* (an education on virtue), and Milton's *Paradise Lost* (which incites more vengefulness: like Milton's Satan, "when I viewed the bliss of my protectors, the bitter gall of envy rose within me").

But all those years earlier, having fled Dr. Frankenstein's laboratory, he happens upon a cottage in the woods. Living undetected in a shabby, abandoned annex, he watches the family inside through a crevice in a boarded-up window, developing a lexicon of semantic fundamentals: "familiar objects of discourse" (*fire, milk, bread, wood),* relational terms *(father, sister, brother, son)*, and abstractions he can't yet deploy *(good, dearest, unhappy)*. When, sometime later, the children teach a foreign visitor how to speak and read, the creature

> improved more rapidly than the Arabian, who understood very little and conversed in broken accents, whilst I comprehended and could imitate almost every word that was spoken. While I improved in speech, I also learned *the science of letters* as it was taught to the stranger, and this opened before me a wide field for wonder and delight.

Frankenstein's artificial creature, in other words, learns through observational data. And it's a more impressive student than its human counterpart—hideous and vengeful, maybe, but this AI outstrips us when it comes to language.

Ginsberg's artificial creature will have a similar arc of development—at ten times the speed. In Shelley's book, Frankenstein's creature takes a few months to learn to speak and read. Its science of letters is still humanoid, built on glacial, perceptual accretion, accessed through a "small and almost imperceptible" eyehole. But Dr.Fill's science of letters is more athletic: Big Data, rapid computation. Stuffed inside it, at the time of the creature's birth, are the solutions to 47,693 crosswords and the text of 3,819,799 clues (1,891,699 of which are unique; clues are often reused) compiled from *The New York Times,* the (now defunct) New York *Sun,* the *Los Angeles Times, USA Today, The Washington Post,* and many other venues.

Dr.Fill does speak more than crossword. Alongside those clues are a set of dictionaries: a skinnier bucket with 8,452 "common," basic English words, and a kitchen-sink list of 6,063,664 that includes rarer words. To decode morphological information in clues, Ginsberg tossed in a list of 154,000 words tagged by part of speech and grammatical root, from Princeton University's WordNet initiative. To help with proper names and phrases, Dr.Fill contains the title of every single Wikipedia page (some 8,472,583 items at the time of first upload) and a list of every pair of consecutive words found in Wikipedia articles (76,886,514 distinct pairs). In *Frankenstein,* the creature knows that its training data limits it, that if instead of the lawful patriarchs of Plutarch's *Lives* its "first introduction to humanity" involved tales of soldiers "burning for glory and slaughter," it'd see things differently. Inside Dr.Fill, too, is a hideous, ultra-specific subset of manmade language: crossword clues, dictionary definitions, the depths of Wikipedia.

Two thousand twelve was Dr.Fill's crossword cotillion. Ginsberg barely slept the night before the tournament; Dr.Fill, powered off, had no such trouble.

That year, for the fifth time, the ACPT unfolded not in the modest matte of the Stamford Marriott but in the grander, glossier Brooklyn branch. The reason was practical—after the 2006 release of the crossword documentary *Wordplay,* tournament registration soared, and the organizers needed more space. But there was also a rightness of fit, holding the tournament coordinated by Shortz and his team in the *Times*'s home turf, an urban grid with Checker cabs, towering spreadsheet edifices, panels of lambent light: Big Data would get its hearing in the Big Apple. On Saturday night, once competitors had completed six of the tournament's seven puzzles, Ginsberg, who'd asked Shortz if he could introduce his creature to attendees, gave what would become his inaugural Dr.Fill address to the Grand Ballroom.

He opened with a joke. Ginsberg had laryngitis, and his voice—his own human language faculty—was failing him. As he left Oregon for New York, his wife had told him that the next time he was unable to talk, she'd like it to be at home, so she could enjoy it. Vengefulness, or a fantasy of it, it seemed, ran in the family.

Then Ginsberg demonstrated how Dr.Fill solves. Hundreds of us crossword faithful gazed at a giant projector as Ginsberg fed his salivating AI a puzzle. Instantly, the screen looked as if the Matrix's green kinetic typography had taken a merry dose of LSD; letters of different colors kept blinking on and off in the crossword's cells. Ginsberg explained that the colored letters represented the AI's confidence in each mapping from clue to answer. Green meant two thumbs-up: in the millions of clue-answer pairs it had ingested, Dr.Fill had encountered that exact clue for that exact answer. Blue, a shoulder shrug: the clue as written was unfamiliar, but certain words in it appeared in other clues for that answer, so the system was gently optimistic. Black was a shake of the head: clue and answer didn't seem to correspond, but the answer appeared in Dr.Fill's dictionary, so that was something. The same for purple, just more frantic: clue and answer again didn't jibe, and the answer itself was unfamiliar, but it was—like neologisms, new book titles, or the entries in some crossword themes—at the very least a sequence of words. And red was a derisive digital raspberry: nothing about the clue-answer connection computed.

Behind the psychedelic interface, Dr.Fill rifles through a puzzle's clues and computes a probability that a candidate answer is correct, a function that weighs the text of the clue (is this clue-answer pair likely?) and the neighborhood of letters in the grid (are these crossing words both legitimate words?). Wordplay-based clues, typical of a Friday or Saturday puzzle in the *Times,* frequently tripped the program up. In a tournament puzzle by Robyn Weintraub, for instance, Dr.Fill's attempt log for a 10-letter word clued as [Wise offering] included SAGE ADVICE, SMART MONEY, SMART ALECK, and RHEESEHUEL, a random string of letters that resembles the correct answer: CHEESE CURL, a product offered by the company Wise. And when either clue or answer involve not just ambiguity but modern language unlikely to be in its database, Dr.Fill struggles even more, all but unraveling at clues like Rose Sloan and Norah Sharpe's [Doing shots?] for SEX SCENES or Paolo Pasco and Erik Agard's [Drag to court] for SWIPE RIGHT.

But Dr.Fill's real kryptonite is themes, the more dastardly the deadlier. The program does have several routines on alert for the tamer mechanisms of wordplay. It knows about anagrams: if, for instance, its algorithm suggests THE SATANIC SERVES might be the answer to the Lynn Lempel clue [A novel about wickedly good aces? (1988)]— not because it gets the gimmick, but because the crossings look good— and it finds other answers that anagram to items in its dictionary (say, LORD OF THE FILES and A FAREWELL TO RAMS), it will pause, take a silicon breath, and solve the puzzle all over again, allowing any answer that anagrams to something already in its dictionary (ultimately uncovering GULLIVER'S VARLETS and TENDER IS THE THING).

Over the years, Ginsberg hard-coded additional scenarios for Dr.Fill to look for. He did so resentfully, like outfitting a child with helmet and training wheels and shin pads while secretly hoping it'd learn how to ride on its own. Initializing a game AI's system, Ginsberg says, was colorful, imaginative labor, like sketching plans for a summer garden, but fashioning paranoid code for edge case after edge case—sweating the details—was tiresome spadework. Ginsberg added add-a-letter themes, like *Simpsons* character SIDESHOW BOB turning into SLIDESHOW BLOB [PowerPoint image that's just a shapeless mass?]. And he added rebuses, in which a series of letters is squished into a single box, like JIMI [HEN]DRIX in a puzzle called "Chicken Little." But in both cases, the theme entries are still composed of real words, not a random string of letters. Add-a-letter themes and rebuses look like kazoos next to the orchestral boom of some Thursday *Times* themes. And ACPT themes are often on another level still: mind-bending, you-gotta-hand-it-to-'em free jazz.

These hard-coded theme types also live in a different part of the AI's brain. If Dr.Fill's database is *Frankenstein*—a creature created in the image of past clues and definitions—its theme detection is something out of *Alice in Wonderland*: a world of whimsy built on enumerable rules, Lewis Carroll's nonsense wrung from the rigid sensibility of Charles Dodgson's (Carroll's birth name) symbolic logic. This is how the era of "good old-fashioned AI"—sometimes called symbolic AI—approached gameplay: searching through and ranking a set of *if-then* rules, wielding them in well-defined, ruly contexts like chess.

But language games are too elusive, too slyly human, for that tactic to always work: there isn't really, at bottom, a science of letters, only a science of probability, a science of search, a science of rules. "The hardest thing about crosswords," Ginsberg has said, "is that there are no rules." To the constructor Brooke Husic, comparisons to games like chess or poker—and thus to the AIs that "solved" them—don't compute; those games run on known rules that an AI, trained on past game logs, has already seen, but "great crosswords," says Husic, "are precisely the ones that show you something you've *never* seen before."

Ginsberg cites a 2010 puzzle by Andrew Zhou in which the clue [Apollo 11 and 12 (180 degrees)] gives the seemingly nonsense answer SNOISSIWNOOW. We human solvers might realize that, remarkably, if you rotate that string 180 degrees, you get MOON MISSIONS: every single capital letter in the original phrase remains a letter after rotation. But Dr.Fill throws up its hands, sticks out its tongue. "It doesn't know that letters have shapes," Ginsberg sighed.

There was another revenge plot afoot at the 2012 ACPT. Ginsberg sensed the tournament constructors were out for blood.

Shortz was jocular if skeptical, as if a nephew had challenged him to an arm wrestle, and he'd been amenable to the experiment. Ginsberg described the green light as "Sure, show up. Get pasted." But the *Times* editor seemed undeniably on team John Henry. He'd had buttons made that read "I Beat Dr. Fill" (incorrectly including the space in the machine's name) and, Sunday morning, distributed them to anyone who outperformed the AI in Puzzles 1 through 7. Before each puzzle, Shortz announced how Dr.Fill fared on the previous grid. If it did well: a boo or two, the scrape of chairs, the hacking of pencil sharpeners like the sharpening of pitchforks. If it made a mistake, though: hoots, hollering, more exuberance than six hundred more-or-less test-takers ought to be capable of. In the back of the ballroom, Ginsberg clicked his tongue at the MacBook Pro on his table.

That year, both Puzzle 2 (usually ACPT's second-hardest) and Puzzle 5 (the tournament's most devious) were what Ginsberg called "howitzers." Puzzle 2, by Patrick Merrell, was titled "Boustrophedon," a Greek word derived from an ox turning at the end of a furrow; *bous* and *cow* are cognates. It refers to writing alternate lines in opposite directions, one line left to right and the next right to left, handy for

2 — BOUSTROPHEDON

```
Y E L P S ■ S C A R S ■ C L E F T
E L O O T ■ T O R A T ■ A I P E S
A M U S E M E N T P A R K R I D E
■ ■ I S P E P ■ Y T L A E R ■ ■ ■
E R S E ■ A P P ■ ■ A I M ■ B A S
D E X ■ D L E I F A G N I W O L P
T V V C R ■ N O R ■ ■ X A C T O
■ ■ R E R B ■ U E I L ■ S C A T
■ O N E W A Y O R A N O T H E R
A N O W ■ D E R M ■ E G R U
S T R E W ■ I A N ■ ■ I P A S S
N W A L E H T G N I W O M ■ S K O
O O H ■ B A H ■ ■ T E M ■ P H I L
■ O C S E N E ■ T N U A H ■
D O T M A T R I X P R I N T E R S
E V R E S ■ O N A D A ■ I S A U Q
F A I N T ■ N O M S G ■ T Y P E S
```

masons carving inscriptions in high places. Veteran solvers sussed out the gimmick before too long—answers were to be entered forward and backward in alternating rows—and while Dr.Fill had no problem with 72-Across ([TV's Dr. ___] for PHIL) it would be haunted by nearby 76-Across ([Stay with, in a bad way] for TNUAH).

Merrell, a kindly cartoonist, graphic designer, and author, insists he didn't intentionally write a puzzle to flummox the AI. "Real solvers were the focus!" he wrote in an email to Shortz before the tournament. Still, he admitted a desire to see the AI fail. "Did I want to beat Dr.Fill? Yes. Some wrong answers would be satisfying. I mean, who doesn't like to beat a computer." (Dr.Fill tanked Merrell's puzzle.) But Merrell also says he was inspired enough by Ginsberg's invention to make an "unsolicited donation": he illustrated Dr.Fill's logo. Squint one way, and you'll see a stoic set of boxes printing out the word FILL; squint another, and there's the raspberry again, the machine taunting us with its insentient tongue.

In Brooklyn, Ginsberg's science of probability underperformed. Dr.Fill was trained in part on past tournament puzzles and, in simulations of the previous thirty-four ACPTs, it would have won three outright. Ginsberg predicted a top-50 finish; the program came in 141st.

Shortz, as it were, got the science of probability just right. He'd only ordered 150 "I Beat Dr. Fill" buttons.

At his Saturday address, Ginsberg was cheery but clearly disappointed. He removed a sweater to reveal a shirt with a bull's-eye decal, as if to get ahead of it all, cast himself as the villain so no one else would get the satisfaction. He joked that the ACPT judges ought to *at least* select Dr.Fill for the "Best Handwriting" award, a nodding consolation at a speed-solving tournament in which many competitors shift from a four-stroke capital E to the one-stroke lowercase, saving precious seconds in a makeshift human science of letters. The tournament winner has never won Best Handwriting.

Ginsberg's Saturday Dr.Fill update became a yearly tradition, a Christmas card depicting a bratty cousin's latest achievements, packaged up by the doting aunt. Ginsberg loved his monster even as it made, given the boos and the buttons, a monster of him too. Besides, like Deb Amlen's Alice—once upon a time there was an AI who loved doing difficult crossword puzzles, who relished a challenge. Ginsberg and his creature would learn persistence, a clear mind. They'd be back.

How do humans know letters have shapes; what can we do that AI, at least for now, flails at? In *Reading in the Brain,* the cognitive neuroscientist Stanislas Dehaene describes how psychologists have begun to "treat reading like a computer science problem." Human readers and our eyes resemble less a *Frankenstein* facsimile than "a robot with two cameras." Our retinal foveae ingest visual information, then forward it for decoding to the left lateral occipitotemporal sulcus, a part of the brain Dehaene calls the Visual Word Form Area.

That neural circuitry represents a sparkling crossroads, unique to reading, linking the visual system (located in the occipital lobe, at the back of the head) with the system devoted to speech (in the temporal lobe, between our ears). Because it's built atop the neural architecture for vision some millions of years in the making, the evolutionarily younger function of recognizing letters—some five to ten thousand years old; crosswords have been around for just over a hundred— "recycles" the hardware our primate ancestors developed to recognize objects. As a result, the neuroscience of letters is practical: T's might indicate the edge of an object, something jutting and grabbable; a Y junction occurs at the corner where three edges meet; O's, of course, look like eyes. "We did not invent most of our letter shapes," writes Dehaene. "They lay dormant in our brains for millions of years, and were merely rediscovered when our species invented writing and the alphabet."

The scientists Mark Changizi, Qiong Zhang, Hao Ye, and Shinsuke Shimojo argue that these survivalist pressures furnished the world's writing systems with a strikingly similar distribution of contours. From Arabic to Cyrillic to Korean to Somali, the world's nonlogographic scripts—where individual characters don't stand for entire words, as in Chinese—have essentially the same number of L-shapes, T-shapes, and X-shapes. What's more, they tend to have more L's than T's, and more T's than X's—the *inverse* of those shapes' likelihood in nature. Throw two sticks on the ground, and the most probable result is they cross, forming some kind of X; next most likely, they make a T; and the rarest outcome is kissing at a single point, as in an L. Across culture and eras, our letters are meant to stand out, look nonaccidental, and arrest our attention.

Lacking a lesson in this Darwinian alphabet, orthographic trickery is beyond Dr.Fill's reach. But crossword constructors, given this neural instinct, are natural graphic designers. Zhou's SNOISSIWNOOW / MOON MISSIONS puzzle is part of a genre. The week of October 17, 2011, the *Times* ran six puzzles in a row by veteran constructor Patrick Berry; the only O's in each grid—four in Monday's corners; one smack in the middle of Tuesday—represented eyes on the side of a die. J's have been fishhooks, I's the length of a spider's web. O's atop a V were once scoops of ice cream on a cone.

An AI can look up facts (kind of), associate clue words with answers, but it can't treat letters like mutable lines; it won't see shapes in the clouds. That ice cream cone theme, in a puzzle by Patrick Blindauer, was inspired by seeing his toddler, Maggie, playing with physical letters at the library. Maggie was learning two things at once: the way meaning proliferates from letters huddled together, and the way the contours of letters are images all on their own.

Developing a crossword theme relies on another property of reading in the brain: bottom-up processing. Our brains construct images from neural circuits responsible for increasingly complex stages in the hierarchy of shape: lines, then contours, then polygons, and so on. This dendritic assembly line is hidden; we see only the finished commodity. Dehaene believes a similar process underlies reading: neurons that churn through letters, then digraphs, then syllables, and so on. The mind's factory sputters at breakneck pace, occasionally producing a dud:

> Our reading apparatus dissects the word "department" into [depart] + [ment] in the hope that this will be useful to the next operators computing its meaning. Never mind that this does not work all the time—a "listless" person is not one who is waiting for a grocery list, nor does sharing an "apartment" imply that you and your partner will soon live apart. Such parsing errors will have to be caught at other stages in the word dissection process.

Like a Freudian parapraxis, these "parsing errors" might be useful for something else. One neuropharmacological theory of psychedelic drugs posits that LSD or psilocybin don't generate fractal patterns where there was only humdrum landscape; rather, they pull back the curtain on earlier stages of visual processing our brain had sanded away. The crossword constructor, by lingering in Dehaene's "parsing errors" (absent chemical intervention, your honor) is similarly touched, and often irrepressibly so: the constructor Ross Trudeau once noted on Twitter that

> a fun thing my brain does when i'm reading is to interpret any adverb ending in -ally as a type of friend [. . .] educationally = study buddy recreationally = playmate algorithmically = facebook friend animalistically = furry companion.

Crossword construction trains the human brain to deconstruct; we can't not do this.

All this gimmickry might seem less the remit of AI than the province of artists and mathematicians. Lewis Carroll, after all, was both. Published in 1856, one of Carroll's early fictions, "Novelty and Romancement," springs from the kind of parsing error Deheane describes. In it, a man sees a sign for "Roman Cement," which, hapless lover that he is, he misreads as "Romancement." When he wasn't researching or lecturing on symbolic logic at Oxford (under his given name, Charles Dodgson), Carroll was inventing word ladders, strings of one-character shifts that evolve a starting word into a concluding one, like genetic twitches in a molecule of DNA:

```
A   P   E
A   R   E
E   R   E
E   R   R
E   A   R
M   A   R
M   A   N
```

One might continue: MAN -> MAT -> BAT -> BOT. Carroll published these "Doublets," as he dubbed them, in a weekly column for *Vanity Fair*. He popularized a proto-version of Scrabble. And he would've made, like today's crossword constructors, a dedicated graphic designer. He obsessed over the contours in *Wonderland*'s text—punctuation, italics, line and section breaks, illustrations—even issuing a revised edition whose amendments only touched the hyphens, dots, and commas.

Today, scholars take *Wonderland* to be more than a vehicle for two of Carroll's loves, wordplay and symbolic logic; rather, it's seen as a wondrous unity of the two. As the scholar Anna Kornbluh writes in *The Order of Forms,* Carroll's tale constructs its form from the "tension between *proliferating meaning* and *the stark contour of the letter*"—the pun and the image, two of the crossword constructor's great loves—a tension that produces both "estrangement from and enchantment of the letter." X isn't a letter but a variable; meaning nothing, it can, unfettered, mean anything.

Wonderland, on this reading, gives us surrealist nonsense (a Mock Turtle dancing to the Lobster Quadrille; a sham trial helmed by the King of Hearts) to make us make sense of literary realism (which, being fiction, is always a construction of the world, not the world itself); *Wonderland* is a "pure" realist novel because it shows the convention of verisimilitude to be unnecessary. Ginsberg, a mathematician like Carroll, feels the same way about crosswords: some odd-looking puzzles (say, ones with asymmetric black square patterns) make us make sense of a crossword's constraints (e.g., grids should be rotationally symmetric); asymmetric grids are "pure" crosswords because they show the convention of symmetry to be unnecessary. Black square patterns are arbitrary, the logician tells us. The words are the thing.

Ginsberg also, like Carroll, considers himself an aesthete. After Wesleyan but before Oxford, he first began graduate school at Caltech. "I hated it," he says, "because they weren't artists." The physics department there solved problems with fortitude, not finesse; he'd get problem sets back with threatening red ink, as if written by the Queen of Hearts, shouting "Not enough equations!" He dropped out, crushed.

Ginsberg ended up at Oxford, where his advisor was physics Nobelist Roger Penrose. One day, he confessed his depressing episode at Caltech to his new mentor. Penrose, a frequent correspondent of the artist M. C. Escher, smiled, went to his shelf, and pulled down a recent article he'd written, "The Role of Aesthetics in Pure and Applied Mathematical Research." *At last,* Ginsberg thought. *I can do that.*

"People look at me and they see a mathematician and a computer scientist," Ginsberg says, "but I'm an artist. The crosswords are art, computer programs are art. It's all art."

In April 2021, after the 2020 tournament was canceled due to the COVID-19 pandemic, the ACPT was, for the first time ever, held virtually.

Will Shortz worked with the software firm Amuse Labs on a platform thousands of remote solvers could use without it crashing, and with the Canadian broadcast firm Waveform to livestream the event. Though they wouldn't be scribbling elbow-to-elbow in a ballroom, and in fact retreated to their suites to solve on laptops, a handful of tournament regulars arrived (fully vaccinated) at the Stamford Marriott to participate on-site and, per Shortz, to "schmooze."

In pictures, the Marriott has the post-apocalyptic campiness of pandemic-era Late Night: unnatural ratio between space and population, hosts emoting to empty soundstage. The Pavilion at the hotel's rear, usually home to the ACPT's Friday wine-and-cheese soirée (cheddar cubes, laminated name tags) had been converted into the virtual tournament's command center. It was manned by producer Justin Hosek, whose credits include the World Rubik's Cube Championship and whose online presence is all Red Bull, neon, and floodlight. Shortz, in an uncharacteristic impression of a tech CEO—black blazer over black tee—emceed seated on a plush olive-colored wingback, positioned before a real wrought-iron gate that guarded a mural of the Italian countryside; the virtual background for the virtual tournament captured the drive to be outside the way paintings in a doctor's office capture the desire to see good art. Wonderland it wasn't.

On Friday, April 23, 2021, some 1,300 remote solvers keyed into the tournament platform. A ringtone-like marimba track greeted them; in a digital waiting room, a slideshow showed us images from when we were younger.

There was the year that, to crowdsource reactions to the World Palindrome Championship, the ACPT team distributed hundreds of signs reading WOW! on one side and HUH? on the other. There was the year someone made a RRRRIPSTEIN! THIS IS THE YEAR! banner to cheerlead perennial top finisher (and onetime Long Island majorette) Ellen Ripstein, who finally won the whole shebang in 2001. There was the year the championship puzzle had ZEBRAFISH at 1-Across and the year it had ZOLAESQUE there instead. There was the year long-time solver Kurt Vonnegut came, saw Hinman speed-solve, and called him, it seemed lovingly, a "freak." The marimba ended; the smooth jazz began. The whole thing had the cozy but hiccupping aesthetic of a home video, a VHS your dad got the guy at the Apple Store to digitize.

One of the 1,300 solvers was once again a machine—but not the Dr.Fill competitors had come to know and love and hate. In March, just a month before the virtual tournament, a Berkeley computer science PhD student named Eric Wallace reached out to Ginsberg. Wallace worked in Dan Klein's Natural Language Processing Group; he and other members of the lab had, like so many, nurtured a crossword habit in the COVID-19 lockdowns. Klein wanted to join forces. Since summer 2020, another of Klein's graduate students, Nicholas Tomlin, had been "re-implementing" Dr.Fill—essentially trying to rewrite the program from scratch—as a "fun side project." When Tomlin couldn't recapture Dr.Fill's accuracy, he brought the project to the broader lab, who agreed it was a good testbed for their techniques. Together the group generated a sophisticated neural network called the Berkeley Crossword Solver (BCS).

On reading the email, the computer scientist in Ginsberg saw an opportunity; the businessman in him jumped in to project-manage it. "I said, 'We better get on it,'" Ginsberg recalls. "Everyone worked pretty hard for a few weeks."

Luckily, the codebases fit together neatly. The resulting Franken-solver—where that prefix refers by turn to godless modification of the "natural" (frankenfood, frankengrass) and to mere hybridity (frankenstorm, FrankenBike)—represented a bionic handshake between Ginsberg's grid handling and the Berkeley team's clue deconstruction. Ginsberg's creature knew about crossing letters and themes, but the Berkeley team employed natural language processing's state of the art; where Dr.Fill's database held some millions of clues, definitions, and Wikipedia articles, the Berkeley solver recruited BERT, a language model trained on some three billion words scraped from the web. The Berkeley solver, in other words, was even more Frankenstein than Dr.Fill—its "eyehole" had dilated to the hideous expanses of human-generated internet text. Only days before the tournament, the hybrid solver—still named Dr.Fill—awoke.

This new creature was formidable. Early on Saturday, Shortz announced that Dr.Fill had finished Puzzle 1 in 34 seconds and Puzzle 2 in 41 seconds, with both grids 100 percent correct. The tournament chat thundered with virtual boos.

Hours later, after what Shortz called "the bitch-mother" of Puzzle 5, he told attendees, "Humans everywhere will be happy to hear that Dr.Fill made a mistake." Then Shortz, who had played table tennis every single day since October 3, 2012, drove forty minutes back to New York, exchanged his Steve Jobs getup for workout shorts, and played a few games at the table tennis club he owns. Then he returned to the olive wingback in Stamford to introduce Ginsberg's yearly talk, this time a panel among Shortz, Ginsberg, and Jonathan Schaeffer, creator of that apostate checkers champ, Chinook.

For the first time ever, six puzzles in, Dr.Fill was beating the humans. And badly—the distance between Dr.Fill and the top human was about the difference between first place and tenth place. What had changed?

For one thing, brawn: Dr.Fill ran on a more powerful machine than the laptop Ginsberg usually ported from Oregon to Connecticut. Now, the AI could contemplate alternate solutions even faster; swiveling in his chair like Dr. No, Ginsberg cheerily indicated the flashing lights of his custom desktop, with its 64-core processor and two GPUs. Adrienne Raphel, in her book *Thinking Inside the Box,* describes Ginsberg "tot[ing] Dr.Fill in a briefcase around the Marriott like a Chihuahua in a purse"; the device behind Ginsberg now was all Doberman, glittering with digital slobber.

The second and by far largest factor was brains: Berkeley's help. Through machine learning, the Frankensolver occasionally cottoned to the second or third senses of words in the trickiest clues, which is how it unraveled, e.g., [Trip to watch the big game?] for SAFARI.

A third: in 2021 the themes were easier. Ginsberg would later chalk this up to "the constructors got sloppy." No entering answers backward or outside the perimeter of the grid—no curveballs, all fastballs over the plate. Dr.Fill's first error of the tournament came on Kevin G. Der's Puzzle 5, in which certain entries, according to the introductory text, "broke the sound barrier." The clues [Crazed] and [Deduces] went with the consecutive answers MANNEQUIN and FIRS. But [Crazed] clues MANIC, not MANNEQUIN, and [Deduces] goes with INFERS, not FIRS. The sound "in" has broken across the barrier of a black square, from one answer to another: MANIC to MANNEQUIN (where "in" is added), INFERS to FIRS (subtracted). The AI went with FIBS, not FIRS, because, according to Ginsberg, it wanted a present tense verb to match [Deduces]; the crossing of IBIS instead of the correct IRIS [Blue-violet shade] seemed iffy but passable. Still, Dr.Fill dispatched other puzzles' punny themes, deducing for instance that [Pasta dish at the center of a murder mystery?] was POISON PENNE.

Shortz said as much to Ginsberg. "You've explained Dr.Fill so many times over the years," he joked, "that if I wanted, I could design a puzzle that Dr.Fill would fail at miserably. We didn't do that this year."

Like the slippage between Dr. Frankenstein and his nameless monster, Shortz's swap of "I" for "we" struck me. If the hammer came down, it'd be Shortz as king slayer; it was the collective goodness of the community—of CrossWorld, as it's called—that held him at bay. He mentioned that other tournaments, like the British National Crossword Championship, impose a sharper penalty for incorrect squares. "I could," grinned Shortz, gripping a trapdoor lever offscreen, avuncular mustache thinning into villainy, "change the rules of the contest, which would also destroy Dr.Fill."

"Your ability to be mean does keep me up at night," smiled Ginsberg.

As the talk wound down, Schaeffer, who'd mostly watched Shortz and Ginsberg spar, wanted to make a point. He teased Ginsberg for a kind of human error—hadn't he anthropomorphized Dr.Fill more than usual tonight, used more "he" than "it," bid his creature come to life? To my surprise, Ginsberg apologized. He's usually more careful than that, he said; the AI's performance must've thrown him off. Actually, it was important we avoid that mistake: these were tools, not people. After all, he said, "we don't call a 'hammer' he."

Don't we? Ginsberg and Schaeffer had named their programs,

Schaeffer with a personal touch. Yachts, swords in stone, hot rods, guitars, and hamsters—to everything along the spectrum of consciousness we pinned a name; the pronoun "it" was no garrison against the siren song of personification. Ginsberg didn't refuse Merrell's logo on the grounds it'd force us to let our guard down. And for every rascally pedant who remembers Frankenstein's creature goes unnamed, here's four hazy silhouettes happy to have him inherit his human creator's, four more installing the prefix Franken- in front of another noun, as though once again naming a monstrosity for a human. Our flexible science of letters is anthropocentric, in a way that feels protective just as much as it can feel indefensible. Faced with an all-knowing, encroaching AI, this assertive whimsy—hallucinating faces on the moon; rotating MOON MISSIONS to get SNOISSIWNOOW; inventing a character like the Mad Hatter; imagining Dr.Fill has a silly little face and a PhD; indeed, playing the very games the AIs now beat us at—can feel, at times, like a kind of revenge.

There's a concept in AI known as "the bitter lesson." Time and again, researchers tried to build the best of human thought into an algorithm's foundation, only to be outdone by unthinking computation and Big Data. We tried to teach an AI the shrewdest chess maneuvers; but no, searching millions of movesets in a matter of seconds proved to be the winning strategy. We tried arming Google Translate with rudiments of syntax and grammar; but no, ingesting massive amounts of bilingual text, like the English-and-French Canadian parliamentary proceedings, gave machine translation its quantum leap.

The same thing happened in crosswords. The hybrid Dr.Fill "won" in 2021—though Shortz prefers "outperformed the humans"; its rank in official standings is not 1 but 0.5—finishing a measly 15 points ahead of Erik Agard, 12,825 points to 12,810. It did so harnessing not the clever theme recognition Ginsberg had built, or knowledge of crossword grid conventions; the Berkeley system, a Frankencorpus of billions of books, articles, and other texts, put it over the top. In the end, *Frankenstein* outperformed *Alice in Wonderland.*

There's an asterisk, here, of course. There are, and may always be, crosswords AI can't solve, whether because they have groundbreaking themes or because they solicit hard-to-verify or context-specific information. (Brooke Husic suggested the banal clue [Current U.S. President] for a 5-letter word; in 2012 that'd be OBAMA, in 2016 TRUMP, and in 2020 BIDEN.) Dan Klein, the Berkeley lab's head, believes this arms race benefits everyone: constructors aiming to outgun the AI will inevitably produce puzzles that pleasurably confound humans too. And asterisk or no, the fact AI can beat humans at a game demanding nimble, language-based modes of thought—as opposed to the purely mathematical tactics of a game like checkers—does feel like it might augur a new world, in games and beyond.

Ginsberg, for his part, is "retired from crosswords." After Dr.Fill's 2021 win, he consulted Murray Campbell (of the Deep Blue team), Dave Silver (AlphaGo), and Schaeffer again (Chinook). They all said know when to hang up your cleats. There's no upside: if you keep winning, everyone hates you for beating the feeble humans. If you lose, everyone thinks when you *did* win, it was a fluke. So he did. "I got my fifteen minutes of fame," he mused.

Over the pandemic, he started talking to X—not Twitter but the "moonshot factory" at Google—confessing a distaste for the "bitter lesson." He had a still insatiable drive to be the one who figures it all out. "All I want from life," he told me, "is to solve problems that are so hard that everyone else thinks they're insoluble." Ginsberg had even written this desire into a self-published novel called *Factor Man,* in which his autofictional double solves computer science's hardest problem and discovers "God's algorithm." When I learned that Ginsberg's father had died suddenly of a heart attack when he was a junior at Wesleyan, I thought of Victor Frankenstein: his mother's sudden passing, the son's anxious fantasy of conquering death, harnessing science to create life.

Google asked Ginsberg to unbox his cleats. He feigned surprise:

"They actually said, we have that job. They pay me like a baseball player to fill it." Since summer 2021, he has focused his optimizing gaze on "real world" issues—no more of that games nonsense; now he was decarbonizing the electricity grid and designing waste-minimizing supply chain routes, wielding techniques that looked less like God's algorithm, and more like the machine learning tools he gleaned on his journey down the crossword rabbit role.

Ginsberg's orbital-hopping career reminds me of a story about Lewis Carroll. After the publication of *Alice's Adventures in Wonderland,* Queen Victoria, charmed by the book, asked that she receive the author's next work, and was sent a signed copy of Charles Dodgson's mathematical tome, *An Elementary Treatise on Determinants.* Having looked it up, it turns out this particular fable is false—Carroll didn't do it—but like an unruly AI, I confess I prefer the nonsense.

PART II

The Crossword Should Be a Soapbox

CHAPTER 4

A Familiar Form of Madness

[Where posters can hang?], 5 letters*
—PAOLO PASCO, *Grids These Days*, 2022

F|or years, Hadas Reich shared a *New York Times* crossword account with her brother, Ben. They lived in different cities and worked the puzzle alone: Hadas polishing off a Wednesday between anatomy lectures at Albert Einstein College of Medicine in the Bronx; Ben, a start-up founder splitting time between D.C. and California, speeding through a Monday between conference calls. In the *Times* app, no alert pops up informing one of the other's solving: *Your sister is halfway through the grid! Your brother could use a hand with 4-Down!* The rewards arrive post-solve: a gold star appears, a nine-note jingle called the "San Jose Strut" plays, and, if you've solved the puzzle correctly multiple days in a row, your streak is shown. Hadas and Ben were casual solvers and busy professionals; between the two of them, they rarely strung together more than a few days of consecutive solving. Seeing the streak was thin, uneasy metadata, an indication that, maybe, start-up work had been light (or maddening, requiring a release); maybe, hospital rounds had been straightforward (or cruel, driving one to the app's Pavlovian bell).

In the spring of 2018, Hadas and Ben's mother, Yael, was diagnosed with pancreatic cancer. For the first year and a half of her illness, she continued her work as a visiting nurse in Queens, educating younger practitioners on the ins and outs of home diabetes care, her specialty. In the fall of 2019, she was hospitalized. Ben came to New York, and the siblings spent as much time as possible at her side. It was a big room, in a recently renovated wing at NYU Langone, where Hadas had done her residency. She knew the nurses who came by to tend to Yael, and glanced quizzically at Ben as he plugged wires into the room's enormous television. To pass the time between conferences with doctors, family visits, and treatment sessions, the siblings did the *Times* crossword together every day, projected onto that expansive screen so Yael, from her bed, could see it too.

That first hospitalization lasted two weeks. After her discharge, the siblings' streak was the longest it had ever been (fifteen days), and they decided to see how far they could extend it. Ben went back home, but each day, he'd send Hadas a Zoom link, then share his screen as the two completed the puzzle as a team. The streak grew: thirty days, then sixty. In that span, their mother was hospitalized a few more times, and each time Ben returned to New York and solved with his sister under the dim fluorescence of a hospital room, the jingle mixing darkly with the sonic wallpaper of a beeping vitals monitor. Occasionally, when awake, Yael offered an answer of her own. Mostly, she was just happy to see her children collaborating.

When the streak was around one hundred days, Ben and his partner, Gauri, who'd planned on getting married soon anyway, decided to push up their wedding. Before the ceremony, the Reich siblings told the best man and officiant that he had one supreme duty that weekend: to ensure the streak persisted. Then, at two hundred days, Yael passed away. Hadas and Ben were by her side in the final days of hospice. She died on March 13, 2020; the siblings arranged a funeral for the next day. It was early in our understanding of COVID-19, before mask mandates and gathering restrictions; one of Hadas's co-residents offered a box of surgical masks, shrugging: "Give this to whoever looks like they need it." By the next week, the world had shut down, entering a streak of travel prohibitions and extended quarantine; much of the Reich family was unable to come to New York to grieve, sit shiva, and embrace the siblings.

With Hadas, Ben, and Gauri in New York and travel impossible, the three of them ended up quarantining in Yael's now empty Forest Hills home for some five months, a somber reversal of the empty nest. Each morning, they spread to different corners of the house to work from home; each evening, they convened to do the crossword, Ben hooking his laptop into the living room TV. In the madness of pandemic quarantine, the familiarity of ritual, the assemblage of chaos and information into solution, felt like an anchor. The streak grew linearly as caseloads grew exponentially. They formed a group chat with childhood friends who became occasional co-solvers via Zoom, renaming the group for each new milestone: "200 club," "300 club." They scoured internet forums to confirm: if you completed the puzzle at 1 a.m.—still before midnight California time—did that keep the streak alive?

In summer, with caseloads at a relative lull, Ben and Gauri decided to return to the West Coast. Old friends from elementary school invited the pod to a restaurant they owned for a COVID-safe sendoff. It was the first time they'd been out in half a year, the first time they'd been indoors with anyone but themselves, the first time Hadas or Ben had felt, since their mother's passing, like there was anything worthy of celebration.

Friends who own restaurants are often friends bestowing free drinks, and in a restaurant emptied of other patrons, the pod cut loose. Hadas hadn't had a margarita in months. At breakfast the next morning, Gauri was the first to realize it. They forgot to do the puzzle. Immediately, Hadas started sobbing. About the streak and the fantasy of normalcy it offered, now shattered; about her brother and sister-in-law leaving; about how the puzzle's tinny jingle, in her mother's hospital room, had felt like a miniature incantation, something small to try over and over in the hopes it would gather the choral voices of solution.

They did the puzzle anyway and they did the one they had missed and then, delirious maybe, back at this rickety bargaining stage of a grief they'd long thought cemented into acceptance, they wrote to the *Times*. They tried the general customer service inbox as well as a reporter friend's email, asking if he could forward it to the powers-that-be. They waxed poetic, they stretched the truth—suggesting it was their mother's dying wish, who knows why, that their crossword streak reach a year; claiming that actually they'd done the puzzle and the app, who knows how, had failed to register their solution. The *Times* reinstated the streak.

It's gone now, of course. They got to almost two years, some six hundred days, but once the streak lost its transfiguring promise, it began, like spellbook cursive stiffening into print, to feel like homework. They forgot one day and that was that. For the siblings, the streak had shown them one solution for closeness, but now, on opposite coasts again, they'd invent new ones.

In the 1920s and '30s, as crossword mania swept America, one newspaper in particular was unimpressed: *The New York Times*.

Worse than unimpressed; they found this whole crossword business unserious, even dangerous. In a November 17, 1924, "Topics of the Times" column entitled "A Familiar Form of Madness," the *Times* attacks the crossword in tones of pseudoscientific alarmism. You can hear the thwack of a boardroom pointer against a jagged graph, demonstrating the public's descent into hysteria, then off the chart and into hell: "Latest of the problems presented for solution by psychologists interested in the mental peculiarities of mobs," the alarum thunders, "is created by what is well called the craze over cross-word puzzles."

To the sensibility of the post–World War I *Times,* America was in an episode of cultural excess. Why couldn't everyone behave, moaned the paper, like an atomized, rational adult? Why did the masses continuously, nearly neurotically, invent a streak of pleasurable obsessions, distracting them from respectable matters? Didn't they know dancing crossword to a grid with blue, gold, and green boxes, like Dorothy's slippers shifting from silver in the book to ruby in the film, to read more vividly on-screen.

▬

The *Times* puzzle editors need a new clue for ASTAIRE. It's August 2023 and Joel Fagliano, senior puzzles editor, is sharing his screen. On the call are Wyna Liu, Tracy Bennett, and Christina Iverson. The four are group-editing the Sunday puzzle set to run on October 15.

ASTAIRE. Great letters that appear in scores of English words, but that means it's always in puzzles. Hard to find a new angle. The last time she'd needed a new clue for ASTAIRE, Tracy had fallen down a YouTube rabbit hole of dance videos: muted trumpets, tap shoes, coattails, and skirts in orbit. The constructors, Juliana Tringali Golden and Jeff Chen, went with [Rogers's dancing partner], but that's a little easy, Joel thinks. He's wondering if Fred Astaire has ever said anything quotable.

Tracy, with a quick google: "Dancing is a vertical interpretation of a horizontal intention." There are oohs and aahs at the abstract insight, and perhaps its association with a crossword's rows and columns; there is the muted tap dance of the other editors typing the quote into a search bar, trying to verify it's real.

Joel sighs. "We've got a Quote Investigator," he says, in the tone of a near-retirement traffic cop, referring to a website whose raison d'être is, essentially, disabusing you of the notion that everything witty was said by Mark Twain. Both George Bernard Shaw and Oscar Wilde have been credited with the supposed Astaire quote, and there isn't great evidence for either. Still, a quote would be nice. "It's a bit much," says Joel, "but what about 'I don't make love by kissing, I make love by dancing.'" There is, after this, what I can only call an uncomfortable silence.

Tracy, who's been here before, wonders if the group really needs to be spending so much time on just the sixth Across clue: "I would just name a movie he's been in and move along." Fair enough, this is was the first red-toed step toward communism? The *Times* went on; it's worth reading this first shot across the bow in depth:

> Scarcely recovered from the form of temporary madness that made so many people pay enormous prices for mah jong sets, about the same persons now are committing the same sinful waste in the utterly futile finding of words the letters of which will fit into a prearranged pattern, more or less complex.

> This [. . .] merely is a new utilization of leisure by those for whom it otherwise would be empty and tedious. They get nothing out of it except a primitive sort of mental exercise [. . .] irrelevant to mental development. The claimed merit of sending the puzzlers to the dictionary and so gaining an increased knowledge of its contents has little basis in fact [. . .] for the words are looked up for a single purpose and no study of the derivation, history or meaning of the words involved. Nothing except their existence is discovered.

> The amount and quality of intelligence utilized in the working out of cross-word puzzles almost precisely equal those that were revealed some years ago when an amazing—and discouraging— army of Americans filled the newspapers that cater to such folk with triumphant solutions of an arithmetical problem concerning the age of a suppositious Ann—a problem that any eighth grade boy or girl who is "all there" should have solved in his or her head in about thirty seconds.

The Gray Lady doth protest too much, methinks. Every line here forges some impure nugget of psychic conservatism into a shining sword of chastisement, tropes familiar to historians of 1920s America. Despite the postwar boom economy, spending money on games wasn't just mindless; Mah Jongg boards' "enormous prices" showed it was fiscally irresponsible to boot. In a moment of moral reorientation in the wake of the Great War, solving crosswords wasn't just idle trifling; it was "sinful," it was "primitive." Here was America mounting the world stage to flex its newfound geopolitical might and monologue its bloody coming-of-age; and yet here was an "army of Americans" "triumphant" about a newspaper riddle, when obviously that was the province of children. And if *the war to end all wars* was a full-throated wager about the future, what could be worse than refusing etymological determinism—rejecting the "derivation, history or meaning" of language and its power—and meditating instead on the sonic or orthographic capacities of words, the pleasure of the words themselves? *Nothing except their existence is discovered*—that doesn't sound bad, it sounds like a Buddhist mantra.

The madness metaphor would proliferate in the *Times*. In a review of Simon & Schuster's 1924 *The Cross Word Puzzle Book,* the *Times* claimed the puzzle was "act[ing] with a peculiar stimulus on the mass mind," and "seem[ed] to be as catching as the 'flu,' and as certain in its conquering power." In another 1924 column, it included the opinion of one J. C. Squires of the *London Observer,* arguing the puzzle was among "the various drugs to which the American people are reputed to have taken as a substitute for hard drink." In 1925, the *Times* forwarded the advice of W. R. Baker, president of the British Optical Association, who noted the "prevalence of headache arising from eye strain caused by cross-word puzzles." That same year, it ran an interview with British anthropologist Sir Arthur Keith, who feared the crossword malady might press the species into regression; the very paper interviewing him, Keith noted, though it was the "most intellectual" of its class, nonetheless devoted precious inches to base matters like sex, gambling, and sports. "Even crossword puzzles," said Keith, "I regard as an ebullition of an animal nature." In a letter to the *Times* editors begging the nation's laboratories to develop a "serum" for a new "epidemic," Philip Skrainka of New York finally named the disease: "crossworditis."

Why all this puffed-up pathologizing? For one thing, innovations in public health had educated the public on the argot of health. World War I, and the outbreak of the Spanish flu, had occasioned a revolution in medical research and technology, with typhoid vaccines, tuberculosis screenings, tetanus treatment, surgery disinfection, and mobile field hospitals replacing world systems of "fairly archaic" pre-war medicine. Gone were the days of quack solutions to real conditions; peacetime, then, meant—could finally mean, as though it were a luxury—proposals of real-sounding solutions to quack conditions like crossworditis. (In true *New York World* form, ads for specious panaceas crowded the page where its puzzle appeared; one issue touted cures for eczema, asthma, and tobacco addiction; other medical miscellany promised to teach you to throw your voice or how to "develop your bust.")

It's notable that the naysayers cited in the *Times* were by and large from across the pond. As historian Hal Barron describes, crosswords were so popular in 1920s America precisely because "they stood at the cultural crossroads of Victorianism and modernism," appeared to be both labor and time-waster, productive and nonproductive, in a postwar nation drawing, for the first time, a bright line between work and leisure. In a culture "still informed by Victorian sensibilities," the *Times* was happy to act as a British mouthpiece, out of which poured a Morse code of *tsk*s and *tut*s. For the Brits, the crossword "epidemic" was insidious because people solved instead of doing their jobs. The epidemic metaphor was thus a useful frame, suggesting as it did a rapid exogenous spread that, like all plagues, both dismissed any materialist or hedonist origins *(You don't like or need the crossword; rather, a parasite's gotten hold of you)* and hinted at top-down redress *(Have no fear, the government's here, to lobotomize those pesky districts of gray matter where your puzzle addiction lives)*.

The fear for "American industry" was as condescending as it was hyperbolic. The London *Times* titled a December 1924 article on the puzzle "An Enslaved America"; the crossword, it bellowed, was "making devastating inroads on the working hours of every rank of society." "It is estimated," the article continues, "that not less than 10,000,000 people have caught the infection, and that they spend half an hour daily, on the average, with the insidious pastime; that is to say 5,000,000 hours daily of the American people's time—most of nominally working hours—are being used up in unprofitable trifling." Word games were as toxic as unions: "This loss to productive activity [was] far more time than is lost by labor strikes."

Naturally, the authorities stepped in. Libraries barred the grids from their stacks; newspapers were "censored" before filing, the puzzle pages "blotted out so as to prevent puzzle addicts from lingering too long over the black and white squared mysteries, thus keeping the papers from other readers." These institutions claimed a right to defend themselves—and their serious patrons—from unseriousness: when "puzzle 'fans' swarm to the dictionaries and encyclopedias so as to drive away readers and students who need these books in their daily work, can there be any doubt of the library's duty to protect its legitimate readers?" Professors at the University of Michigan banned the puzzle in their classrooms. Magistrate Earl A. Smith ordered "court attendants, policemen, lawyers and their clients to cease pondering over cross-word puzzles" so traffic court could be respectably convened. Also in the U.K., "police magistrates [were] sternly rationing addicts to three puzzles a day, with an alternative of ten days in the workhouse."

All this ruckus over a game. If the crossword was a measly gimmick, then its critics furnished a master class in gimmickry: a Rube Goldberg machine stringing cavil and nostrum and up-turned nose one after another, to little cumulative effect. We can see the detractors getting the puzzle to do too much for their condemnations. The crossword was a menace, it was diseased, it was too modern, it was an affront to hard work. It was the idle plaything of a child, it was so dangerous everything must be sacrificed lest a child get their hand on one. When Simon & Schuster's *The Cross Word Puzzle Book* appeared in Britain, the sardonic preface gave instructions "as officious as a surgeon general's warning":

THIS IS NOT A TOY!

To Fathers, Mothers, Uncles and Aunts:

It is just possible you may pick this book up thinking of it as
a present for younger children. Will you please do us this one

favour—in the name of humanity? Just solve half a dozen of the puzzles, taken at random, yourself, before you pass it on. It's a small thing to ask—you'll be able to go back to your work in about a week.

The paper whose puzzle Shortz would go on to not only edit but spirit into the twenty-first century was, throughout the early twentieth, stalwart in its puzzle allergy. By 1941, the *Times* was the only major metropolitan daily paper in America that didn't have a crossword, the last adult in the newsroom. "Strictly a *News*paper," it advertised in 1925, in both senses of the word "strictly." "*Without* Comics, *Without* Puzzles." Shortz, who in his younger and more vulnerable years already wanted to make puzzling his work, encountered precisely this kind of resistance. In the eighth grade, he wrote an essay called "Puzzles as a Profession," sketching a career path and citing the (decidedly extracurricular) work of Dmitri Borgmann's *Language on Vacation*. "Making puzzles is a great life from my point of view," Shortz concludes, "easy life, fun and leisure[ly]." He got a B+. In the margin, his teacher wrote, "I thought you would connect this to the topic of becoming an adult. Obviously, you did not understand me."

Whether the buttoned-up *Times* understood its readership or not, eventually, like a father chided once too often for being unfun, it rolled up its shirtsleeves to show the world (and the *World*) how it was done. And if the Great War was the impetus for the roaring and jazzing and lindying and puzzling the *Times* so resisted, it took the fracture of World War II for the paper to come around.

Eleven days after the Japanese attack on Pearl Harbor, on December 18, 1941, Lester Markel, the editor of the Sunday *Times*, sent a memo to Arthur Hays Sulzberger, the paper's publisher. Markel had had a number of meetings with one Margaret Farrar "on the cross word puzzle thing." He left those meetings convinced of two action items:

1. That we ought to proceed with the puzzle, especially in view of the fact that it is possible that there will be bleak black-out hours—or if not that, then certainly a need for relaxation of some kind or other. [. . .]
2. That we ought not to try to do anything essentially different from what is now being done—except to do it better.

He included a memo from Farrar as well, and closed his note with three words: "Shall we proceed?"

The first *New York Times* crossword appeared three months later, on February 15, 1942, constructed by Charles Erlenkotter of the Bronx and edited by Farrar. "I don't think I have to sell you on the increased demand for this kind of pastime in an increasingly worried world," Farrar had written in her memo to Markel. "You can't think of your troubles while solving a cross word."

But that puzzle treats those troubles as impossible to ignore. Perhaps inevitably given the onset of World War II—or perhaps as a subconscious tactic to dampen the doom, see the names and consequences of conflict reduced, made mere monospace capital letters in a game, like alphabet blocks in a kindergarten. The clue for 1-Across was [Famous one-eyed general], for WAVELL, Sir Archibald Wavell of Britain, who lost that eye in the First World War at the Second Battle of Ypres (1915) and whose World War II victory against Italy at the Battle of Sidi Barrani (1940) "shattered the illusion of Axis invincibility." 117-Down was [Nazi submarine base in Belgium]: OSTEND. 54-Down was [Reluctant allies of Germany]: FINNS. 103-Down was [Port on Zuider Zee, occupied by Nazis]: AMSTERDAM. No old-boy mentions of the Schermerhorns of New Amsterdam here; there was a war on, damn it.

Even the fill-in-the-blank clues, many of which rummage for literary quotes (Shakespeare, naturally) to fluff up utilitarian words, arrive decidedly dour. (In 1925, the columnist Arthur Brisbane, perhaps unaware of how often the Bard appears in the grid, wrote, "Young people who want to increase their vocabulary should not deceive themselves with crosswords. Let them read Shakespeare.") The clue for SLEPT isn't [Reposed] or [Got some shuteye] or [Definitely didn't dream about Nazis], it's ["I have not ___ one wink."—*Cymbeline*], the servant Pisanio's insomniac lament on being ordered to murder Imogen. LIVE isn't [Exist] or [Not die], it's ["Men's evil manners ___ in brass."—*King Henry VIII*], the usher Griffith's hung-head assurance to sickly Katherine that our misdeeds never disappear, while our "virtues / We write in water." SIR doesn't reference "Little Sir Echo," the children's song popularized by Bing Crosby in 1939 ("You're a nice little fellow / I know by your voice / But you're always so far away. (Away)"); instead we get ["I am ___ Oracle"], Gratiano's taunt to sullen Antonio in *The Merchant of Venice*. You can only think of your troubles, it would seem, while reading Shakespeare. But then, Shakespeare disagreed, and punned in the gravest of circumstances. Mercutio, in *Romeo and Juliet*, bleeding to death: "Ask for me tomorrow and you shall find me a grave man."

■

If the clues in the inaugural *Times* puzzle can't help but cry havoc, future puzzles would quickly drop any pretense and let slip the dogs (and dogmas) of war. "Margaret Farrar practically enlisted the *New York Times* crossword in the Allied war effort," says John Farmer, a crossworder who helped digitize *Times* puzzles from the pre-Shortz era. While doing so, he came across clues from 1943 like [One of the gangster nations] for JAPAN, [Marine junk yard for Nazi subs] for ATLANTIC, and [Hitler's alibi in Russia] for RAIN, a reference to the autumn downpours (*Rasputitsa* in Russian, "quagmire season") that turned dirt roads to mud and slowed German formations advancing to Moscow on wheeled and horse-drawn transport. As with its first puzzle's mining of Shakespearean melancholia, vocabulary words with broader clue possibilities were, in the *Times* puzzle's debut decade, often routed back to war. TODAY is ["___ Europe, tomorrow the World"—Hitler]. APPEASER is [He thinks he can do business with

Hitler]. ELITE is frequently [Crack Nazi regiment]. And so on, often with that same tonal cocktail of jocular, triumphal sarcasm ("junk yard," "he thinks . . . " "crack") that sounds like neurotic blurting.

Eighty years on, the faraway but all-consuming cacophony of war was, in the era of the COVID-19 virus, transmuted twice: first into the maddening and mournful din of ambulance sirens; and then, once stay-at-home measures were instituted in 2020, into the silences of lockdown. In the gray streak of quarantine, games became a refuge. A million new subscribers signed up for Chess.com each month in 2020, once lockdowns began. Hours spent playing games on Nvidia's graphics platforms jumped 50 percent during quarantine, and spending on video games by Americans hit a record $10.86 billion in the first quarter of 2020. "Americans are stocking up on dry goods, toilet paper . . . and puzzles," reads a March 2020 headline in *The Washington Post,* as if diversion in a world at standstill might be deemed an essential good. "At the height of the pandemic," writes Oliver Roeder, "more games were being played than at perhaps any time in human history."

As it did for Hadas and Ben Reich, this gaming instinct had a social aim. Slews of families and friend groups—mine included—stayed in touch by convening board game nights on Zoom, playing web-based party games like JackBox, or texting each other their Wordle grids. Writing about Wordle in the *Los Angeles Times,* C. Thi Nguyen, a philosopher of games at the University of Utah, described the "steady stream of small communions" on seeing another player's 5-by-6 yellow and green grid, announcing the specific way they struggled, in one sliver of their day, toward victory. "In normal life," writes Nyugen, "other people's cares and goals are diverse—and often opaque." This was an opacity that social distancing had only amplified, adding the silicate film of a screen to the means of separation. But by "giving everyone the same objective," Nguyen continues, "games artificially align our interests. This designed narrowness is what enables the strange intimacy of game-playing."

And as it did for Hadas and Ben, the crossword, and the crossword streak, each played a remedial role in pandemic life. Like other games, the crossword could be cast as uncomplicated solace: the psychologist Namrata Malhotra told *The Times of India* "puzzles and problem solving games have the ability to keep the player distracted from the madness . . . affecting their lives [during] the COVID-19 pandemic." But they could also serve a more profound purpose. In Nguyen's book, *Games: Agency as Art,* he argues that more than simple diversion, "games are part of our human practices of inscription." In the tradition of philosopher John Dewey, Nguyen is interested not in how games or puzzles resemble fiction or visual art, but how they stand apart as their own medium, enabling medium-specific effects: "Painting lets us record sights, music lets us record sounds, stories let us record narrative, and games let us record agencies." Games ask us to accept and strive for designed ends (points, a solved puzzle) in order to reveal new sets of means, a library of dormant agencies. The simple rules of basketball produce a roster of possible actions, and strategic choices among them: bounce vs. chest passes, inside game vs. shooting threes, 1-on-1 coverage vs. zone defense. And these strategic choices in turn produce an evolution of the circumstances in which one or the other is called for, a metagame of compounding, newly discovered agencies. "Just as novels let us experience lives we have not lived," writes Nguyen, "games let us experience forms of agency we might not have discovered on our own."

Crosswords are no different. They help us discover a madness that "defamiliarize[s] the familiar," writes Adrienne Raphel, by which she means they let us do things with language beyond making sense, often by letting letters briefly dissolve into unsignifying signs. At times when language fails to adequately represent the madness of life, the crossword defamiliarizes language in the grid as solvers build up words letter by letter, as though making language anew. This defamiliarization occurs whenever a constructor notices a favorite phrase is 15 letters long (MAKE IT MAKE SENSE, HIDDEN BALL TRICK) or capitalizes on linguistic happenstance (e.g., by punning on "eye rhymes," which look like they should but don't actually rhyme, as in KOSHER NOSHER or BASELINE VASELINE). Constructing a grid is so arithmetical a task that one frequently forgets the true meanings of words once they've become puzzle entries. I always see DUAL IPA (what is that? some beer I'd hate, twice as much?) before the singer DUA LIPA comes into view. Once, the constructor Brooke Husic requested that we remove the word GROPE from a grid we were building together. I suggested an A instead of an O. "What's *grah-pay*?" she asked.

This defamiliarization is part of the solver's toolkit too. Knowledge of orthography might lead one to pencil a tentative S at the end of a clue asking for a plural noun, or an ED for one asking for a past tense verb—a strategy the game designer, the constructor, will exploit in turn. [Ancients, for instance] isn't a plural, it's ANAGRAM, since "ancients" is a rearrangement of—an anagram *for*—"instance." [Taken control] isn't a verb phrase, it's PLACEBO.

Nguyen prefers purer strategy games like Go (in which a vast agential plain opens out from simple rules) and deception games like Mafia or *Secret Hitler* (in which the full sweep of human suggestiveness is deliciously manipulable) to word and especially trivia games (in which background knowledge, and its inevitable biases, can predict success). Crosswords, by their nature, traffic in these skewed demands for knowledge, and reversing this exclusivity—a campaign led by many of the figures in this book—would make crosswords not just a fairer game, but a deeper one.

But the crossword's epistemological frame, along with its status as a daily, social pandemic balm, is no coincidence. If the content of crosswords is, as constructor Laura Braunstein has put it, one answer to the question, "What do you need to know in order to be a person of the world?," then solving the crossword is affirmation that, having demonstrated your knowledge, you can continue to exist in that world, even trust it. Will Shortz likes to say crosswords challenge us to "create order out of chaos." In the COVID era, in which misinformation and disinformation and informational overload and panicked uncertainty all proliferated in an expanding universe of public health directives, knowing how to manage the data of a crossword was to create order out of a kind of chaos that, up to now, had been unimaginable. In a *New York Times* "solver story" by Italian writer Cosimo Bizzarri, he remarks: "Right now in Italy, a country where governments change frequently, citizens are in desperate need of someone to trust." His solution was a weekly Italian magazine with crosswords, quizzes, and logic games. "With its long history, immutable layout and fixed set of contents, *La Settimana Enigmistica* is looked upon by many as one thing they can depend on to reassure them." Wash your hands, stay inside, solve crosswords. If you have to get sick, crosworditis may be the lesser evil.

The combination of these two features of crosswords—defamil-iarization of the letter and daily requests for familiar knowledge—produced, for many, an outré soothing. In a literal 15-by-15 frame of reference, words could be playfully, safely divested of their frames of reference, each word wearing a mask over its mouth, its meaning muffled, its tongue sticking out at you underneath. When the *Times* announced, in April 2020, that it would expand its print puzzle options (adding among other offerings a "tweet-sized riddle" called a Brain Tickler), Shortz recognized that solving could be a salve in troubled times. "People feel stressed," he said. "You feel in control of life when you've finished a good puzzle." If the timing was meant to ease the burden of the pandemic, the content would mask it: the puzzle page would "not even contain the word 'coronavirus,'" according to Shortz. Where the early *Times* puzzles frequently mentioned, even sometimes spotlighted, the current events grimly addressed in the paper's reportage, in 2020 the puzzle page drew a boundary: "This will be the one coronavirus-free part of the newspaper."

And then there's the crossword streak. I confess that I have never much tended to my own crossword streak, possibly a nostalgic snobbishness from my time as a paper-and-pen solver. But its curative powers in lockdown are undeniable. There were countless people, like Hadas and Ben, for whom the streak seemed to generate a quiet but substantive momentum, as though all those gold stars and jingles might swell into galactic explosion, a Big Bang inaugurating the New Normal. For many, the streak assessed their daily cognitive readiness, an evaluation, however imprecise, of just how fast their minds were or were not rotting in quarantine; I have heard from dozens of people who refused to start their day without solving the *Times* crossword, or attaining the Genius level in Spelling Bee. And there were people for whom the crossword could stand for productivity in a moment of nonproductivity, of forward motion as everyone sheltered in place, of pseudo-work amid mass layoffs and furloughs. Wordplay can feel like last-ditch frivolity, as with Mercutio's final quip, or when Cosimo Biz-zarri's friend Marina informed him that CORONAVIRUS is an ana-gram of CARNIVOROUS, as if the pair were rearranging deck chairs on the *Titanic*. But crosswords can be more than played. They can be solved, day in and day out. They can become the familiar stuff of ritual.

❑■❑

When I interviewed Nguyen, I half-expected him to rail against the streak. In his work, what he calls the "value clarity" of games is pre-sented as a respite from, not a solution for, the messiness of real life. In an echo of Will Shortz, Nguyen describes how our daily problems are often misshapen: either far beyond our ability, or else frustratingly simple. Games, on the other hand, offer obstacles of precisely the right size and shape. In the same way, real life asks us to be value pluralists: we might want to be a good friend, a diligent researcher, a gentle par-ent, an ethical consumer, a happy person, and so on. This is a dense thicket of values in itself—what would winning even look like?—and some of them are in hard-to-resolve tension, even mutually incom-patible: we value convening with family for the holidays, we owe it to our community to be COVID-safe. A primary pleasure of games, per Nguyen, is that they simplify the value landscape: solve this puzzle, save that princess, collect these coins, and win.

But Nguyen worries about what happens on exiting the "magic cir-cle" of the game, the philosopher Johan Huizinga's term for the con-secrated, ritualistic zone of play. "The value clarity of games," writes Nguyen, "might bring about an expectation for value clarity outside the game, and attract players to those real world systems that present values with game-like simplicity." That is, as he's said more strikingly elsewhere: he isn't worried first-person shooter video games will pro-duce more violent children, he's worried they'll produce more money-obsessed adults; the single-minded striving for points can too easily become the single-minded striving for quantifiable status; Nguyen loves games but is suspicious of gamification. Where gamified systems rule, value pluralism and the richness of activities are thinned out in favor of a single, portable metric: you get a FitBit to exercise more, but end up obsessed with step counts. You seek a ranging education with pillowy outcomes like wisdom, curiosity, and breadth, but feel forced to optimize for grades. You join Twitter, earnestly if naively in search of conversation, but become occupied only by follower counts, likes, retweets. Everywhere, process cedes to product, experience to commodity. It's not that these measures are universally empty or bankrupt. It's that their proliferation is built on their trackability, their family resemblance to existing data, and participants' manic pursuit of them to the exclusion of the unquantifiable: a madness, then, of the familiar form.

Nguyen acknowledges the crossword streak has an element of this manicured addictiveness, and that streak obsessives might be accordingly less impressed by a given puzzle's inventiveness (the same way FitBit users might be more enamored of their step counts than the physical feel of running, the views on their route, and so on). But the streak might also be another game altogether. Timing your solve or extending your streak are, on that view, analogous to the distance between chess and blitz chess, or the way tournament players might lose a game on purpose, to match with a lower-ranked opponent in later rounds.

Whatever its addictive underpinning, Nguyen saw the crossword streak as an enriching ritual. He cited the philosopher Simon Scheffler, whose essay "The Normativity of Tradition" describes rituals as one attempt, poetic as much as practical, to carve out a home in time. Our physical homes establish a sense of belonging; when we're outside them, they hold the possibility of return. But we are all "homeless in time," says Scheffler; rituals and traditions are one method of domesticating time, "enabl[ing] us to feel, as we engage in the routine activity, that we are making contact with other stages of our lives." We lack temporal mobility, and the "twin urges to revisit the past and to see into the future can be almost unbearably powerful." In lockdown, when we lacked physical mobility as well, when time seemed all of a sudden doubly indomitable, the streak's power would only grow. All the more so since traditions, more than personal routines, are "public, collective enterprises," implicating us in a "custodial chain" that's both forward- and backward-looking.

In the hospital, or locked down in their childhood home in Queens, Hadas and Ben Reich could do the crossword every day, an attempt to lock down time—create a future in which, if their mother couldn't exist, at least her memory might be held aloft. The psychotherapist Deborah Sosin, whose father died in 2015, describes finding, among piles of her father's papers, a two-pocket folder labeled "A Portfolio of Puzzles." It contained seventy-six *New York Times* Sunday crosswords, some blank, some partially completed by him. Her father was the one who, in his Queens accent, had tutored her in crosswordese, what the two of them called the Crossword E's: "fancy words like ETUI or EFT or EWER or EPEE or EKE." Encountering her father's work in progress, Sosin commits to solving every unfinished puzzle. She will thrill on seeing his answers for clues she wouldn't have known herself, on subjects like poetry or mythology. Occasionally, she'll mask his wrong answers, her blue pen gliding over his ghostlike pencilings. She'll do it carefully. "It's a collaboration across time," she'll say.

The COVID-19 pandemic refashioned many people's relationship to solving crosswords; it would do the same for crossword construction.

To many, this was a long time coming. In the decade before the pandemic, the *Times* crossword app, launched in 2009, began exposing a younger, tech-savvier audience to the puzzle, who wondered in turn why their pop culture sensibilities rarely appeared in the grid. In 2013, Sudheendra Hangal, Jaya Hangal, and John Temple (two computer scientists and a newspaper editor, respectively) founded Amuse Labs; their PuzzleMe product let crossword-makers embed a solvable grid directly onto a webpage, rather than link to a downloadable PDF. A spate of indie crossword blogs launched in this era, with punny names like *Glutton for Pun* (Erik Agard), *The Grid Kid* (Sam Ezersky), *Grids These Days* (Paolo Pasco), *Jenna Sais Quois* (Jenna LaFleur). Many of these sites modeled themselves on the blog of Brendan Emmett Quigley, who since 2008 has published what he calls "locally-foraged puzzles," borrowing an aesthetic partway between dumpster diver and artisanal coffeemaker. Quigley, with his gravelly voice, catholic musical taste, and mad-lib-sounding hobby (he's in a percussion ensemble called the Boston Typewriter Orchestra), is a first-wave crossword gentrifier—though the gentrification here is happening in reverse, like if Lou Reed moved to a doorman building on the Upper East Side.

Like Quigley before them, the indie blogs wanted to publish puzzles in response to current events, more tweet than retrospective essay—a spontaneity bedeviled by the years-plus gap between acceptance and publication at venues like the *Times*. To see Quigley pay tribute to Sonia SOTOMAYOR days after her 2009 confirmation to the Supreme Court was to understand that puzzles didn't just solicit common knowledge, they had a hand in affirming it.

Also like Quigley, indies wanted to make puzzles weirder. Sometimes that looked like gentle trolling. In 2019, Quigley ran a blog puzzle called "Do Me a Solid." 1-Across was [Even-money roulette bet]. 8-Across was [Gass's partner in Tenacious D]. 36-Down was [Tell-tale sign of a goth, outfit-wise]. Solvers eventually realized that every single clue had the answer BLACK, and that, once filled in, the grid could be imagined as a solid black 15-by-15 expanse. "Dark humor," said one blog commenter. "You win Quigley!" said another.

The blogs became virtual watering holes, not only for collaborating with other puzzlers (by, say, writing puzzles together then cross-posting on each other's sites) but also for bringing new puzzlers into the fold (by, among other mechanisms, offering one's services as a mentor). As it had with the Reich siblings' solving, this turned puzzle-making into even more of a social phenomenon. Of course, crossword lovers, and slingers of wordplay generally, have always sought one another's company, even in calamitous times; the pun requires the assent of the groan.

The craze of the 1920s was propelled in part by the barbed wits seated like knights around a table at the Algonquin Hotel, on 44th Street in midtown Manhattan. The very first meeting of the Algonquin Round Table was planned around a pun, born of good-natured ribbing: Alexander Woollcott, the *New York Times* theater critic who signed his column A. Woollcott, had antagonized his literary coterie by opening many of his reviews with a piece of self-serious shrapnel: "From my seat in the theater of war . . ." ("Must have been the last row near the exit," quipped editor Art Samuels; Woollcott never saw battle, and instead worked on the military newspaper *Stars and Stripes*). In 1919, Woollcott's friends—including Franklin Pierce Adams (F.P.A.), Dorothy Parker, and Ruth Hale, the last of whom would go on to cofound the Amateur Cross Word Puzzle League of America in 1924—staged a catered intervention: they invited Woollcott to lunch at the Algonquin in order to welcome him home from the war, a year after his return. Snickering, they put up a banner in the hotel dining room:

AWOL
cot

A. Woollcott had gone AWOL; he was furious at the joke and the misspelling; these quipsters would return to the Algonquin at 1 p.m. nearly every day for a decade. As they had with Woollcott, the Round Table threw verbal elbows, then praised one another; an entente of entendres would ensue. They played charades, they punned mercilessly, they called the group the Vicious Circle, the Luigi Board. Dorothy Parker, their Guinevere, the "grande dame of cleverness," eventually attempted a distinction between witticism and criticism. "You can't teach an old dogma new tricks"—one of her more famous puns—was as much a joke as affirmation of the unfamiliar madness of postwar modernity. Parker would lend her sharpened tongue to causes beyond the literary: in 1927, she raised defense funds and wrote moving appeals on behalf of Nicola Sacco and Bartolomeo Vanzetti, the Italian anarchists arrested for murder in 1920 on flimsy evidence. Later, she'd become a socialist, and cofound the first-ever screenwriters' union ("Union is not a four-letter word!"). Like many in this book, she wanted her language games to be both *leisure* and *license,* to allow space for play that might solidify into social vision: "There's a hell of a distance," she said, "between wisecracking and wit. Wit has truth in it; wisecracking is simply calisthenics with words."

The crossword puzzle has long straddled that distance. Born of wise-cracking, perhaps, but drafted, sometimes clumsily, in service of wit, of delivering truth, only to go AWOL again among a chorus of groans. The various dens of cruciverbalism tended to emphasize one of these ends over another. Cruciverb.com, an early online forum, was a space to discuss puzzles, bounce theme ideas off one another: a pasture for grazing wisecrackers. On the other hand, initiatives like the Crossword Puzzle Collaboration Directory, established in 2018 by constructors Erik Agard and Will Nediger at the urging of the *Times*'s Deb Amlen, focused on diversifying the bylines normally seen in newspaper and magazine puzzles: a mentoring system for novel wits.

Indie blogs did both, commenting on yesterday's news, punning on whatever. When the COVID-19 lockdowns began, a new community developed: a crossword puzzle "server" on the social platform Discord, called Crosscord.

◼

The members of the Algonquin Round Table, writes historian Jennifer Ratner-Rosenhagen, "became famous for being famous"; online communities, on the other hand, prize anonymity and democratization. When Crosscord launched in January 2019, it boasted a handful of newer puzzle lovers in discussion with old salts. (Tyler Hinman, in 2005 the youngest-ever ACPT winner at twenty years old, goes by "Tyler Hinman, Aged Prodigy" on the platform.) But when lockdowns began in 2020, hundreds flocked to the site. A new crossword craze was born.

The zeal of these converts was a digital recursion of the 1920s, a century on; a familiar form of madness, told through memes, GIFs, and emojis. These new cruciverbalists developed a shorthand, distinguishing between "indies" (blog puzzles; nonmainstream venues like the American Values Club, which once was published by the satiri-cal outlet *The Onion*) and "syndies" (for those solving widely syndi-cated puzzles like the *Times*'s in local papers). They shortened the phrase "unchecked squares" to "unches"; they called grids with black square asymmetry "asyms." Through their elders (Hinman again) they learned the terminology of their forebears: black squares added to a crossword grid that don't affect the word count and only make existing words shorter (and so make the grid, it's hoped, easier to fill) are called "helpers" (by the generous) or "cheaters" (per the purists). Merl Reagle, forever getting words to shed their outermost skin, called them "black adders." Leonard Williams, an anarchist, calls them "black blocs." Like astrology lovers on a dating app, Crosscord users asked one another if they'd solved the *Times* puzzle published on the day they were born, and if so what it all means. They talked about cutting the silence of lockdown with background noise as they'd solve or construct: one lis-tened to commercials from the 1960s and '70s, another binged *Fra-sier,* a third put on jazz. They nurtured a dramaturgical obsession with identifying real-life crosswords used as props in television and movies.

Ben Bass, an attorney in Chicago, August 2022: "Tony Soprano's biggest crime—not starting with the crossword." He'd posted a screen-cap from a 2004 episode of *The Sopranos* ("Where's Johnny?," Season 5, Feech La Manna tries to muscle Sal Vitro outta the neighborhood). Tony, smug, hunches over a newspaper's puzzle page, the commuter's accoutrements flanking him: Dunkin' Donuts coffee, bagel with cream cheese. He appears to be working a jumble, not the crossword above the fold. "A challenge," says one commenter, "identify the puzzle." Someone figures it must be the *Star-Ledger,* the New Jersey periodi-cal a squinting and robed Tony fetches in the series pilot. Another suggests the episode was likely shot in 2003. In a matter of days, in a rare combination—buzz of an online hive mind, industriousness of a library's worker bees—the Crosscord sleuths had phoned multiple New Jersey libraries, unearthed scans of the *Star-Ledger* from 2003, determined it *wasn't* that paper, then with help from the Archives Department of the Newark Library ascertained it was, in fact, another New Jersey paper called the *Courier-News,* which on April 26, 2003, ran a puzzle by one Josiah Breward. It was the grid Tony was looking at, appropriately called "Spinoffs." Evan Birnholz, the Sunday crossword writer for *The Washington Post,* solved the decades-old puzzle. "I love the internet," beamed one of the server's moderators. (Librarians, a century ago the crossworder's natural enemy—remember the censored papers, the guarded reference books—are here restored to their natural role as puzzler's ally.)

Why do they do this? Ben Zimmer, a lexicographer and linguist who helps lead Crosscord's "gridspotting" efforts, has described how shows like *Mad Men* treat language just as meticulously as its retro set dressing. Creator Matthew Weiner was known to halt that production "over matters as subtle as the size of fruit in a bowl," lest an anachronism sneak in. And Weiner told Zimmer he still regretted allowing Joan to say "The medium is the message," four years before Marshall McLuhan introduced the idiom in print. Vintage dresses, bowls of fruit, turns of phrase, and crosswords—all of it is an index of time and place.

When Margaret Farrar retired from the *Times* in 1969, loyal solvers and constructors rushed to pay tribute in the language she'd taught them: crosswordese. On January 26, 1969, the *Times* printed a poem by Don Parks of Cranston, Rhode Island, with lines like "The ern upon the Azov Sea, / Sing ave and adieu to thee!"

The crossword as a print object is time-specific, but crosswordese is often presented as timeless: words that, because they feature certain letter combinations, are—have been, will be—overrepresented in crossword puzzles, relative to their obscurity. At a macro scale, this lexicon is trackably stable: in 2013, the software developer Noah Veltman calculated a "crosswordiness" score that weighs how often a word appears in a crossword puzzle *against* how often it appears in the Google Books database. From 1996 to 2012, ERA, AREA, and ERE were the most common crossword answers (each appeared over 250 times), but ASEA, SMEE, and URSA had the most *crosswordiness,* maddening in their simultaneous familiarity (ASEA is in the puzzle again, ugh) and unfamiliarity (wait, wouldn't you say "At sea"?).

But at a micro scale, Crosscord users—younger, newer to puzzles and so lacking the baggage of decades of solving that would inure them to words like INURE—brought fresh perspectives to the crossword's stale fill. Malaika Handa, a software engineer who writes puzzles for *Vulture,* in 2021: "My favorite game is 'which crosswordese did I know before solving crosswords?'" ECRU was common knowledge to her; the color is a plot point in one of Sydney Taylor's *All-of-a-Kind Family* books. Musicians chimed in to say ARIA, the opera solo, never seemed a rarefied term. Jazz banders knew OLEO as the title of a hard bop tune written by Sonny Rollins, recorded by Rollins and Miles Davis, and deemed a standard by goateed bandleaders nationwide. People who'd spent time in the corporate world didn't think IDEATE was strange; someone once bought their New York-baseball-loving mother one of Mel OTT's bats for Christmas; someone's dog was named after ASTA from *The Thin Man;* art lovers had encountered not just DALI and MIRO but ARP, ERTE, KLEE, and ENSOR. To see one's knowledge reproduced in the grid—not once or twice but constantly thanks to its letter composition—was to be reminded that the knowledge demanded of a crossword solver is incidental, and malleable. And to begin, as so many Crosscorders did, to write their own clues for musty, inherited crosswordese—as an internet-savvy twentysomething, say, stuck at home in the pandemic—was to step into Simon Scheffler's "custodial chain," try to shake off its rust, and bring some madness to the familiar.

There was Ada Nicolle's OREO Cluing Project, an effort by Nicolle, a trans comedian and constructor, to crowdsource as many clues as possible for the stalwart crossword cookie. Starting in September 2020, she stacked 238 of them from fifty contributors. The clues showcased not only a widening aperture of cultural reference, but also experimentation with clue syntax, by breaking the fourth wall or rambling irreverently. Here's fifteen cookies, one sleeveful:

- Its website says "Our site uses cookies. We make them too."
- Cookie split by Ross and Rachel in the first "Friends" episode
- Brand with a "Twist, Lick, Dunk!" game on the App Store
- "Parent Trap" treat eaten with peanut butter

- Edible poker tell in the film "Rounders"
- Brand known in China as 奥利奥 (Àolì'ào)
- Dunker's dunkee
- Cookie that Ben Carson confused with a foreclosure-related term
- Brand whose jingle is G-Bb-G-Bb-C-Bb-Ab-G-F
- You gotta really soak it in milk to get that perfect soft texture, in my experience
- Crème blue-gray? (clue for ___ if it weren't black and white)
- ___ Collins (tuxedo cat on Wikipedia's "List of animals with fraudulent diplomas")
- Cookie whose filling can be replaced with toothpaste, in a cruel prank
- Cookie whose Twitter account recommends eating all the cookies from the middle sleeve, then filling the empty sleeve with milk for dunking, which, what the HELL
- Apt rhyme for "gory, yo" (because it's real messy when I eat them)

In a similar vein, a pandemic-era indie blogger going by meatdaddy69420 created the Tabula Rasa Project. They constructed a 15-by-15 grid and sent it to whoever agreed to clue it. Seeing how different people clue the same entries, they wrote in a blog post, is an "intimate moment where you get a curated peek inside someone's brain . . . indie puzzles are where most of this magic happens, as the 'rules' imposed by larger publications aren't a thing out here in this wild, wild, west." They described the guiding principles behind the project: puzzles "are designed to be fun—not stuffy homages to Puccini operas or whatever"; "everyone is secretly a huge freak"; and "fun is more fun when you get more people involved." One person would clue OTHER as ["Eating the ___: Desire and Resistance" by bell hooks, 1992], another would go with [Common third option in a dropdown menu for choosing one's gender (they can do better than this)], a third with [___ Mother ("Coraline" character)]. To clue his version, Alex Boisvert, a software engineer with a PhD in math from UCLA, used a scoring algorithm called TF-IDF (term frequency-inverse document frequency). For a given crossword answer, the "term frequency" measures how often a word appears in clues for that answer, highlighting, say, how regularly "bird" appears in clues for HERON, or "lake" in clues for ERIE. The "inverse document frequency" suppresses words common to clues for *other* answers—words like "the" appear in clues for so many answers that they don't reveal how that particular answer is uniquely clued. Boisvert's program lists the four "most important" words in clues; that list becomes the new clue, like an AI-generated poem:

Bulb light invention thought	IDEA
Longoria Mendes Peron Gabor	EVA
Buildup stuff yucky filthy	CRUD
Generation cop's drummer's route	BEAT
Copy command fine fabric	PRINT

Ricky Cruz, who established Crosscord and never expected it to get so popular, has seen it spin into a roundtable not for high-society journalists but for cruciverbalists young and old, rich and poor, neophyte and veteran. Cruz, a twenty-five-year-old from Rancho Cucamonga, California, has loved puzzles since he was a kid, but thought crosswords were "the boring ones." Then in college he came across a crossword whose conceit involved the game Tetris; he remembers the grid's black square clusters were all valid Tetris blocks, and moving the black squares around revealed a hidden answer. "That was amazing," he told me. "I didn't know you could do that with a crossword." He encountered the rambling and acerbic cluing style of Paolo Pasco, the independence and verve of Brendan Emmett Quigley's themes, the sleek and boundary-pushing grids of Kameron Austin Collins. A college kid on a shoestring budget, he would read crossword review blogs to see, without paying for a subscription, what kinds of puzzles the *Times* was running, since bloggers always include a solution grid in their writeups. He was just out of college, living in L.A. with friends from undergrad and working at Papa Johns, when he got his first *Times* acceptance. He'd heard from others on Crosscord what the subject line looked like in the email, and when he saw it, he let his coworkers see the email on his phone: *Crosswords—Yes!*

When that first puzzle ran, on October 3, 2019, Cruz drove to the Barnes & Noble in a Glendale mall to get a hard copy of the *Times* and show his coworkers. His excitement was about more than just prestige: "The $500 for it is basically a month of rent for me," he posted on Crosscord. The puzzle's theme was fitting, given how the explosion of interest in crosswords in the 2020s mirrored the first crossword craze of the 1920s: words that precede "mirror" were literally reflected in the grid, so [Dressing room staple] was VANITY YTINAV and [London tabloid that Piers Morgan once headed] was DAILY YLIAD. Since then he's had six more puzzles in the *Times,* and published dozens more on his blog. Occasionally, Cruz worries he's "falling out of love with crosswords." But then a new idea will strike. It's something that's never been done before, and he's not sure it'll work. He opens up a blank grid, and the streak continues.

CHAPTER 5

Except for the Marabar Caves

[Hot take?], 9 letters*

—ERICA HSIUNG WOJCIK, *The New York Times*, 2023

O n February 17, 2020, Sally Hoelscher published her first crossword puzzle in *The New York Times*. It was Presidents' Day; the theme was memoirs by first ladies. The crossword puzzle's buzzing ecosystem whirred into action. Hoelscher posted a photo of the newspaper her husband had risen early on his day off to buy, and old salts offered congratulations in the Facebook group that develops constructors from underrepresented groups. Some of the *Times*'s million-plus digital crossword subscribers finished Hoelscher's puzzle with their thumbs, extending their solving streaks. Crossword bloggers favorably reviewed the puzzle's theme, nonthematic vocabulary, and clues.

In comments sections on crossword blogs, under off-color riffs on hypothetical titles for a Melania Trump memoir, a debate raged. Jenni Levy, an internist and writer on the review site *Diary of a Crossword Fiend,* applauded how roundly Hoelscher's puzzle "passe[d] the crossword Bechdel test." But Levy bemoaned a "missed opportunity."

"I went through looking for men's names with mounting excitement: What if there weren't any?" she wrote. But 66-Across, DEE, was clued as [Billy ___ Williams], not as the letter or the grade. (It's worth noting this disappointment is associated with a clue referencing a Black man, another unfortunate rarity in mainstream puzzles.) Responding to Levy, a commenter wondered: "Why is it desirable/necessary to have women's names predominate in crossword puzzles. . . . I ignore the male/female body count." Levy's response was a full-throated call to arms:

> Because women are underrepresented in puzzle content and cre-
> ation. Clues and answers that are stereotypically masculine are
> "general interest"; clues and answers that are stereotypically femi-
> nine are "niche" or "obscure." . . . We're so far from [parity] that
> a few puzzles with exclusively women's names wouldn't get us
> there . . . [and feminism here means] we acknowledge the systemic
> forces that threaten women, we speak up when we see those forces
> represented in crosswords, and we call on our community to do
> better.

Hoelscher appeared, replied to Levy, and said she'd submitted the puzzle with no men, but wasn't surprised when the *Times* editors changed that.

◼

Crossword editors are strange arbiters of cultural relevance. Read tweets by Awkwafina or Olivia Wilde on learning they've been immortalized in the black-and-white grid—it's the bookish version of handprints on a slab outside Grauman's Chinese Theatre. But any pub trivia attendee—exposed to categories on craft beer or things that smell like sourdough or whatever the emcee is into—will tell you personnel is policy. That crossword mainstays like *The New York Times, Los Angeles Times,* and *The Wall Street Journal* have largely been written, edited, fact-checked, and test-solved by a single demographic—older white men—dictates what makes it into the grid, and what's kept out.

When editors review a puzzle submission, they mark it up—minus signs next to obscurities or variant spellings, check marks by lively vocabulary. But one editor's demerit is another solver's ambition. Constructors constantly argue with editors that their culture is puzzleworthy, only to hear feedback greased by bias, and occasional outright sexism or racism. MARIE KONDO wouldn't be familiar enough "to most solvers, especially with that unusual last name." GAY EROTICA is an "envelope-pusher that risks solver reactions." (According to Xword Info, the blog that tracks *Times* crossword statistics, EROTICA has appeared in the *Times* puzzle more than forty times since 1950.) BLACK GIRLS ROCK "might elicit unfavorable responses." The rapper FLAVOR FLAV, in a puzzle I wrote, earned a minus sign.

"Popular music," crossword editor Ben Tausig told me, "where lots of young women and people of color are visible, is regularly dismissed as too ephemeral for a Great Crossword Puzzle . . . ephemerality is the code word, exclusion is the result."

And while some corners of culture are kept out of crosswords, some troubling aspects of language creep in. The *Times* puzzle weathered deep sensitivity issues in the 2010s, including allowing a racial slur in a grid in January 2019—despite protestations from those who saw the puzzle prepublication. Clues can reek of mischaracterization disguised as description: consider clues for MEN [Exasperated comment from a feminist] and HOOD [Place with homies]. In many cases, editorial changes warp a constructor's original, inoffensive clue.

Will Shortz, *Times* editor since 1993, has cited low submission rates from underrepresented groups as one reason for lack of constructor parity. But tone-deafness and opacity can put constructors off the newspaper. In a 2020 Facebook thread with Shortz and other commenters, constructor Rebecca Falcon posted: "I can't feel good about putting my work into an outlet that I feel has very different values than my own [. . .] is there anything being done to address these issues?" Shortz gave a thoughtful answer citing recent increases in women bylines, saying parity was "an important issue for us." But when prodded about insensitive edits, he denied them, adding: "If a puzzlemaker is unhappy with our style of editing, then they should send their work elsewhere (or publish it themselves to keep complete control)."

And so they did. The rise in indie puzzles was as much about instant gratification—publishing a puzzle days, not years, after making it— as it was dissatisfaction with mainstream editing norms. In the Wild West of the internet, puzzle anarchy could reign. Rebecca Falcon could run a puzzle themed around the answer SIDE BOOBS, in which the letters BOOBS extended beyond the sides of the grid—too bodily, too tittering, for a mainstream puzzle. Grid art could skew cartoonish, as in puzzles in the shape of a donut or a Minion from the movie *Despicable Me*—both of which, because posted online, arrived in color, with yellow squares for the Minion's body and pinks, greens, and reds for the donut's sprinkles. These puzzles could get as niche as they wanted: in that donut puzzle, by Alex Boisvert, every single clue is a reference to a joke on *The Simpsons*. Swapping column inches for infinite digital space, they could go long on clues, hyper-contextualizing entries dear to them, or experimenting with lankier versions of the *Times*'s dad jokes: that Minions puzzle, a collaboration between bloggers Crosstina Aquafina, meatdaddy69420, and Kate Chin Park, has the clue [my cry as my cannibal boyfriend tells me he's going vegan and then breaks up with me] for WHAT AM I CHOPPED LIVER.

If this was a politics of thumbing one's nose at the buttoned-up *Times,* there were attempts at direct intervention too. This same era saw the rise of the puzzle pack: crossword bundles whose proceeds help fund progressive causes, as in *These Puzzles Fund Abortion, Queer Qrosswords, Puzzles for Palestine,* among others. (It's true that, to date, there is no *Minis to Stop the Steal* or *January 6th Xwords: 1-Down with the Government,* but in 2023, *Reason* did start "a weekly puzzle for libertarians," if a "pro-capitalism, pro–free market" puzzle is your bag.)

Young, politically minded constructors also intervened upstream. It was the editors who were old-guard, selecting puzzles from constructors they knew; outlets like the American Values Club launched a "bite-sized" crossword whose roster was selected through a partly anonymous submissions process. It was because constructing was so intimidating that younger solvers didn't try their hand at it; initiatives to pair veterans with newbies from underrepresented groups (Crossword Puzzle Collaboration Directory) and create free constructing software (Ingrid, for building grids; Spread the Wordlist, for building a crossword dictionary) lowered the barriers to entry.

For many, the tide shifted when Erik Agard became the editor of the *USA Today* puzzle, at the end of 2019. In a few short years, he "brought something pretty radical," per Andy Kravis, a queer constructor, onetime assistant for the *Times* puzzle, and now an editor for *The New Yorker*'s Puzzles & Games Department. Because of Agard's active recruitment, in 2020, nearly 70 percent of *USA Today* puzzles were made by female, nonbinary, or gender nonconforming constructors, compared to around 25 percent for *The New York Times* and 19 percent for the *Los Angeles Times,* according to records kept by speed-solver Matt Gritzmacher. "It's a model people would talk about as—surely you can't mean this, [surely we'll] compromise along the way," says Kravis, and yet, under Agard's stewardship, the *USA Today* puzzle has become unwaveringly diverse.

Part of that diversity is procedural, the millennial tendency to scrub hierarchy for collaboration. Agard has workshopped grids countless times with newer constructors, providing "a level of support and mentorship that no other editor offers," says Rachel Fabi, a bioethicist and crossword constructor. "The construction process [with Erik] is so much more efficient and respectful," agrees constructor Stella Zawistowski, arguing that editors like Agard prove collaboration need not be cumbersome or slow, or sacrifice authorial voice.

Solvers noticed. Agard, who once wore a PUBLISH MORE WOMEN shirt to a crossword tournament, does think Shortz and other legacy editors "could snap [their] infinity gauntlets like Thanos, and 50 percent of puzzles would be by women." But for now he is focused on making puzzles for communities rarely represented in puzzles—a project of expansion, not education. A solver lauded Agard for using "they" pronouns for singer Sam Smith in a *USA Today* clue. He clued WIFE not as [Meghan, to Harry] but as [Ali Krieger, to Ashlyn Harris], hat-tipping two members of the U.S. women's national soccer team, and causing a solver to gleefully tweet, "USA Today Crossword making me feel ALIVE!" Even cluing fusty crosswordese like OLE via the song "Big Ole Freak" wins converts and bridges generations; as one person observed on Twitter, "Megan Thee Stallion was in my grandmother's crossword today."

Agard, who speaks in a gentle monotone, sounds one minute like a wizened revolutionary and another like a beloved English teacher. He has a rascally streak. He was on *Jeopardy!* in 2018, and answered the Final Jeopardy clue that stumped him with a reference to a meme—"What is you doing, baby?"—reveling, as did the studio audience, in Alex Trebek's attempts to parse the phrase. ("What is you doing, baby? Well, I'm responding incorrectly," Trebek stammered.) In a *USA Today* puzzle, he clued OREO as [Cookie that some people eat with mustard], which led to another public figure doing something embarrassing: Hoda Kotb, she of the crossword-friendly first and last name, ate an Oreo dipped in mustard on the *Today* show. His Twitter bio, referencing the notably fustier *Times* puzzle editor before Will Shortz, could be a line out of either Sondheim or MF DOOM: "gene maleska but statuesquer."

In more grandiose moments, Agard might take to Twitter and wonder at the crossword puzzle's "liberatory potential." Can a puzzle, he thinks, in an era in which trans rights are being dismantled, at the very least refuse the trans community's most vicious or visible antagonists? (Agard, like many younger cruciverbalists, now bans Harry Potter references in his puzzles, given J. K. Rowling's record of anti-trans vitriol.) Could a puzzle that highlights members of the trans community do more than act as a reference for those in the know—more than feeling "seen," could it make one feel the opposite of ephemeral or disposable, not so much plucked as enshrined? And would any of this affect the old guard?

The first time INDIA appeared as an answer in the *Times* crossword under Shortz, in 1994, it was clued as [Kipling story locale]. The next time, the clue called on solvers to know Ashley Wilkes's sister in *Gone with the Wind*—India Wilkes being, of course, Scarlett O'Hara's high-society rival in the Margaret Mitchell classic. Throughout the 1990s, the *Times* cycled through white lenses on the subcontinent: INDIA is ["Gunga Din" setting] and ["The Jungle Book" setting], reviving Kipling's caricatures. INDIA is [Where George Orwell was born], his father a minor official in the Opium Department of the empire's Indian Civil Service; Orwell and his mother moved from Motihari to Henley-on-Thames when he was a baby. The clues repeatedly reference E. M. Forster's novel *A Passage to India,* a book that Edward Said once argued "culturally refused a privilege to India nationalism" and "made one see Indian politics as the charge of the British." In over two hundred appearances in some eighty years of the *Times* crossword, allusions to the British Empire, Vasco da Gama, or outsourcing are much more common than trivia on South Asia's rich history, its linguistic diversity, or its cultural contributions to the world. "Except for the Marabar caves," goes the first line of Forster's novel, "the city of Chandrapore presents nothing extraordinary."

Crosswords aren't novels, but Said might blanch just the same at these clues; the refusal of what's extraordinary, and the narrowing of what counts, matters as much in paraliterary forms as in literary ones. When solvers come to the black-and-white grid, they expect a black-and-white, objective relationship between clue and answer. But as in any linguistic pursuit, crosswords can reproduce the blind spots of their writers and editors.

Today's constructors argue the stakes of flushing out those blind spots are clearer than ever. To many, the harm is hardly abstract: media workers now draw straight lines from op-ed doublespeak and passive-voice depictions of police violence to the endangerment of Black people, to take one well-documented example. And the *Times* Games app has some million digital subscribers, a nontrivial reach. The crossword is often a solver's first look at certain words, scaffolding their window into a culture with characterizations that either miss the mark, or paint too narrow a picture. While the crossword puzzle has come a long way from, say, relying on Kipling to mediate South Asian experience, many constructors believe there's more to do. "The bar," as Agard has said, "is on the floor."

What would a better crossword look like, on these terms? One whose entries, for once, were all references to women or nonwhite cultural icons? Whose words were drawn not just from English but from Spanish, Mandarin Chinese, and Swahili? Whose clues avoided tokenizing or outright inaccuracy in a puzzle's clues—and, having accomplished that, used the clue as a device, less as an intimidating flashlight, rummaging for illustrative bits of arcana, and more as a spotlight? "When," asks constructor Ashish Vengsarkar, "did RANI become more a princess than a queen?" To him, most South Asians think of the word as being closer to "queen," though the princess definition is much more common in crosswords. Constructor Sid Sivakumar told me that since 1993, of the sixty-plus times RAGA has been an answer in a *Times* crossword, "by my count it has been given an inaccurate clue at least fifty times," treating it as a style rather than a melodic framework, "a shame because there are so many rich cluing opportunities that have been overlooked." Constructor Vega Subramaniam agrees, noting entries such as TAJ, RAJ, ROTI, and NAAN appear so often it's easy to get "tired of the sloppy, tokenizing cluing." (Despite being different, ROTI and NAAN frequently receive the same vague clue: [Indian flatbread].)

Constructors often roll their eyes when faced with cluing another morsel of crosswordese. But a new line of thinking sees NAAN as an opportunity: in one of the many Wikipedia rabbit holes she's liable to fall down during clue-writing, the constructor can do her research and clue NAAN in an interesting, instructive angle—[Peshwari ___ (raisin-filled fare)], say, or [Chapati alternative]—that way, not only will she learn something, but the solver will too.

And why not learn something? Eugene Maleska, the *Times* editor before Shortz, conceived of the puzzle as a kind of test, assent from a former school superintendent that indeed you still had your Latin, your geography, your Shakespeare ready to hand. By contrast, Agard thinks modern puzzles are "about viewing the crossword as a place to learn something new rather than simply confirm what you already know." Confirmation is easy, self-flattering. Of course, quotidian habits have a slippery tendency to recede into the background, to resist the disruption that learning requires. That goes double for games—come on, how sinister could the crossword be?—and triple for one whose habituation nets clicks and subscriptions—who wants to disrupt the dopamine hit of a solving streak to talk politics? But one material effect of the increased recognition of constructors, for instance—it was Shortz who added bylines to the daily puzzle—is solvers associate a constructor not only with grid shape, cluing style, or theme creativity, but with their missteps too.

This has happened to me, in ways more and less serious. The funny story first: in March 2022, I had a Saturday puzzle in the *Times* that included the answer THONG SONG. My original clue, [Sisqó #1 hit with the lyric "Ooh that dress so scandalous"] was changed by the editors to [2000 Sisqó hit with a rhyming title], presumably hoping those who didn't know the song could now, given they had some letters from the crossings, infer the remaining ones. Three weeks later, back in the Stamford Marriott for the first in-person American Crossword Puzzle Tournament in three years, I was at the lobby reception desk when Peter Gordon came up to me with a bone to pick. Gordon, a longtime editor and prolific constructor, and a quick-talking and surly man—like if Will Shortz was a bookie—said, in his Great Neck, Long Island, accent, "'Thong' and 'song' don't rhyme!" That was news to me, but luckily the crossword community counts among its ranks many linguists (not to mention pedants); a few group chats and audio recordings later and the Great Thong-Song Divergence of 2022 was confirmed. The going hypothesis by the linguists was, not unlike the Northeast corridor's resistance to the Cot-Caught merger, the frequency of the words was at play: more common words (like "song") are more resistant to vowel shifts, but less common words ("thong"; but say it more often, why not) lack this pressure, and so the Long Island vowels have freer rein: "thahng sawng," in the unrhyming dialect. If linguistic micro-communities could shake their fists at the accuracy of this kind of clue, surely they'd shake two when the stakes were higher still.

It wasn't so. In 2015, I published a puzzle cowritten with a crossword construction class I teach for a senior services nonprofit, the Jewish Association Serving the Aging. The grid had ANWAR in it, which has nearly always been clued by way of former Egyptian president Anwar Sadat. That's how we'd clued it in the submission, but when we looked in the paper, the clue had been changed by the *Times* to [___ al-Awlaki, terrorist targeted in a 2011 American drone strike]. It was a perfect storm, featuring many of the reasons crossword-making would come to be politicized: first, if anything violates Farrar's "Breakfast Test" surely it's extrajudicial murder. And there were students in my class who'd worked as civil liberties attorneys and were horrified—as was the ACLU—at this first drone killing of the Obama era. It seemed strange too to call the drone strike American (as opposed to "U.S. drone strike"; as if personifying it) while neglecting to mention that al-Awlaki himself was American, born in Las Cruces, New Mexico. Whether or not al-Awlaki (who'd never killed anyone himself but indeed spread and organized anti-American sentiment) was a terrorist was at the time hotly debated. I don't like the inflationary use of the term "terrorist," I'm against killing terror suspects, even more so absent due process, and yet here was a puzzle with my name on it, all but claiming, since this was a clue in the country's premier crossword, that facts were facts and thus they were unremarkable. Literally so: a few people reached out to me saying they imagined the clue wasn't mine, but the fracas, such as it was, was confined to a subculture debating internal norms.

In just a few years, with hundreds of thousands of additional Games subscribers, the public would involve itself in these clue politics. In 2022, Lynn Lempel, known as "Queen of the Mondays" for her uncanny ability to make engaging and witty Monday puzzles (the easiest of the *Times*'s offerings to solve, but for many the most difficult to make), published a puzzle in the *Times* with the entry CLEAN COAL. This, per *Vice News*, caused a "mini-scandal." The clue read [Greener energy source]. "Clean coal is not a 'greener energy source,'" tweeted Molly Fisch-Friedman, a senior manager of survey research at the communications outfit Climate Nexus. "Do better." The Sierra Club fired off a few fist-shaking tweets, huffing that they "[a]pplied this rage into today's Wordle instead, which was difficult but featured no fossil fuel industry greenwashing." Sara Hastings-Simon, a University of Calgary physicist and *Times* crossword aficionado, told reporters there was "such a violent reaction" to the crossword clue because promises of "clean coal" have been used as "this delay tactic, as a way to say we don't need to do anything else" to address climate change. "The fact that that filtered down to something like *The New York Times* crossword puzzle is an example of how these approaches by industry are ultimately successful at influencing our discussions and approach toward climate."

Those are fighting words—is there another discernible straight line, however faint, connecting dirty-energy lobbying to crossword clues? Fisch-Friedman noted at least "how easy it is for misinformation to spread." The puzzle is famous for reflecting the biases of the paper it appears in; the same bigwigs pushing anodyne climate copy hired the puzzle editors too. In the same way that one would never have seen the entry CLEAN COAL decades ago, crossword clues serve as a micro-historiography—a barometer for not only how specific language won't be clued, as with the stubbornness around INDIA, but also the allowable band for how it can be clued. As a bouquet of shimmering and supposedly neatly trimmed facts, the crossword could demonstrate how those facts were always subject to recontextualization, as with the case of the entry MAU MAU.

Now understood as an anticolonial uprising against British rule, the Mau Mau (also called the Kenya Land and Freedom Army) were tarred as violent extremists by the foreign correspondents of the time. The crossword followed suit: clues in the 1950s and '60s denigrate the movement as [African menace], [Kenyan terrorists], or [Dreaded name in Kenya]. A few decades later, clues began to mention "rebellion" and call the rebels a "phenomenon." It wasn't until 2013 that the clues spoke any modicum of truth to power, when the MAU MAU, as they're currently treated in history books, were clued as [Fighters for Kenyan independence]. Their first appearance in the puzzle was in 1953—that's sixty years of misclassification, spilling over from *Times* international coverage into its own miniature almanac, the crossword.

[Greener energy source]—that clue wasn't Lempel's, and those politics aren't hers, either. When Lempel submitted the puzzle, the original clue for CLEAN COAL read [Dubious term for a greener energy source]. Lempel had a back-and-forth with the editors, sending an email explaining that "[i]f you Google 'clean coal,' there seem to be a lot of questions as to whether it's actually clean. That's why I used the qualifier and I wonder if it should stay in there." The *Times* reply was that Shortz "still finds the clue better as it is without any hedging."

After the puzzle ran, the response was so forceful that it led to that rarest of things, a crossword correction:

> The clue for 47 Across in the Monday puzzle implied incorrectly that coal is a viable source of clean energy. While it is possible to capture and sequester some of the greenhouse gas emissions and other pollutants from coal-fired power plants, the technology has never been used on a large scale because of its high cost.

For those couple of days, a crossword clue was being talked about with a fervor normally reserved for corporatist propaganda or outright racism. What's more, longtime crossword solvers were learning that Lempel wasn't exactly to blame. It was an editorial choice, and recognition was dawning that Lempel's original clue calling clean coal "dubious" was just as much an editorial position as extracting that context from the final clue. "There's been more politics in puzzles lately," Lempel would later say, "about what people should include in puzzles and what people shouldn't include and the way clues should be directed. . . . I don't disagree with a lot of that. But it's a puzzle, you know."

❑■❑

I don't know, not really. I might know how to narrate my own stumbling through a life in puzzles, that at the outset making crosswords felt about as political as shuffling around Lego blocks, that as a high school kid part of the puzzle's appeal was how it simultaneously held language at bay (treating the letter more as construction material than a unit of meaning) while meaning proliferated (in puns; in newly gathered knowledge). I know that if I first made puzzles for myself, the first people I tried to impress were other constructors and the then nascent blog scene, that because the blogger Rex Parker (Michael Sharp, a literature professor at Binghamton, who reviews the *Times* puzzle every day) liked *The Simpsons* as much as I did, I was delighted to debut the answer NED FLANDERS in a grid, even more delighted when he thrilled to it.

I know that as the puzzle became more politicized—a shift I had a hand in shaping—the proliferation of new norms didn't always make sense to me, that the *Do no harm* ethic seemed admirable but often contradictory or inarticulable. Puzzles were to exclude the names of celebrities accused of sexual assault, but many of history's greatest monsters were okay; it would be bad manners to exile REAGAN, IDI AMIN, STALIN from the grid but CHRIS PRATT might need to go for his associations with Hillsong Church. (Just him; never mind the countless celebrities also affiliated.) The instinct here was to treat the puzzle as a cultural force; what went in it approached endorsement. And if the puzzle was a release from real life, *any* reminder of the political world outside was an invasion; we had our solvers to think of. This too was a kindness taken revealingly far: I once heard an editor would reject a puzzle with the answer SHOOTING GUARD because that first word might remind a solver of the ongoing crisis of mass shootings. This is an editorial stance difficult to evenly apply (is CANCER okay? clued as the zodiac sign? Why is IED okay? because those deaths happen far away?) but it also presumes to know the solver's reaction in advance, a move that can go quickly from caring to infantilizing, its own version of taking away someone's language (*in-* "not" + *fant-* "speaking").

I know in weaker moments when I've tested *It's just a puzzle* with newer constructors, their fiery rejoinders have made me not ashamed but envious. I know every time I've published an article saluting the efforts of more politically minded puzzlers, the far right has seized on it ("Oh, so now the *crossword puzzle* needs to be woke!?"), as good a proof as any that it's *not* just a puzzle. (In Vienna in 1925, crosswords had to be submitted to government censors: "The measure has been promulgated because . . . a Legitimist [royalist] newspaper published a crossword puzzle with the solution: 'Long Live Otto.'") I know that as a young crossword writer I wanted to make politics, not puzzles, my job, and have; I know that among the people I admire most in the crossword world are those who left strenuous, overtly altruistic jobs (as lawyers for LGBTQ+ rights, as teachers, as therapists) for full-time roles as puzzle editors—not because I think puzzles are more or less moral than those industries, but because I sense in these people a decision to finally make good on their desires, and what could be more moral than that?

I know that all this happens not just because the puzzle is a media cash cow, or only because it's made up of language, though those are both crucial. The puzzle encourages a certain brand of attention. To wit: every so often someone suggests a crossword's grid—the negative space of its white squares, framed by the black square placement—resembles a swastika. The best response in such instances is not to deny what people see, or to issue expert dismissals. *(Well, if only you understood . . . lots of crosswords have this shape, in fact . . . it's never intentional, of course . . .)* It's to make sure the discussion ends at the shape: when a Sunday *Times* puzzle whose white squares looked to many like a swastika ran on December 18, 2022—in an awful coincidence, the first night of Hanukkah—outraged solvers began looking for clues in the clues. 60-Across read [Style of column at Berlin's Brandenburg Gate] for DORIC. Nazi soldiers marched through those columns in 1939 to observe Adolf Hitler's fiftieth birthday, and the gate was a symbol of the party. It's also where Ronald Reagan delivered his famous

1987 "Tear down this wall!" speech, and where Napoleon, on defeating the Prussians in the 1806 Battle of Jena-Auerstedt, first used the structure as a site of triumphal procession. And so on. SIXES was clued as ["Boxcars"]; rolling two dice and getting double sixes is so-called because the dots' crosshatching resembles the sides of a freight train. When I saw solvers close-reading this clue as a surefire indication that the puzzle—and, crucially, its author—*meant* to reference not just the Nazi symbol but the actual transport to death camps, I was, to put it lightly, alarmed. It wasn't just that the ensuing Twitter attack inevitably found its way to the puzzle's writer, who deleted his account. It was also a negative image of exactly what the crossword encourages: searching for clues where they're least expected, misreading language in pursuit of a deeper code. In the context of a puzzle, or a pun, or a session of Kabbalah, this linguistic defamiliarization can border on the spiritual, letting meaning proliferate unbounded for a bounded span of time; in the context of charged political debate, it can feel like paranoia.

These principles of inclusion and exclusion, this fight to make the puzzle kinder and more interesting—it made its way back to the *Times*.

Sometimes the argument was straightforwardly to do with clues or entries in a grid. Sid Sivakumar, who curated a list of South Asian words yet to appear in crosswords, despite their popularity and cultural relevance—everything from ALOO to longer terms such as GAJAR KA HALWA—had a 2022 *Times* Saturday with the word ATTA clued not as ["___ girl!"] but as [Flour ground in a chakki]. He also debuted the entry MODEL MINORITY in a *Times* grid, in a collaboration with Brooke Husic—an entry that likely wouldn't have been accepted only a few years ago—with the clue [Demographic myth often used with respect to Asian-Americans].

But sometimes this debate is downstream of the puzzles themselves. At the same time as the *Times*'s in-house puzzle blog, Wordplay, got off the ground, the site XWord Info began offering more than just puzzle statistics and clue databases. Billing itself as "the essential resource for crossword constructors and enthusiasts," XWord Info played host to its own daily commentary on the *Times* puzzle, written by prolific *Times* constructor Jeff Chen. As with the rest of the site, Chen's write-ups were positioned as technical—an insider's look into what sacrifices the constructor had to make in the nonthematic fill to support an ambitious theme, say, or a constructor's take on what worked and what didn't. (Most puzzle critics are not, on the whole, also puzzle writers, or at least not as productive as Chen, who has written more than 125 puzzles for the *Times*.)

But behind the technical guidance and proffering of resources was—how could it be otherwise—a point of view. Chen tended to like his puzzles apolitical. When issues of social justice found their way in, the review wrinkled its nose. He flinched when WHITE PRIVILEGE appeared in the Saturday, March 11, 2017, puzzle, stacked atop the feminist writer GLORIA STEINEM: "Although I think it's an important concept more people ought to learn about, I wonder if some solvers will feel like the puzzle is trying to shame them. I wonder how I'd feel if I were white." When Agard had a *Times* puzzle deliberately built around HAUDENOSAUNEE [Native name for the Iroquois Confederacy], Chen worried the answer would be "alienating." (Agard's response: "Making a point of calling out 'hard-to-spell' names in puzzles is a classic example of something that may seem inherently 'colorblind' to you on paper, but really is racist in practice. . . . Whether you're an editor rejecting a name from a puzzle for that reason or a blogger 'just asking questions' about someone's gridworthiness, understand that bigots are cheering you on.")

XWord Info allows constructors to comment on their own puzzles too; Agard's comment accompanies his Friday, February 5, 2021, puzzle, when the *Times,* for the beginning of Black History Month, recruited seven Black constructors to make that week's puzzles. The Saturday was written by Kameron Austin Collins, who had also wrestled with Chen's commentary in the past. This time, Collins had had enough. Instead of the usual four lines on how excited one is to debut this or that entry in the grid, Collins wrote an essay, which reads in part:

I am tired of how some entries and constructors are accused of "alienating solvers." It's a claim that Jeff makes too often and applies unevenly, in glaring ways. If Byron Walden's HEPPLEWHITES—a great entry! referring to the antique furniture style—isn't earning him any lecturing on solvers being "alienated," then Pete Wentz publishing the far more contemporary TANEHISI COATES (public intellectual; multi-time bestselling author; MacArthur fellow; TV talking head) shouldn't either. Nor should Nam Jin Yoon publishing COATES, just the last name, become an occasion for Jeff to once again argue for cultural gradualism: "This is by far the best way to work in names like COATES, gently introducing solvers to more recent influential persons. Other puzzles have risked tainting solvers' first associations with someone new to them."

Arbiters like Chen and editors like Shortz have long judged a puzzle's merits against the imagined reactions of an "average solver"—a shadowy fabulation that not only seems to flatten a constructor's voice in the name of maximum reach, but denotes a deliberately moving target. As Collins says, "Why cater to a solver who'd sincerely finish a puzzle with a bad taste in their [mouth] because—despite apparently knowing all about HEPPLEWHITES—they've never heard a CHAKA Khan song? . . . Why do I get the sense that Jeff's idea of the average solver could never be someone who looked like me."

On August 23, 2022, Trey Mendez published his first crossword puzzle in *The New York Times*. Crossword constructors, like many creatives, tend toward the autobiographical. As a self-described "New Yorker with a mailing address in California who currently lives in Zagreb, Croatia," his puzzle's theme answers were phrases about air travel, whose first and last two letters were state abbreviations, as though the answers linked those two states in flight. FLYING TIME, which starts with Florida and ends with Maine, thus was clued as [Duration of air travel from Miami to Bangor?]; VAPOR TRAIL as [What follows a plane going from Richmond to Chicago?]; and so on, out into the horizon.

This theme was appropriate not just for Mendez's jet-setting modus vivendi but as a stand-in for this puzzle's long trajectory from inkling to ink. Mendez was the first mentee to be published from the *Times*'s Diverse Crossword Constructor Fellowship, a program launched in early 2022 with the aim, as the *Times* announcement put it, of "creat[ing] grids that reflect a range of cultural reference points." Free wordlists and constructing software helped new puzzle-makers get their sea legs; solver feedback and newer outlets gave them newer opportunities; now the *Times* would make its own upstream intervention. Everdeen Mason, the inaugural editorial director for Games at the *Times,* and the brains and bureaucratic brawn behind the fellowship, laid out the cohort's first-class itinerary for me: Mendez and the other four fellows were matched with *Times* editors for one-on-one mentorship, attended *Times*-produced seminars on Crossword Theme Development and Clue Writing, and were ushered into a Slack workspace where they could pepper the editorial team with cruciverbal questions. All five fellows emerged from the three-month process with publication-worthy puzzles on file, and the *Times* would release one a month until they ran out, then, per Mason, do it all over again. In his notes on the *Times*'s "Wordplay" column, Mendez thanked the mentor he happened to be paired with, puzzlemaster Will Shortz.

While the archetypal solving or constructing session might seem like a lonely pursuit, a new generation of puzzle lovers prizes collaboration. On the Crosscord server, newbies and veterans alike bat theme ideas back and forth and, like a haiku contest, write comments that have either 15 or 21 letters (and so would fully span the grid on a daily or Sunday puzzle, respectively). On Twitch, the video game livestreaming giant, new solvers and tournament-winning speed demons broadcast themselves polishing off a crossword—some challenging themselves by using only the Down clues, ignoring the Acrosses—as digital cheerleaders shout punny encouragement in the chat. The Crossword Puzzle Collaboration Directory, created at the suggestion of the *Times*'s Deb Amlen and run by Agard and Will Nediger, continues to match would-be constructors from underrepresented groups with mentors; this was the group that congratulated Hoelscher on her February 2020 debut.

Agard, for his part, continues to have a knack for reimagining stale crossword fill for the modern day. In his hands, the answer ONT— normally clued as the abbreviation for Ontario—is recast as ON T, as in, taking testosterone, and so becomes one of the few crossword entries geared toward the trans community. Kameron Austin Collins pointed to TOP SURGERY as a quintessential Agardian answer: "politically persuasive," "inferrable" (because solvers who don't know the phrase can piece it together from its constituent parts), and "powerful" (because solvers who *do* know the answer might finally feel like the crossword was made for them too). On the very same day as Mendez's *Times* debut, Agard's crossword in *The New Yorker* featured DIGITAL BLACKFACE [Modern-day form of minstrelsy] stacked on top of ANISHINAABEMOWIN [Language in which "boozhoo" is a greeting]. Part of the bid of the wide-ranging crossword grid is that the solver develops the same curiosity *after* solving that the constructor had *before* the puzzle was published, as she was building the grid and writing the clues. Part of the crossword's power is lucky juxtaposition, seeding connections and semantic rhymes that feel unbidden yet natural when words are side by side in the black-and-white grid.

As a constructor, it's those moments of serendipity that can give the crossword an almost spiritual linguistic aura. Researching clues is a lot like researching a book, and while panning through dozens of browser tabs I googled Trey Mendez, only to find the debut crossword constructor shares his name with the mayor of Brownsville, Texas. I recognized the name—he'd been in the news then for coming out in favor of ending Title 42 immigration restrictions, and for gladhanding with billionaire Elon Musk, who located a SpaceX facility in nearby Boca Chica. On the one hand, a creator of a language game and a newsworthy mayor were linked through a trick of homography; on the other, the doubling was a reminder that crosswords have their politics too. Still, I tried not to read too much into it.

CHAPTER 6

The Melting Pot of the Crossword

[Love thy neighbour, say?], 4 letters*
—CHRISTINA IVERSON, *Los Angeles Times,* 2022

R oot around in the alphanumeric soup of the U.S. visa system for long enough and you'll discover the EB-1A, sometimes known as the Einstein visa. Among the most coveted and hardest permanent-residency benefits to obtain, it's reserved for noncitizens with "extraordinary ability." John Lennon got a forerunner of it in 1976, after a deportation scare that nearly sent him back to Britain. (His case, which spotlighted prosecutorial discretion in immigration law, forms the legal basis for Deferred Action for Childhood Arrivals, or DACA.) Modern-day recipients include the tennis star Monica Seles and, in 2001—in a telling irony—the Slovenian model Melania Knauss, four years before she became Melania Trump. To secure an EB-1A the U.S. Citizenship and Immigration Services requires that applicants fulfill three of ten criteria for extraordinariness, or else provide evidence of a major "one-time achievement." "Pulitzer, Oscar, Olympic Medal" are the agency's helpful suggestions. *No pressure,* says the government, behind crossed arms and blinks of bureaucratic prose. Of a half million permanent-residency visas issued in 2022, only one percent were EB-1As.

One went to Mangesh Ghogre, forty-three, of Mumbai, India, whose extraordinary ability is writing crossword puzzles. I first met Ghogre in March 2012, in Brooklyn, at the American Crossword Puzzle Tournament. I entered the Marriott ballroom grumbling because subway delays had made me late; just then, Will Shortz was announcing that Ghogre was, by a few thousand miles, the person who'd traveled the farthest to be there.

In early 2021, Ghogre came across a *Forbes* listicle titled "Seven Ways to Get Your Green Card in the United States." Most were familiar—"marry your way in" (the IR-1 or CR-1 visa), "invest your way in" (EB-5, for those with a loose million dollars)—but the EB-1A ("achieve your way in") was news to him. As he read the specifications, his twenty-year crossword journey flashed before his eyes: the criteria seemed like a puzzle to which he was the perfect solution.

Q: Was there press on his accomplishments? A: Yes; among the lone creators of American crossword puzzles outside North America, he'd been profiled in *The New York Times* and *The Times of India*. Q: Had his work "been displayed at artistic exhibitions or showcases"? A: It had; at the 2014 Hindustan Times Kala Ghoda Arts Festival, some of his finished grids colorized and enlarged, every square the size of a fist. Q: Were his contributions of "major significance"? A: Ghogre had published a newsworthy tribute crossword in *The New York Times*, marking the 150th anniversary of Gandhi's birth. In it, the string GANDHI, put through the puzzle-maker's literalizing wringer, is reinterpreted as "G AND H I"; the trigram GHI appears squeezed into a single box in phrases like WEI[GH I]N, LON[G HI]STORY, and NOTTIN[G HI]LL.

Ghogre told only his wife that he intended to apply for the visa. He dashed off a form email to some twenty-five immigration lawyers, expecting silence. Instead, he received a handful of enthusiastic replies; one attorney offered a full refund of his fee if Ghogre was rejected. "Suddenly, my immigration puzzle was solved," he told me. "Today, when I look back, it looks like it was all destined to happen."

Ghogre's crossword and immigration stories began around the same time, twenty-six years ago, when he was an engineering student at Veermata Jijabai Technological Institute. Born to a middle-class family in Chandrapur in 1980, he was thrust into the business-and-STEM marching orders of global mobility. Ghogre, like many of his classmates, began studying for the GMAT (the de facto entrance exam for U.S. graduate programs in business) immediately on entering university. Too poor to attend college abroad, he and his peers hoped to trade a high test score for a scholarship to a top U.S. MBA program—but first they had to conquer the Verbal section. Ghogre started doing crosswords to broaden his English vocabulary. He lived with a dozen or so hostel-mates, most of whom spoke and wrote English as a second or third language, on a campus where *The Times of India*—with its syndicated *Los Angeles Times* crossword—was delivered daily. (The entire back page, like that of many international outlets, was a low-cost collage of syndicated Americana: Dilbert, Garfield, a jumble.) Each morning, a handful of students clustered around the puzzle, honing their English on a borrowed crossword, in a periodical with the largest daily English-language circulation in the world.

This was in 1997. In a couple of years, the dot-com bubble would burst; the NASDAQ ticker would run red with loss-studded listings that looked like crossword entries with a single letter amiss (IPET for Pets.com, ASKJ for Ask Jeeves). Thousands of would-be immigrants pursuing the U.S.'s putative silicon riches would shelve their plans, and stay put. Ghogre was one of them. He wound up obtaining his MBA in India at Narsee Monjee Institute of Management Studies (motto, "Transcending Horizons"). Until recently, he worked in Mumbai as an IPO banker, for the Japanese firm Nomura, the firm that acquired Lehman Brothers in the aftermath of the 2008 crash.

In the meantime, he was hooked on crosswords. He was thrown out of an engineering lecture for smuggling a puzzle into class, more rapt by the black-and-white grid than the matrix grids of linear algebra.

His mother recalls him crosswording while waiting in queues, solving in pen while standing. Ghogre delighted in crossword themes that backlit the malleability of the English he was rapidly mastering: the wordplay reminded him of his fascination, in the eighth grade, with Sanskrit, whose morphology could be deconstructively shucked into root, affix, and ending. The dictionary he carried around *(Random House Webster's)* offered merely rote learning, but crosswords felt like engineering, a tactile means of putting his learning to use.

As Ghogre improved, he found he could grok a puzzle's linguistic quirks even if, some eight thousand miles away from the United States, he didn't always understand their context. Crossword lovers, like joke lovers, have a quick-draw inventory of memorable puzzle themes; Ghogre remembers a quip puzzle by Vic Fleming featuring the answers PIG-TIGHT, BULL-STRONG, and HORSE-HIGH—the archetype, in old cowpoke parlance, of a good fence. Ghogre had never seen a pig, let alone an Indian village with a Western-style enclosure. "We don't have fences," he told me, chuckling.

Soon Ghogre was using graph paper and pencil to sketch his own crossword constructions. He submitted his early work not to *The New York Times,* then considered the gold standard of the grid, but to the *Los Angeles Times,* the puzzle syndicated on a three-month lag in *The Times of India.* Between airmail and courier fees—this is before frictionless digital submissions—it cost more to shop around his grids than he'd be paid on publication ($85). In India, he was the only one of his peers for whom the crossword had alchemized from leaden pedagogical tool into a gleaming obsession; in the online forums and message boards of the American puzzle community, Ghogre found a string of mentors, collaborators, and friends.

He began corresponding with Nancy Salomon, a legendary constructor and also a generous mentor. (Cruciverb.com featured a post of hers with "instructions for working with me.") Over email—Ghogre couldn't afford international phone calls—Salomon workshopped his theme proposals. She'd let Ghogre know when a phrase he suggested as a theme answer wasn't, as crossword people say, "in the language." Occasionally, they disagreed: Salomon had never heard of CHALK

AND CHEESE, which Ghogre was pairing with BREAD AND BUT-
TER and COOKIES AND CREAM in a puzzle whose theme was MID-
DLE AGE SPREAD. "Chalk and cheese" describes two things that are
superficially alike but, on inspection, utterly different. From Salomon's
confusion, Ghogre deduced that the expression was a Britishism, current in India but not in the United States.

Salomon also coached Ghogre on another unfamiliar language:
crosswordese. A good crossword grid should avoid words like STOA
and ANOA—the Greek colonnades and Celebes oxen, whose common
consonants and felicitous diphthongs mean they're overrepresented
in puzzles, relative to their obscurity. Ghogre absorbed the dicta of
the American crossword just as he'd absorbed American idioms. *A
good crossword fence should be IBEX-tight, ANOA-strong, and OKAPI-
high.* . . . After dozens of attempts, one of his puzzles with Salomon's
imprimatur was accepted by the *Los Angeles Times*. It was the MID-
DLE AGE SPREAD puzzle, with Salomon's revisions. Ghogre's thank-
you missive to Salomon is jittery with elliptical gratitude:

> . . . you cant imagine how happy i am . . . after 12 yrs of dailysolv-
> ing . . . this is a fitting fruit for all the effort and passion . . .

> many thanks to you Nancy . . . in Indian culture, one expresses
> their gratitude to teachers/seniors/elders by touching their feet . . .
> one day i want to touch you feet too . . . if u dont mind . . . as token
> of my appreciation of your kind gesture to help am unknown
> like me . . .

How American is the crossword puzzle? For all its aura of sophistica-
tion, the black-and-white grid has also been seen as hokey, anesthetiz-
ing American kitsch, one more anodyne neon sign on a featureless
roadway. In the Weird Al parody song "The Biggest Ball of Twine in
Minnesota," a family piles into a '53 DeSoto with "crossword puzzles,

Spider-Man comics / and mama's homemade rhubarb pie." Far from a nourishing educational aid, the puzzle is just more sugary, plasticky entertainment, letters to be mindlessly filled in on the way from point A to point B, like Muzak for words. The America in the song, just like its crossword, is of a specific time and place, but the mythos is familiar: a big-box store point-of-sale kiosk hawking crossword books, glossy tabloids, processed foods. Dead Kennedys, in their 1980 song "Drug Me," lump the puzzle in with markers of insensate consumerism, as though the black-and-white grid were a bar code:

> *Drug me with your sleeping pills*
> *Drug me with your crossword puzzles*
> *Drug me with your magazines*
> *Drug me with your fuck machines*

Jello Biafra delivers his verses at a frenetic clip, spit out like the fine print at the end of a drug commercial, as if the hundreds of letters, dozens of clues, and orthographic tricks of the crossword were meant not to inform, but overwhelm. Who could understand all that pharmacological jargon; who could know everything in the crossword? "I don't want to think, don't make me care," "Drug Me" begins. Head down in a crossword, you may as well be asleep.

Whatever its narcotic middle-class charm, the crossword—like many American triumphs—is the invention of an immigrant. When, in 1910, Arthur Wynne left Liverpool for Pittsburgh, he was one of forty million migrants from Europe to America between 1830 and 1930, nine million of whom would leave Liverpool in particular for the "New World." And Wynne's instructions on the inaugural "Word-Cross" read like guidance for immigration paperwork: "Fill in the small squares with words which agree with the following definitions." Like much cultural work, sieving the in-crowd from the out, that first American grid even conducts a background check: the clue at square 6 asks [What we all should be]; the answer is MORAL.

The crossword's success led Stanley Newman, the longtime crossword editor for New York's *Newsday,* to quip: "Liverpool's two greatest gifts to the world of popular culture are the Beatles and Arthur Wynne." The crossword craze of the 1920s often took on a particular American sheen. A solver with a penchant for needlework sewed a quilt composed of forty-eight different puzzles, one for each state in the union. The crossword was becoming a mass movement in an era of mass movement: the Pennsylvania Railroad printed crosswords on its menus; the Baltimore and Ohio Railroad stocked its seat backs with dictionaries.

Wynne's native Britain looked on with horror, moving to close its borders to the crossword. As we've seen, British papers warned of the puzzle epidemic on the horizon: "In a few short weeks, it has grown from the pastime of a few ingenious idlers into a national institution." The crossword, likened to wildly proliferating hyacinths, was cast as an invasive species, indigenous to the States, but contagious; to prevent its spread, the authorities should erect a good fence. Nevertheless, in February 1925, the London *Times* announced that crosswords had made it across the Atlantic. "The nation still stands before the blast," the *Times* said, "and no man can say it will stand erect again."

When Ghogre and I first met at the 2012 tournament, it was his first visit to the United States. He had come on the invitation of Will Shortz to volunteer as an official at the ACPT. Ghogre imagined, between his obligations at home and the headache of the visa system, that it would be his first and last tournament, telling Shortz it was a "once in a lifetime opportunity." Days before flying in, he wrote a letter to his fellow conventiongoers, which he sent to Shortz. After not hearing back for some thirty-six hours—Shortz, an efficient and fastidious correspondent, is the first adult I met who'd mastered inbox zero; his former email address, in a nod to ANOA, was celebesox@aol.com—Ghogre zipped over an apologetic follow-up, worrying he'd overstepped. "Are you kidding?" replied Shortz. "I loved your piece. I already passed it along to the ACPT webmaster for posting on our website."

Ghogre's letter begins:

For someone like me, who has come all the way from a small town on the outskirts of Mumbai in India, attending this occasion is close to attending the Oscars of the crossword world. Though my heart is beating at twice the speed, my chest today swells with humble pride. Being the first from India to be a part of this tournament as one of the judges is not just a milestone in my life. Back home, a number of souls has taken inspiration to dream big and achieve even bigger.

At the tournament, the six-hundred-odd competitors sat in rows in the boxy, corporate Marriott ballroom as if in office-park pews, scribbling furiously behind cardboard dividers. Shortz was at the dais emceeing like a boyish preacher. In 2012, nearly four times as many competitors solved in the Westchester geographic division as in the entire Foreign division, which was mostly Canadians. When he wasn't whisking grids from the ballroom to the subterranean judges' room, Ghogre spent the weekend sampling Americana he'd encountered only in crosswords. He tasted his first PBJ and BLT, saw his first TPK, ate his fill of OREOS, overheard someone say MY BAD (though not EGAD or NEAT-O, both of which, from crosswords, he thought were still commonplace).

Since 2000, Ghogre has kept a crossword diary ("my personal Wikipedia"), detailing the lexicon that solving American puzzles has revealed. There is a section on biblical names (ENOCH, HOSEA, ENOS, ESAU) and one on American lakes and rivers (ERIE, MEAD, HURON, GILA). There is a section with clues for ERNE, TERN, and EMU ("birds which I have never seen, but I meet every day"). When Ghogre showed me the pages—dutiful tick marks next to commonly occurring answers, in the stocky, diligent handwriting of an engineer—they seemed like flash cards for a fun-house citizenship exam. I imagined Ghogre raising his right hand, swearing—AVOWING—upon an EPEE or SNEE, reciting lines from Melville's OMOO. When he told me the date he began journaling, March 4, I couldn't help but notice the serendipitous whiff of mobility in the date's homophone—*March forth!* "It's been an eight-thousand-mile march," Ghogre laughs. To both of us, every pun is a crossing: a refusal to let a run of letters mean only one thing. When he was solving, Ghogre says, "I could not physically travel to the U.S., but I was traveling every day in my mind."

■

"Something there is that doesn't love a wall," begins Robert Frost's "Mending Wall," as though the line of poetry were a riddle. The crossword ignored the refrain muttered by the poem's neighborly bellyacher—"He says again, 'Good fences make good neighbors'"—and crossed overseas, assimilating to the language games of the places that, reluctantly or not, took it in. In the U.K., a variant called the cryptic now reigns supreme. Where, for difficulty, modern American-style puzzles might resort to arcana or forbiddingly laconic clues, British cryptics build an answer up from riddle-like instructions. In a *New York Times* crossword, MIGRATE might be the solution to the clues [Move] or [Emulate Albert Einstein in 1933]; in a *Guardian* cryptic, MIGRATE could be clued by [Move to noodling ragtime]. Here, "Move" is a straight-ahead definition of MIGRATE, while "noodling" indicates we should rearrange the letters of "ragtime," which anagrams to "migrate."

Solvers exposed to both styles might emerge bilingual, literal code-switchers—but with preferences. Stephen Sondheim, an avid cryptic-solver, whose stamp of approval helped the style find an audience in America, and thus enacted a reverse Atlantic crossword crossing, wrote in 1968: "There are crossword puzzles and crossword puzzles. The kind familiar to most New Yorkers is a mechanical test of tirelessly esoteric knowledge: 'Brazilian potter's wheel,' 'East Indian betel nut' and the like are typical definitions." His fantastical examples imply that esoterica is often dredged up from far-flung countries with far-fetched definitions. When the British poet W. H. Auden, another noted crossword lover, moved back to Oxford from New York, he published a farewell letter to America in the *Times*.

> People ask me if I shall miss the "cultural life" here. My answer: I have never taken part in it. . . . My cultural life is confined to read-

ing, listening to records of classical music, and solving crossword puzzles. . . . At this point I must say that the crossword in *The New York Times* frequently drives me up the wall with rage because of the lack of precision in its clues. . . . The clues in British crosswords may be more complicated, but they are always fair. E.g., *Song goes dry for a ruined Dean.* Answer: *Serenade.*

Whoever invented the myth that America is a melting pot? It is nothing of the kind and, as a lover of diversity, I say thank God. The Poles, the Ukrainians, the Italians, the Jews, the Puerto Ricans, who are my neighbors, may not be the same as they would be in another country, but they keep their own characteristics.

In Auden's image of America, crosswords, culture, and immigration are inextricable. He invokes the original sense of "melting pot," in which, as an 1875 article put it, "the individuality of the immigrant" melts into uniformity "in the democratic alembic like chips of brass." The contextless alembic of the crossword does something similar to foreign languages, burning off information like punctuation, spaces between words, capitals, and diacritical marks, until they are made uniform. (There is an instinct among some modern constructors to cross Spanish words containing an *ñ* with one another, AÑOS intersecting JALAPEÑO, since *ñ* and *n* are different letters in the Spanish alphabet. In many cases, the tilde entirely refashions a word; without it, the clue ["Cien ___ de Soledad" (García Márquez classic)] has a much raunchier solution.) And where English itself is a melting pot, its gravitational tug naturalizing loanwords into satellite moons, the crossword reflects it: an analysis by Charles Kurzman and Josh Katz of 2,092,375 *Times* clue-and-answer pairs shows that words like NADA lose their Spanishness over time: clues go from, say, [Nothing, in Navarra] to, simply, [Zilch]. If anything, Kurzman and Katz conclude, puzzle parochialism is actually deepening: "The [*Times*] puzzle today uses one-third fewer non-English clues and answers than it did at its peak in 1966, and makes two-thirds fewer international references than its peak in 1943." Globalization, waves of immigration, and hiring efforts may have remapped its reporting desks, but "when we turn from the *New York Times* news pages to the puzzle page, the rest of the world fades away."

Non-English words are often, as Auden implied, represented absent "their own characteristics," like surnames stripped of pharyngeal or cedilla at Ellis Island. At best, this is deliberate, even instructive: decades ago, crosswords in the *Jewish Daily Forward* featured a combination of Yiddish, Hebrew, and English—TROUBLE was clued by the Yiddish "tsoris," for instance—and appeared on the same page as the famed "Bintel Brief," which offered advice to assimilating immigrants. At worst, as we've seen, the puzzle inflects a clue or answer with negative, sometimes racist, connotations, as when ILLEGAL was clued in *The New York Times* as recently as 2012 as [One caught by border patrol]. Like Sid Sivakumar, Ashish Vengsarkar, and Vega Subramaniam before him, Ghogre recalls the sense of defamiliarization he felt when, say, seeing the clue [Unstitched garment] for SARI; "un-stitched" appears in the first sentence of the "Sari" Wikipedia page, but he says it's a facet of the Indian clothing no Indian national would notice. In his 2012 ACPT letter, otherwise a friendly salvo, Ghogre describes how American puzzles offer a narrow aperture through which to view Indian culture, citing the "usual suspects": NAAN, RAJA, DELHI, SITAR, RAVI, NEHRU, and so on. It felt flattening, doubly so when clues had inaccuracies, as if the words were tchotchkes bought by the cosmopolitan solver and deposited on the mantelpiece of the grid. Where the crossword was Ghogre's rosy, cherubic language tutor, it could also be his immigration officer, demanding a story distorted into legibility by the shimmering totems of stereotype.

The American crossword's misfires aren't preordained. If the British cryptic is predicated on riddles, its composers looking for words like LOOKING, which they can decompose into slippery cluable units (LOO + KING; an anagram of O.K. LINGO), then the theme, fill, and clues of American puzzles are more pliable zones for constructors to politicize. Kurzman and Katz's analysis ends in 2015; since then, the previous chapter's constructor-activists have devoted a world of effort devoted to making the puzzle respectfully worldly, both within the borders of the *Times* grid and without.

In 2021, the psychologist and puzzle-maker Erica Hsiung Wojcik published the Expanded Crossword Name Database, a "list of names, places and things that represent groups, identities and people often excluded from crossword grids." Because of English's consonant-heavy phonotactics—some eight out of ten words begin with one—you and *moi* speak crossword French; a crossword's rows and columns are outfitted with the vowel-heavy release valves of ETE, OUI, EPEE, nestled beneath trigraph Germanic blends like STRAP, SPLIT, THREE, and so on. That's also, perhaps, why we know Jean AUEL, EERO Saarinen, and all the canonical IRAs. If vowelly nouns are so useful, why not arm constructors with an updated canon: why not put EULA Biss, Michaela COEL, or YAA Gyasi in a crossword? One solver's trivia is another's lived lexicon; what's "fair" to W. H. Auden might keep a crop of newbie solvers on the other side of the fence.

After Eric Albert, most constructors use software assistance to build their grids, including the "wordlist" file, where thousands of entries are ranked by their crossword worthiness, their desirability for that particular constructor. Higher-scored words pop up as suggested fill more often; a new cluing angle might lead a constructor to rescore a word, as if on appeal. Nancy Serrano-Wu, a constructor and immigration attorney, began solving crosswords in the courtroom, waiting for case dates to be set at interminable master hearings. Recently, she clued TPS not as the usual [Festoons with Charmin, informally] (TPS was a lowly 25 in my wordlist; I won't use any word under 50) but by way of [Temporary Protected Status], the immigration relief granted to many Ukrainians, Afghans, and Venezuelans. (I've since bumped it to a 50.) Wojcik clued VIET not as [___ Cong] but as [___ Thanh Nguyen, Pulitzer-winning author of "The Sympathizer"]. And, given the U.S.'s enormous Spanish-speaking population, constructor Brooke Husic often writes clues in what she calls "stealth Spanish," where bilingual crosstalk obviates the need for disambiguation: ["Hand it over!"]

might clue the imperative ¡DAME! [Pies for a social distancer] is SEIS, or six, since "pies" is the Spanish for "feet"; the pun shakes off the othering manacles of italicized, "foreign" words. In all these cases, the editor can override a constructor's original angle—Shortz is known for rewriting up to 90 percent of a submission's clues. To get something new accepted, constructors festoon a clue with the kind of accolades—like Nguyen's Pulitzer—that might adorn an EB-1A application.

Ghogre, for his part, preaches "crossword diplomacy." His second *Times* puzzle, a 2017 collaboration with Brendan Emmett Quigley, ran on the Fourth of July. Its marquee answers are JAY GATSBY, YOU ARE NOT ALONE, ELLE MACPHERSON, and WHY BOTHER. Each begins with a spelled-out version of the letters J, U, L, Y: a fourth of the word JULY. The consul general in Mumbai noticed the puzzle and, in the spirit of interdependence, invited Ghogre to a celebration of America's Independence Day. The consulate asked the *Times* to print an additional five hundred copies of the crossword, to distribute to guests. (Xeroxing would've been verboten, for copyright reasons.) Shortz autographed a copy, as did Quigley, Ghogre, and, at the event, the consul general, who wrote below his signature: "This is a great symbol of U.S.-India dosti." Dosti means "friendship" in Hindi. I didn't know the term, but I'm glad to have learned it. One day, you might see it in a crossword.

Harry Houdini, the most visible escapist in the history of magic, was born Erik Weisz in Budapest in 1874. In *Houdini's Box*, the British psychoanalyst Adam Phillips describes how Weisz's family, "invisible immigrants" who tried and failed to assimilate to the commercial churn of the New World, raised "a child who would defy nature, confound gravity," and "devote his life to the performance of a violent parody of assimilation." Where his parents either couldn't or wouldn't adapt, Houdini "would be the man who could adapt to anything *and* escape from it." After Erik Weisz but before Harry Houdini, he had another identity. Phillips writes:

He called himself—and this self-renaming was crucial to the person he was making himself out to be—Ehrich, The Prince of the Air (as a crossword puzzle clue to his life, it is worth noting that this new given name has "rich" as its second syllable, just as "Houdini" would have "who" as its first).

A "crossword puzzle clue" to a man who escaped boxes for a living, but also a clue to those who escaped immigration narratives and made it into the boxes of the crossword. There, as Ghogre felt about Sanskrit, words and identities can be erected and destroyed time and again. As a crossword writer and the son of an immigrant, I've always found worldmaking through wordplay intuitive, almost fated. My father signs his emails and texts ABBADAD, concatenating the Hebrew transliteration for "father" with the English; the string appears to me as an alien rhyme scheme, the specs of a poetic septet for an as yet undiscovered form. The writer Ocean Vuong has said that his late mother, who neither read nor understood much English, would sit facing the audience at her son's poetry readings, fluent at least in the language of bodily rending, of visible transport and escape. I imagine my mother, a Moroccan Israeli immigrant whose written English is spotty, tottering over to a customer at the restaurant where she waited tables, scowling as they worked one of my crosswords instead of calculating the tip.

Once, a friend remarked that if you were to give a crossword writer a name in a work of fiction, you could do worse than Natan Last. My first name, derived from the Hebrew for "gift," is a palindrome, spelled identically forward and back, a round-trip of letters; my last name is autological—a word that describes itself, like "pentasyllabic." When a customs officer, glancing at my passport, mispronounces my first name, I feel at once like an outsider and like someone else, someone new; if the officer riffs on my last name being Last, I'm quick to develop the joke.

Perhaps this is why the crossword has long kept company with émigré writers. In Berlin in 1924, as the crossword craze raged in America, Vladimir Nabokov published the first Russian crosswords (first called *kreslovitsa*, ultimately *krossvords*) in the émigré newspaper

Rul', founded by his father. The American-style puzzles afford Nabokov a point of view; one clue asks, rhyming with Arthur Wynne's first Word-Cross, [What the Bolsheviks will do], with the answer being "Disappear." Nabokov's fiction brims with what one critic called "ego-alphabetic surrogates," anagrammatic avatars of the author: Vivian Darkbloom (from *Lolita*), Adam von Librikov *(Transparent Things)*, Blavdak Vinomori *(King, Queen, Knave)*, Baron Klim Avidov *(Ada, or Ardor)*. Immigration is an occasion for what Phillips called "self-renaming," exposing, as one of Nabokov's characters notices, that all names—the ones we come into the world with and the ones we make a new world with—are formed from the same set of letters; Vladimir Nabokov knows that Vladimir Nabokov is, too, a fiction. He seems to know it better for having written crosswords. "Definition is always finite," says Fyodor in Nabokov's *The Gift*, "but I keep straining for the faraway; I search beyond the barricade (of words, of senses, of the world) for infinity."

Unlike a crossword puzzle, that search is never-ending. Georges Perec's most famous work is likely his lipogrammatic *La disparition* (in English, "A Void"), a novel composed entirely without the letter E. He also wrote a moving study of Ellis Island and immigration, a weekly crossword for the newspaper *Le Point*, and the novel *Life: A User's Manual*, which features a started but uncompleted crossword grid. When I first saw it, it felt like the ultimate ideogram for the hybrid crossworder-novelist-migrant: the half-finished puzzle, always anagramming, escaping and assimilating at the same time. In that context, it's worth repeating Perec's description of writing crossword clues: "a stroll in the land of words, intended to uncover, in the imprecise neighborhood that constitutes the definition . . . the fragile and unique location where it will be simultaneously revealed and hidden."

When, in December 2022, Ghogre came to the United States on his EB-1A, we met for lunch in midtown. Though I worked for a refugee resettlement nonprofit nearby for three years, I couldn't remember any suitable lunch spots. It turned out not to matter. All the storefronts had, during COVID, anagrammed or rearranged themselves into other eateries: PRET A MANGER had become CHIPOTLE, TWO

FORKS was FIVE GUYS. At a ramen joint with a decent lunch special, Ghogre explained that though this phase of his immigration tale was over, there was much to do. Find an apartment in New Jersey. Enroll his children, Eva (named in part for his favorite crossword answer) and Advait, in school. Though the EB-1A does not require one to have a job lined up in America, applicants must explain how they intend to continue working in their area of "expertise." Ghogre, who like almost everyone began making puzzles as a hobby, is immigrating at a time when a post-pandemic puzzle boom and the success of the *Times* app have enabled dozens (though, it should be said, just dozens) of this book's puzzlers to find full-time work as editors. On his application, Ghogre expressed interest in eventually owning a puzzle company. Since he's an IPO banker by trade, he wants to list his own firm, and he already has the four-letter ticker picked out: CLUE.

Until then, he'll continue to imbue each grid he makes with his own perspective, stretching the horizon of common knowledge. He's proud of a recent clue for EPICS, normally ["Iliad" and "Odyssey," for two] or ["Beowulf" and "Paradise Lost"]. Ghogre's clue was [The Hindu "Ramayana" and others]. These little shifts can add up. "Fill in the crossword grid," suggests the scholar Gareth Farmer, "and you get an epic."

PART III

The Crossword Should Be Art

CHAPTER 7

Old Possum's Book of Schrödinger's Cats

[Words read with feeling], 7 letters*
—DANIEL OKULITCH, *The New York Times,* 2022

C rossword puzzles are quantum, always two things at once. There are puzzle-makers who invest their political essences into the grid; there are those who reject the notion the grid should be anything more than a zone of play, Huizinga's magic circle become square. The crossword traffics in at least two distinct registers of language: the pun clue's dad joke, and the trivia clue's prodding for erudition. And though the puzzle asks its solvers for supposedly canonized information, it is after all ephemeral, anointing a different cast of nouns tomorrow and tomorrow and tomorrow.

This issue of tricky, erudite language—and how seriously to take it—is normally the remit of literature. The crossword is a modernist object, born in the same era—and of the same instincts—as T. S. Eliot and Gertrude Stein. The puzzle's bag of linguistic tricks directly inspired some of modernism's ablest practitioners, just as it fed the fires of modernism's fiercest critics: in the 1920s and '30s, certain clusters of writers were even tarred as a literary "crossword-puzzle school."

Their twinned histories don't necessarily mean crosswords are literature or that literature is best thought of as a puzzle; but allow me to outline the limits and fruits of the analogy. To get a sense of those limits, we first need a detour to another quantum realm, a place whose natural language is itself that of limits, disambiguation, and consequence, but where levity occasionally squeaks through: the courtroom.

The Lord Chief Justice of the King's Bench Divisional Court saw the word "lottery" written all over the scheme. On January 27, 1935, *The People,* a British tabloid, had run "The Great Crossword. Offer, £2000." The "offer" was part of a broader trend: pay-to-play crosswords, in which you mailed a filled grid to a publication along with a small fee, and hoped, if yours was the first correct grid received, for a cash prize.

These contests proved lucrative for newspapers. But there were allegations that puzzle-makers had an incentive for ambiguity, dashing participants' hopes on the rocks of insoluble clues. Eventually, police issued a summons for *The People*'s proprietors (Odhams Press, Ltd., of Long Acre, London) and its publisher (one Mr. Antil Gray) under the Betting and Lotteries Act of 1934. Two infractions were alleged: advertising a "certain lottery" (Section 22 of the act) and, as prohibited in Section 26, offering a game "in which success does not depend to a substantial degree on the exercise of skill."

The lordly crossword, lacking skill? Because puzzles of this era often had "unchecked" squares, if solvers were stuck on a given clue, they had no crossing words to come to the rescue, and thus, the lawsuit asserted, had to resort to guessing. The chief justice, Lord Gordon Hewart, was now presiding over the appeal. A magistrate at Bow Street had dismissed the initial suit, arguing that, when more than one answer might plausibly fit for a clue, the answer the puzzle-maker picked was "the best and most appropriate, having regard to the clues."

That magistrate found "as a fact that a considerable element of skill was required to solve the puzzle."

But the appeal's lawyer, one Roland Oliver, King's Counsel (K.C.), disagreed. Whatever skill solvers deployed was psychological: apprehending which word the editor was likeliest to select, not necessarily the clue's best answer. That, Sir William Jowitt, K.C., contended, was patently false; editors weren't picking words willy-nilly; these were "competent people," choosing the answers with "every reasonable care." A lottery, said Sir William, would be "if you [had] the word 'animal' as the clue for a three-letter word ending with 'at'"—that could equally be CAT, BAT, or RAT. "But cross-words," he said, "are not so simple as that."

The lawyers traded examples of varying ambiguity. Mr. Oliver: "Causes much sadness when this has to be given up," for HO?E, which could reasonably be either HOME or HOPE. Sir William: "Father often loses his temper with one" for CO?K. Just then in London you'd be unsurprised to learn the average father tended to distance himself from domestic labor, a distance that took him to the pub; though the answer could be either COOK or CORK, "The proper word obviously is 'cork,'" winked Sir William, imagining a wrathful father having uncorked yet another bottle of ale, "for a wise father leaves the cook alone; she is mother's department. He concerns himself much more about corks." The courtroom laughed; it really was like that, wasn't it.

Not to be outquipped in his bailiwick, Lord Hewart, new to crosswords, ventured: "Is it not like the case of the blind man in a dark room searching for a black cat which is not there?" It wasn't, really, but more respectful laughter. In his verdict, averring that these contest crosswords had undue ambiguity, Lord Hewart draws a distinction between the crossword and a literary contest. At least the judges in poetry competitions opted for *their subjective idea* of top-shelf work. These puzzle-makers, though, bad news: "There is nothing to suggest, much less to indicate, that the competition editor will seek to . . . prescribe the best solution. There is no clue at all"—Lord Hewart couldn't help himself—

to the qualifications of the editor as to the frame of mind in which he will act or has already acted . . . [and] who may act in an arbitrary, capricious, or mischievous spirit . . . and whose ignorance may be as coextensive as the wisdom of Solomon.

It's this very ambiguity—and a recurrence of the ?AT animals Sir William highlights, not to mention that mischievous spirit—that underpins perhaps the most famous crossword of all time.

The puzzle appeared in the *Times* on Tuesday, November 5, the day of the 1996 U.S. presidential election. Its constructor, Jeremiah Farrell, had noticed the candidates from the major parties, BOB DOLE and Bill CLINTON, both had 7-letter names. 68-Across was MISTER PRESIDENT, and at 39-Across, solvers found the clue [Lead story in tomorrow's newspaper (!), with 43-Across]. 43-Across was ELECTED. But then: 39-Across could be either BOB DOLE or CLINTON; the Down clues all worked regardless of who you picked. The first such clue—39-Down, in an echo of the King's Bench case—was [Black Halloween animal], and could be either BAT or CAT. Crosswords are indeed not so simple as that.

Black Halloween animal.	CAT / BAT
French 101 word.	LUI / OUI
Provider of support, for short	IRA / BRA
Sewing shop purchase	YARN / YARD
Short writings.	BITS / BIOS
Trumpet	BOAST / BLAST
Much-debated political inits.	NRA / ERA

```
          Y
          A  B
          R  I  B
    C  L  I  N  T  O  N
    A  U  R     S  A  R
    T  I  A     S  A
                T
```

```
          Y
          A  B
          R  I  B
[ B  O  B  D  O  L  E ]
  A  U  R     S  A  R
  T  I  A     S  A
                T
```

With this puzzle, the Schrödinger crossword was born. Named for the physicist's hypothetical cat, simultaneously alive and dead in Erwin Schrödinger's famous thought experiment, these crosswords feature squares with more than one correct answer; sometimes called "quantum" puzzles, they exist in two states at once; they court the ambiguity at stake in Hewart's courtroom. Because Schrödinger puzzles violate one of the bedrock attributes of the crossword—the existence of a unique solution—they are often pressed, however clumsily, in service of more serious subjects: the outcome of a presidential election, in Farrell's case, or genderfluidity, in a 2016 Ben Tausig puzzle in which, e.g., [Word that can precede sex] could be either SAFE or SAME, with F as feminine and M masculine. When Farrell's BOB DOLE / CLINTON puzzle appeared, solvers and civilians were outraged: "For a while today, before any polls closed, we thought the *New York Times* had been particularly flagrant. Take a look at the *Times* crossword puzzle," deadpanned one news anchor that November Tuesday. Clinton, an avid solver, found the puzzle "an amazing thing." He solved it, made a copy, and sent it to Dole, after calling his opponent to say, "We both won after all." But serious or not, the Schrödinger puzzle, by having more than one unique solution—by resisting a single interpretation—is the crossword equivalent of modernist literature.

■

On November 15, 1924, T. S. Eliot and Gertrude Stein met for the first and only time, in the latter's Paris salon at 27, rue de Fleurus. Stein's partner, Alice B. Toklas, remembers Eliot as an austere man, endlessly expecting rain, "who, refusing to give up his umbrella, sat clasping its handle while his eyes burned brightly in a non-committal face." Stein remembers the meeting with some animus: the two had "a solemn conversation, mostly about split infinitives and other grammatical solecisms and why Gertrude Stein used them." Before Eliot left, he first informed Stein that were he to print anything of hers in *The Criterion,* the literary magazine he founded, "it would have to be her very latest thing." Immediately, Stein sat down to compose a mordant portrait of her visitor. She called it "The Fifteenth of November," coolly reasoning "that being this day . . . there could be no doubt but that it was her latest thing." The story, as critic Roddy Howland Jackson notes, reads "through squinted eyes, like someone shuttling over the rows and columns of a weekly crossword's clues":

> *In this case a description.*
> *Forward and back weekly.*
> *In this case absolutely a question in question.*
> *Furnished as meaning supplied.*

When Stein's story was published, that puzzle quality wasn't to its credit: as a 1926 review of "The Fifteenth of November" in the *Aberdeen Press and Journal* remarks: "Cross-word puzzles are like eating toffee to this stuff."

This stuff—Stein's and Eliot's poetics—was, per the scholar Marjorie Perloff, two sides of the same modernist coin. Both have a crossword aspect to their craft. There's the Steinian pseudo-aphorism, cryptic and glinting like a difficult clue; and there's Eliot's encyclopedic range, a collagist's grid curated with culture both foppish and popular. In the wake of World War I's destruction—both Stein and Eliot were poets in exile; both had had major publications delayed by the war—the pair were interested in whether language could reconstruct a world; a principle, as Howland Jackson puts it, of "radical reassembly." Or, as Stein avows in *How to Write,* "A sentence means that there is a future."

Failing that, language might assemble some curative solace, difficult lines for difficult times. Writing in the *Daily Mirror* on "Rhymes to Cure the Cold"—on literature as medicine—one critic mused: "Much more modern [medically] and infinitely more powerful in its effects is Gertrude Stein. Up to date disease like cross-word mania can be banished in one dose." In *Tender Buttons,* Stein's plain-language gathering of domestic Cubist still lifes, the author affirms the offbeat tonic of her syntax: "The line which sets sprinkling to be a remedy is beside the best cold." In the very next sentence, we find the respiratory fit difficult literature sometimes brings—clauses Bob Dole might dolefully have bobbed his way through, that other November: "A puzzle, a monster puzzle, a heavy choking, a neglected Tuesday."

Eliot, for his part, would see his 1922 magnum opus *The Waste Land* skewered as too cerebral, too allusive. In a 1939 review in the *Birmingham Daily Gazette,* one critic harrumphed that Eliot's masterpiece "*may* be a great poem; on the other hand it may be just a rather pompous cross-word puzzle." This judgment was as much about its creator as his gung ho code-breakers: in *American Poetry Since 1900,* poet and critic Louis Untermeyer dismissed the pleasure of reading *The Waste Land* as "the same sort of gratification attained through having solved a puzzle, a form of self-congratulation." Eliot himself was an eager solver, smuggling *The Times* of London puzzle into "tedious" editorial meetings and scribbling under the table. He could think of perhaps no grander congratulations than canonization, not in Stein's portrait, but in the black-and-white grid: "The appeal to my vanity," he wrote in a 1958 letter, "is as great as that of finding a reference to myself and my works in *The Times* crossword puzzle."

At the height of the crossword craze in the 1920s and '30s, the puzzle came to stand in for precisely these questions of difficulty and canonization. Stein was a member of the "crossword-puzzle school" of literature because her descriptions were deliberately roundabout, like a clue that asks you to unearth a word's second or third definition.

Sometimes her syntactic experiments prized the sonic over the sense-making, as in *Tender Buttons*'s "Vegetable": "It was a cress a crescent a cross and an unequal scream." And Eliot's poem, famous for its informational gluttony ranging from Whitman to Chaucer to Baudelaire to the Hindu *Brihadaranyaka Upanishad,* promises, like a crossword grid, to frame a certain kind of knowledge for the hybrid reader-solver.

To some, treating a difficult poem or novel as a crossword paradoxically made it easier: the artwork was now "completely explainable through a mechanical procedure of finding a cypher, of filling in the blanks," writes the scholar Leonard Diepeveen. "The difficult crossword puzzle text had none of the resonance of the great work of art." The vibrating wings of a great poem might, on this reading, be stilled and pinned to mounting board by the gloved lepidopterist, taxonomic caption resolving any pesky ambiguity: *Crestos lovitxa Sirin . . . Tender Buttons is about lesbianism.* The author herself might pen the caption: the poet William Empson prefaced his 1940 collection, *The Gathering Storm* (whose poems, like Eliot's *The Waste Land,* arrived with Talmudic self-annotation), with a wryly didactic "Note on Notes":

> No doubt the notes are partly needed through my incompetence. . . . But partly they are meant to be like answers to a crossword puzzle; a sort of *puzzle interest* is part of the pleasure that you are meant to get from the verse. . . . It is clear that you try to guess the puzzle before you turn to the answer; but you aren't offended with the newspaper for publishing the whole answer, even when you had guessed it. . . . And the comparison to poetry is not quite a random one; the fashion for obscure poetry, as a recent development, came in at about the same time as the fashion for crossword puzzles; and it seems to me that this revival of puzzle interest in poetry, an old and natural thing, has got a bad name merely by failing to know itself and refusing to publish the answers.

Who was this puzzle interest for? In an era when the crossword was seen by many as the realm of "idlers," as much a waste as reading

The Waste Land, one might, out to sea with the sources of modern culture, outsource looking them up. In P. G. Wodehouse's 1957 novel, *Something Fishy* (called *The Butler Did It* in its American release), Lord Uffenham, every bit an imperious sneeze as his name suggests, barks at his wittier niece, Jane:

> I'm doing my crossword puzzle, and it's a stinker this morning. Run and ask Keggs what the dickens "Adventurer goes in for outrageous road-speed" is supposed to signify. Tell him it's urgent. And I want some more coffee. . . . Yer can't drink too much coffee. It bucks you up. It stimulates the mental processes.

The answer—DESPERADO, an "outrageous" anagram of ROAD SPEED and synonym of "adventurer"—is supplied by the august valet Augustus Keggs. Then Uffenham proceeds to a second stinker: "Desperado, eh? Capital. Now, go and ask him what the devil 'So the subordinate professional on trial gets wages in advance not without demur' means." For the intellectual or the upper-crust peer, the crossword and coffee must be consumed; who labors for it is immaterial. Eliot's brooder Prufrock "measured out [his] life in coffee spoons," Margaret Farrar called the *Times* Saturday crossword a "two cups of coffee puzzle," Lord Uffenham has his niece make the coffee and his butler solve the puzzle.

The butler did it; but who is there to say, besides Jane, that Uffenham didn't solve it himself? One imagines Keggs following Uffenham on a summery lawn the color of turtle shells, moving the lord's croquet balls, muttering "Very good shot, sir" as he does. The puzzle disorients Lord Uffenham precisely because it's shifted from a knowledge game to a battle of wits:

> [His niece Jane] found him in his study having difficulties with [the clue] "Tree gets mixed up with comic hat in scene of his triumphs," and for a while listened sympathetically while he spoke his mind on the subject of the smart alecks who compose crossword puzzles these days. Lord Uffenham had been brought up in the sound old

tradition of the Sun God Ra and the large Australian bird Emu, and he resented all this stuff about subordinate professionals and comic hats.

In a postwar world, the crossword had morphed from aristocratic to meritocratic; the British cryptic puzzle now sported more tricks than trivia; subordinate professionals like butlers had somehow gotten promoted; homburgs had been doffed and more comic headgear donned. Jane, for goodness' sake, had fallen for a *sculptor*, the oddball Stanhope Twine, that surname another loose and taunting ball of clues. Uffenham—his pedigree, his way of life—was a dying breed. The crossword puzzle, solved and then discarded, was nevertheless an index of timelessness; the unsolved clue lives forever. "I've put in so many enigmas and puzzles," James Joyce said of *Ulysses*, "that it will keep the professors busy for centuries arguing over what I meant, and that's the only way of insuring one's immortality."

◻◼◻

Like Schrödinger's cat, modernist literature and crosswords both flicker between the serious and the unserious, the magisterial and more minor registers—the cute, the naughty, the mischievous spirit Lord Hewart named. A bon mot could emerge from a potty mouth attached to a famous face. It could playfully needle a comrade in letters, via reversal (Samuel Beckett, Nobel Laureate: "T. Eliot is toilet spelt backwards") or anagram (James Merrill, Pulitzer-winning poet: MARCEL PROUST is PEARL SCROTUM rearranged). This quantum nature is biblical in age; an apocryphal tale of Saint Martin features both cross words and a fearsome palindrome: the bishop is walking to Rome when the Devil appears, mocking the man for not riding a donkey. Saint Martin promptly turns the Devil himself into an ass, which he rides the rest of the way; the duplicitous Prince of Darkness curses Martin with a pair of Latin palindromes.

Signa te Signa: temere me tangis et angis:
Roma tibi subito motibus ibit amor.

Cross, cross thyself; thou plaguest and vexest me without necessity;
For, owing to my exertions, thou wilt soon reach Rome, the object of
thy wishes.

The back-and-forth satanic palindrome is attested hundreds of years
before anyone's playing Led Zeppelin in reverse, before the hokier
"Do geese see God?" or the goofier putative first man's first words:
"Madam, I'm Adam."

And about that donkey: it's uncanny how often modernist literature
and puzzles adopt—and then reject—images of cutesy creatures, like
balloon animals let loose in a library. There's Gelett Burgess, the dandy
iconoclast best remembered for his 1895 nonsense poem "The Purple
Cow": "I never saw a Purple Cow, / I never hope to see one; / But I
can tell you, anyhow, / I'd rather see than be one." Burgess, who had
loftier literary ambitions, resented the ditty's popularity. He also introduced French modern art to the United States in his 1910 article "The
Wild Men of Paris" (written humorously but not cutely); coined the
term "blurb" in the dust jacket for his own book, *Are You a Bromide?*,
which featured a fictional Miss Belinda Blurb "in the act of blurbing"
(definitely cute); and contributed crosswords to the *New York World*
(cute?). Years later, when the *New York Times* puzzle bungled a reference to another bit of light verse, it issued a correction on this cutest of
subjects in its classically un-cute even keel:

> The crossword puzzle on Tuesday provided an erroneous clue
> for 1-Down, seeking the answer "Baa Baa." The clue should have
> read, "Salutatory cry to a black sheep, in a nursery rhyme"—not
> "Black sheep's cry, in a nursery rhyme"—because it is the unnamed
> speaker of the rhyme (not the sheep, of course) who says, "Baa, baa,
> black sheep, have you any wool?"

Not the sheep, of course; we regret the error. And nothing cuter, nor more infuriating, than precociousness, in either literary or crossword form. Much to the chagrin of Margaret Farrar, an error in a *Times* puzzle was nabbed by a prepubescent Ahab, grasping after a black-and-white whale:

> Not long ago, a constructor sent in a puzzle that asked for Long John Silver's distinguishing characteristic, in nine letters. The answer, of course, was "wooden leg." Well, we'd just used Long John Silver in a puzzle, so I switched it to Captain Ahab's distinguishing characteristic. After the puzzle came out, I got a letter from an eight-year-old boy complaining that while he'd found that the only answer that fitted was "wooden leg," as a reader of "Moby Dick" he knew that Captain Ahab had an ivory leg. Perfectly true, but I couldn't help wondering, rather testily, what an eight-year-old was doing reading "Moby Dick."

What's an eight-year-old doing solving a crossword, for that matter? Then there's the singsongy clues that replaced the squarer "definitions" of an earlier era: OAT, for instance, clued as [Morsel a horse'll eat], or BEE as [Nectar inspector], whose syntax sounds like Gertrude Stein's. There's the tender cuteness of Stein's *Tender Buttons,* an affect of compactness and domesticity that the theorist Sianne Ngai, in *Our Aesthetic Categories,* pits against the supposedly sharper image of the cutting-edge avant-garde. Ngai describes how poetry like Stein's, invoking commodity culture with its rainbow run of homey objects—colored hats, malachite spoon, white petticoat, cushions, cups, and saucers, and so on—nonetheless resists easy consumption, by reflecting back the same aggression generating its minorness ("A puzzle, a monster puzzle, a heavy choking"). We want to dominate the little crossword to demonstrate our intelligence, but those rhyming clues and winking puns can shame us just as much as unknown trivia. Even the word "cute" is itself a Schrödinger's cat, derived from the fully clawed hunter of "acute" but belly-rubbed by the linguistic process of apheresis into purring, lap-bound submission, Sphinx into kitten. There's Eliot too, crossword lover and cat person, composer of both *The Waste Land* and *Old Possum's Book of Practical Cats*. While preparing to publish Marianne Moore's "The Jerboa," Eliot cutesily wondered if Ezra Pound, whom he'd address in letters as "Dear Rabbit," was "maybe not a Rabit at all but a Gerboa a Little Animil wich I understan does illustrate the Quantum Theory by being at two Places at once even if he don't understand it."

■

Modernism itself was quantum, with simultaneous outposts in America, Britain, France, Germany, and beyond; if Stein and Eliot were its American emissaries in exile, then its Russian attaché was Vladimir Nabokov. It's a moniker he would've hated. Not only as a staunch individualist skeptical of -isms, literary coats of arms that constricted more than they cheered, but also because it was that doctrine of classification that got his books (and many of his modern peers') banned from libraries in the Soviet era—in which writers like Flaubert, Joyce, Kafka, and Proust were deemed insufficiently "socialist realist" by the regime—until Gorbachev's glasnost in the 1980s loosened the screws of state censorship.

What Nabokov loved was words. He has John Shade and Charles Kinbote play "word golf" in *Pale Fire,* a variant of Lewis Carroll's doublets, in which participants change one word into another target word in as few one-letter shifts as possible, making sure every stop on the way is also a valid word. (One could get PALE -> FIRE in three moves, PALE -> PARE -> FARE -> FIRE.) Shade "would interrupt the flow of a prismatic conversation to indulge in this particular pastime"; Kinbote's feats include HATE -> LOVE in three and the Schrödinger-esque LIVE -> DEAD in five. For trilingual Nabokov, *every* conversation was prismatic: he was born with grapheme-letter synesthesia, and saw alphabets in color. The long A in English was weathered wood, the French A polished ebony. In English, the blacks were hard G ("vulcanized rubber") and R ("a sooty bag being ripped"). The whites: N (oat-meal), L ("noodle-limp"), and O ("an ivory-backed hand mirror").

Nabokov was born in 1899 in a Russia boiling over against the czar-ist regime. By May 1905 the countryside was ablaze with riots; by year's end Russia had had more strikes than in the whole of its previous his-tory. Nabokov discovered his synesthesia while building an alphabet block tower in Vyra, the countryside estate of his maternal grandfather, an engineer and gold miner with a name like a rifle: Ivan Rukavishni-kov. Nabokov, his mother, Elena, and his siblings were hiding out in Vyra. His father, a prominent lawyer, was in St. Petersburg in Russia's nascent parliament, the first Duma, as a leader of the anti-czarist Con-stitutional Democrats. By 1917, the elder Nabokov had helped draft the Grand Duke Mikhail's abdication, ending the Romanov dynasty; by year's end the Bolshevik Revolution had forced the Nabokovs to flee, first to Crimea, then England, then Berlin. Vladimir would never set foot in Russia again.

In Berlin, Nabokov's father edited *Rul'* ("The Rudder"), a Russian émigré newspaper whose inaugural issue appeared on the streets on November 15, 1920, four years to the day before Stein and Eliot's meet-ing. In *Rul'*, Vladimir Nabokov published the first known Russian language crosswords. These *krossvords* are less complex Nabokovian nesting dolls than indexes of a youthful exile poet's preoccupations: there's yearning for homeland (in subtle, huffy ways: an insistence on imperial nomenclature for weights and measures, for instance, after the Bolsheviks banned them) and frequent reference to exile (the Caucasus region, where the Nabokovs and many others had first fled, and Nansen passports). There's the quotidian (department stores and movie stars) alongside references to literary lions like Pushkin (though Nabokov does, *tsk tsk,* incorrectly attribute a Knut Hamsun character to Ibsen) next to political rabble (the clue [What the Bolsheviks will do] for the answer "Disappear"). Occasionally, the black squares spell out words in the Russian alphabet.

In Nabokov's case, it's not merely that the crossword is some pre-figurative laboratory for his fiction; he was in his twenties, scraping together odd jobs (giving boxing lessons, translating *Alice in Wonderland* into Russian, tutoring English) so he could focus on writing. It's that the crossword promises the same curatorial power as the novel: the diarist's detritus, the polemicist's dig, the designer's pristine arrangement, the poet's letter of recommendation, the quipster's wink—the crossword puzzle was capacious enough for all of it. It could even, in Nabokov's hands, be a figure of love.

When Nabokov came to Berlin after graduating from Cambridge, he proposed to seventeen-year-old Svetlana Siewart at Berlin's aquarium; she only agreed to marry him because "he seemed so pitifully and uncharacteristically sad." Her parents said okay so long as he left the limbo of freelancing and got a steady job (plus ça change). Gallant Nabokov landed a position at a German bank, at which he lasted "a mere three hours." "He could never be an Eliot," writes his biographer Brian Boyd, referring to Old Possum's stint at Lloyds Bank, where Eliot managed foreign accounts by day. Their one condition unfulfilled, Svetlana's parents broke off the engagement. Nabokov, devastated, wrote poetry ("Finis"). Then in 1923 at a Russian charity ball he encountered a woman in a black mask with a wolf's profile, a few days before he'd decamp to the south of France for a summer as a migrant farmhand. Her name was Véra Evseevna Slonim. Nabokov, enamored, wrote poetry ("The Encounter"). They were engaged by 1924. Many years earlier, Véra had nearly run into Nabokov near Vyra, a word golf of only one, as if embalming a simpler past. She had grapheme-color synesthesia too, and the couple would pass it on to their future son: "One letter which [Dmitri] sees as purple, or perhaps mauve, is pink to me and blue to my wife. This is the letter M. So the combination of pink and blue makes lilac in his case. Which is as if genes were painting in aquarelle."

In 1926, Véra was unwell, and was sent to two sanatoriums in the granite highlands of the Schwarzwald to recuperate. Nabokov stayed home; Véra had him promise to send daily letters, which metamorphosed from larval musings, mostly about the food he ate ("Huge waffles, like corsets"; "lunch: meatballs and a nameless jelly") into a kind of pupal newspaper, with weather reports, advice, and even a puzzle section. From July 1 through July 19, 1926, when Véra returned home, Vladimir added a puzzle nearly every day to his reports. On July 6, he drew a crossword in the shape of a butterfly, clues in the lower wings, grid in the upper: *Crestos lovitxa Sirin,* Sirin being one of his noms de plume. "I love you unspeakably today," writes Nabokov on July 2, in a letter betraying frustration that he's written about 80 percent of the missives. The puzzle is for Véra, but it's also for him; a finished grid would prove she's engaging: "I am curious whether you will solve it!"

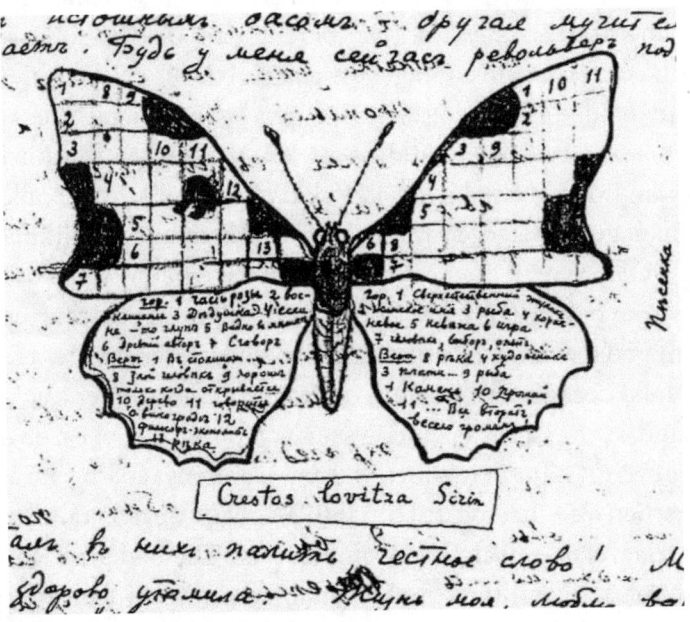

Love might seem difficult to represent in either the crossword or the literary "crossword-puzzle school," with their presumed preference for cerebral collage over direct romantic overture. Where the "average novel reader" cracking open James Joyce's *Ulysses* "expected to find a story of love and ambition and struggle, he finds a bewildering crossword puzzle," wrote Paul Jordan Smith in 1927. It's tempting to treat Joyce's novel as merely encyclopedic: Ezra Pound called it "encyclopedia in the form of farce," not a bad description of a crossword. And if *Ulysses* isn't a crossword, its linguistic artifice is puzzle-adjacent:

concatenations (dressinggown, snotgreen, lovesoft), puns, onomato-poetic runs ("seesoo, hrss, rsseeiss, ooos" for waves; "frseeeeeeee-fronnnng" for a distant train), all of these "wavewhite wedded words shimmering"—another apt image of a crossword grid.

But if a crossword has one solution, and a Schrödinger puzzle has two, the great work of literature is never fully soluble. A crossword can be poetic but never quite poetry because it is, ultimately, single-use. For all the compendia and explainers, *Ulysses,* as the critic Merve Emre points out, citing Sam See, counsels against treating the text as a series of clues or references to be tracked down. Surrendering to what you don't get is the novel's great pleasure:

> This surrender is love. If desire is the pain of ignorance, then love . . . "is the pleasure of ignorance: the pleasure of renouncing our desire to fill the hole of knowledge, to make knowledge whole, to master those to whom we bear relation." To relinquish mastery is to sing, as Molly does, "love's old sweet song."

Or, as Adam Phillips puts it in an essay fittingly titled "On Not Getting It," there's a difference "between words as procurers of experiences and words as consolidators of knowledge." Love bridges that gap in *Ulysses,* connecting the experience of love to the common-sense definition of the word, positioning the universality of emotion against the obscurity of the text: "O, touch me soon, now," crows Stephen Dedalus. "What is that word known to all men?" Then answers his own question, six episodes later: "Love, yes. Word known to all men."

Even if it's no great work of literature, the crossword, seen along-side its modernist littermates, might teach you to love your ignorance. It might spark a desire to be curious, not vengeful, about what you must look up. I like to think the crossword has made me less apt to treat a great novel as if it had a single, verifiable solution; friends and romantic partners as if I could fully puzzle them out; myself as definable by a five-word clue. I'd like to linger over the undefinable: "To define—is to distrust," as Laurence Sterne writes in *The Life and Opinions of Tristram Shandy, Gentleman.* Those that define too readily are, in the modernist canon, easy to lampoon. Take Mr. Ramsay, the tyrant father in Virginia Woolf's *To the Lighthouse,* anxiously linking alphabetic orderliness to the disorder of self-love, but hiccupping at his own limp initial: "He reached Q. Very few people in the whole of England ever reach Q. [. . .] But after Q? What comes next? [. . .] Z is only reached once by one man in a generation. Still, if he could reach R it would be something. Here at least was Q. He dug his heels in at Q. Q he was sure of. Q he could demonstrate. [. . .] R is then—what is R?" For Ramsay, there could be self-love in refusing total self-knowledge, pleasure in leaving oneself unsolved; but alas, he is hell-bent on getting to Z, on solving the puzzle at any cost.

We've seen how literature makes use of crosswords, but do crosswords do their own impressions of Eliot, Stein, or Nabokov? After the crossword craze, "definitions" (one-to-one, buttoned-up, rote) would give way to "clues" (twinkling, taking liberties, implying a give-and-take). The culture solicited in, say, the *Times* crossword would come to look less like the classical education baked into *Ulysses*'s most cryptic episodes, and more like the ranging and personal mode of Molly Bloom's final monologue.

This transition took a long time in part because the man presiding over the *Times* crossword in the 1970s and '80s was himself invested in that tradition of classical education. Eugene T. Maleska was born in 1916 in Jersey City, and began his career teaching Latin and English at a junior high school in Palisades Park, New Jersey. In 1973, he retired as a superintendent in the Bronx, and had I.S. 174, at the mouth of Pugsley Creek in Castle Hill, named for him—the only person to have a New York City public school dedicated for them during their lifetime, a riff on Eliot encountering his own work in the crossword.

Crosswords were Maleska's second career, but he treated the puzzle like an AP Latin exam, bringing "the same knuckle-rapping rigor" to his *Times* editorship. Maleska, went the scouting report, was "an educator first and an entertainer second." His puzzles demanded esoterica like NEMAS [Eelworms], TRETS [Allowances once given by weighers of commodities], ADITS [Entrances for miners], ANILE [Old-womanish], and so on. As a constructor—he'd been selling puzzles since the 1930s—he was early to the multiple-words entry, and Margaret Farrar credits him with debuting an answer that could double as self-awareness: HARD SHELLED CRAB. (Despite being a grump, he'd used puzzles as a love letter too—putting JEAN, his then-girlfriend at Montclair State College, at 1-Across in his first grid, clued as [Most beautiful girl on campus]. In letters to constructor Jim Modney, who'd snuck his wife's name, ANDREA, into a *Times* puzzle, Maleska would refer to Jean, now his wife, by her clue number, as in "1-Across sends regards.") As an editor, Maleska was perhaps more exacting on submitters than on the clues themselves. A review of his book *Crosstalk: Letters to America's Foremost Crossword Puzzle Authority,* notes Maleska "emerges as a smug man who delights in using obscure and archaic definitions in childish games of verbal one-upmanship. This rather unflattering self-portrait may please disgruntled puzzle fans." Things slipped through, of course: Maleska says he learned the hard way that Bambi is a stag, not a doe; that dodecahedra have twelve faces, not sides; that "Et tu, Brute?" were Caesar's penultimate words, not his last ("Then fall, Caesar"); and that the sound of a tuba is *oom,* not *oompah-pah.* "I may have a Polish name," he said in 1987, "but unlike Pope John Paul II, I cannot claim any kind of infallibility."

Then in 1993, there was a shake-up at the *Times.* The papal conclave had convened; black-and-white smoke issued from a midtown chapel; a new crossword editor had been named. Will Shortz was then something of an avant-gardist in the puzzle world. After law school at the University of Virginia—he'd decided not to practice the spring of his first year—he landed in 1978 the editorship of *Games* magazine, a brand-new outlet produced with little to no oversight from its robed and relaxed parent company: *Playboy.* (Shortz and the other puzzlers at *Games* got free copies of *Playboy* every month during their ownership.) Shortz worked the circulation up to six figures and welcomed experimentation from the innovative minds in the National Puzzlers' League. A divide was brewing between the crossword's ancien régime (Maleska; William Lutwiniak, coeditor of *The Washington Post Magazine*'s Sunday puzzle; *New York* magazine's Maura Jacobson) and what was called the New Wave (Shortz; Merl Reagle; Henry Hook, who wrote goofy clues like [Bet middler?] for BOOKIE; Stanley Newman, who organized an annual crossword cruise for the younger set—"Sail Away with Stan!"—on which, donning one of his many Hawaiian shirts, he'd lead passengers in sessions called "Puzzling 101" and "Tackling the Toughies").

"The old guard, like me, say, 'Thou shalt not coin,'" grumbled Lutwiniak, a former cryptologist with the National Security Agency, then in his late seventies. "But these guys go their merry way." The New Wave wanted loopier puns, more culture and brand names not in the dictionary; they wanted to clue OREO as the cookie, not the preposterous Greek prefix ὀρεο-; they'd had it with cobwebbed crosswordese like INEE [Arrow poison] or PROA [Malaysian boat]; they favored less dry clues than [Exsuccous] or [Anhydrous] for the word DRY. Lutwiniak, his NSA fear of overreach hardwired, hallucinated a slippery slope: "I'm afraid that once you open the door to this kind of thing, you can't stop it."

Then, in 1988, Robert Guilbert Sr., a seventy-six-year-old entrepreneur from Milwaukee, invited well-known constructors from both factions to a meeting at the Harvard Club in New York, to discuss the formation of the world's first Crossword Puzzle Hall of Fame. (Guilbert had ulterior motives, it seems: he'd invented a game called Pago Pago, an infinite crossword on a Möbius strip, and wanted to hawk it to the greats.) The group created a board of directors with equal representation, half New Wave, half old guard: Maleska as president and Will Weng, *Times* crossword editor between Farrar and Maleska, as chairman; Shortz as first vice president and Newman as secretary. By the time Shortz was anointed in 1993, he was determined to bring the modernist's dictum—*Make it new!*—to the grid. The very first *Times* puzzle he ran, on Sunday, November 21, 1993, was like slapping a fuzzing black-and-white TV, rendering the image suddenly in color. The puzzle featured rebuses, single squares representing colors of the rainbow, hidden within longer words or phrases, as in SH[RED], [VIOLETS] ARE [BLUE], and SYDNEY [GREEN]STREET.

Under Shortz's watch, the *Times* crossword became more like Stein and Eliot—more syntactically playful, more welcoming of culture once excluded from the grid. In the Shortz era, tricky clues might play with the conventions of written language, hiding proper nouns as in [Law with many parts] for JUDE or a part of speech as in [Love going to different parties?] for POLYAMORY. Constructors like Merl Reagle and Patrick Berry oedipally transfigured Maleska's fatherly "crossword authority" into the paunchier dad joke: [Ex-wife's refrain?] for REMEMBER THE ALIMONY (Berry) and [Séance-loving crime writer?] for RAYMOND CHANNELER (Reagle). The conventions that Margaret Farrar had established, her successor Will Weng had gamely maintained, and Maleska had tightly gripped could, in the Shortz era, be massaged into softness. Crosswords have odd-by-odd dimensions, 15-by-15 (dailies) or 21-by-21 (Sundays); here's a 1995 puzzle by Bob and Sharon Klahn in which, poking his head above the 15-by-15 grid as if out of his burrow, emerges the 16-letter PUNXSUTAWNEY PHIL, the initial P bearing news of six more wintery weeks. Crosswords feature all-over interlock, the idea you could draw a line into every section of a grid without picking up your pencil, and a proxy for ease of breaking into certain sections while solving; here's a 2011 puzzle by Jeremy Newton and Tony Orbach called "You'll Get Through This," in which the grid is a maze, walls of black squares carving it into 16 mini-puzzles. To get from one to the next, the solver must realize that certain black squares actually represent the word DOOR; 25-Across is [Done for, finito, kaput] for the entry DEAD AS A [DOOR] NAIL. NAIL stays perfectly hidden at first with its own clue at 26-Across, [Execute perfectly].

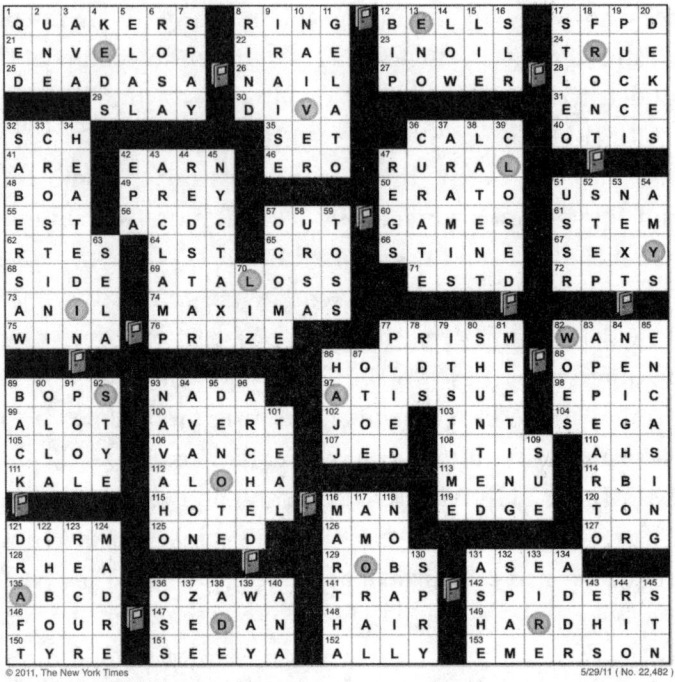

© 2011, The New York Times   5/29/11 (No. 22,482)

The innovation that Shortz encouraged would then see its post-modern equivalent on crossword blogs and in subscription puzzles, which proliferated at the turn of the twenty-first century. Metafiction was all the rage in literary circles; one of my favorite crosswords ever is an example of what's called a metapuzzle, in which, after finishing a crossword, the solver must "extract" a final answer from the completed grid and the constructor's hints. The puzzle, which ran in May 2009, was part of Matt Gaffney's weekly "Crossword Contest," a dastardly metapuzzle he's offered for some fifteen years. Called "Clues Are Clues," it asked solvers: "Somebody killed Mr. Boddy—but whodunit, which room did they do it in, and with what weapon?" The only hint in the grid was the strange answer EIGHT THAT END IN 2, in the center row. Solvers were to look at the clues whose clue numbers end in the numeral 2. Those clues and their answers were:

2-Down	Ark. Neighbor	OKLA
12-Down	___ fever	RUNS A
22-Across	Fashionable	MODISH
32-Down	Word in the name of the band that did "London Calling"	CLASH
42-Down	___ card	HIGH
52-Down	Accompanying	ALONG
62-Down	Hot drink in France	CAFE
72-Across	Hitchcock film	TOPAZ

Each of these clues works with one or more additional answers—Arkansas also borders Missouri, Tennessee, Mississippi, Louisiana, and Texas, for example—and substituting other answers yields the following:

2-Down	Ark. Neighbor	MISS
12-Down	___ fever	SCARLET
22-Across	Fashionable	IN
32-Down	Word in the name of the band that did "London Calling"	THE
42-Down	___ card	LIBRARY
52-Down	Accompanying	WITH
62-Down	Hot drink in France	THE
72-Across	Hitchcock film	ROPE

On the culture side, Shortz's main intervention was allowing more of it—brand names, modern movies, sports, up-to-date changes in language. When Shortz took over at the *Times* in 1993, Jack Rosenthal, the editor of the Sunday magazine, told him that if references showed up in the puzzle from the most recent twenty-five years, "it came as a shock." Shortz changed that, particularly with music, and early grids in his tenure feature ELTON JOHN, the Michael Jackson–Paul McCartney collaboration SAY SAY SAY, and the R&B singer ASHANTI. He didn't always have his finger on the pulse, though. In the early 2000s, the constructor Peter Gordon sent him a puzzle featuring OOPS I DID IT AGAIN—a grid-spanning 15 letters, and at the time a #1 song. "Lots of hits come and go," recalled Shortz. "Why would you put that in a puzzle when, three months from now, no one's going to remember it? So I rejected the puzzle for that reason." Six months later, Gordon tried him again with the same entry, and by that time Britney Spears, and the song's impact, were unavoidable. Shortz ran the puzzle.

These blind spots, as we've seen, are political. But they're real cultural preferences, crossed with imagined pandering: just as Paul Jordan Smith dreamt up an "average novel reader" in 1927, for whom *Ulysses* had one puzzle too many, Shortz, and the crossword mainstream generally, stake any editorial gatekeeping in defense of an "average solver." It's a frustrating strategy, not least because it's often wrong on its own merits (as when one reviewer dinged a Kameron Austin Collins puzzle for the "unfair" and "not ubiquitous" OLIVIA POPE, Kerry Washington's character on *Scandal*; the show, at its peak, had an average of more than twelve million viewers). Or it's just bafflingly, almost endearingly blinkered, and out of step with solvers (as when Shortz rejected a puzzle with the theme answer EVERYTHING BAGEL, which he said he didn't recognize; this entry, too, finally made it into the Gray Lady). It can also drain the puzzle of color; whoever this average solver is, worrying too much about him (and it seems, from the culture in mainstream crosswords, inevitably to be a him) can, at worst, produce inartful pap, to the extent that trying to please everyone often results in pleasing no one at all.

When editors act like music labels, then, constructors turn to mixtapes. Forget being mainstream; indie puzzles give you the space to canonize in black-and-white all the bands a *Times* editor or *Wall Street Journal* solver might not know; like a burned CD, a crossword can function as a curated collection of meaningful words. (It's like a poetry collection in that way too. Constructors' wordlist scores amplify words the constructor likes, though one can imagine a grid crowded with top-scoring proper nouns to be overwhelming, like wading through a particularly citational thicket of *The Waste Land*. Similarly, John Ashbery apparently evaluated his poems with letter grades, but when collecting them for a book, didn't want to have all A poems. A book of A poems was a boring book, he thought; some B's or even a C or two would make the texture of the book more interesting.)

In a way, this is demographic destiny. The cohort of solvers who grew up with Shortz's puzzle, already far more welcoming of pop culture than his predecessors', would start blogs where they could put whatever they wanted in a crossword—especially if it was unwanted in a *Times* grid. Then, when the second crossword craze came around in the 2020s, and outlets were adding crosswords left and right, those same culture vultures (Erik Agard, Amanda Rafkin, Malaika Handa, and more) were installed as editors or staff constructors at legacy publications (like *USA Today, New York* magazine, *The New Yorker,* and others) where they could turn the cultural insurgency up to eleven. Today you can find musician BEBE REXHA in a *USA Today* puzzle or YouTuber JACKIE AINA in *The New Yorker.* Agard and Rafkin in particular, both millennials, have breathed new life into the *USA Today* puzzle, which before them was underwhelming fare. In fact, the cultural supremacy of the *Times* puzzle inflected even the supremely countercultural: the indie rock scene.

On the 1995 Lollapalooza tour, Hole's Courtney Love was always challenging Pavement's Stephen Malkmus to battles of wits. An indie rock quiz, a discussion of lyrical muses (Malkmus, demurring, kept calling them "mooses"), even an essay-writing contest, but Malkmus wouldn't bite. Someone suggested they race to solve the Sunday *Times* crossword, and that was amenable. They bet on it. If Love lost, she'd be condemned to a very un-Love-ly outfit, going onstage in X-girl corduroys, an X-girl tee, Pumas with no laces, a bit like putting a conical birthday hat on a sorceress. If Malkmus lost, he had to do shots of tequila, play a Pearl Jam song "with absolutely no irony," then stage-dive.

Love hadn't solved the *Times* in a year; on the tour bus she got out the *USA Today* puzzle for drill, supposedly "as dopey as *TV Guide*'s . . . clues like 'Lennon's widow,' or 'Morrison's band,' but there was still shit I couldn't figure out." Love panicked. She went to a store and got one of those high-fructose point-of-sale crossword books; being a good sport she bought one for Malkmus too. "Courtney," Malkmus sighed on seeing the gift, "I need you to know that I've been doing the *New York Times* crossword puzzle every Sunday of my life." "Well, Steve,"

Love shot back, "I want you to know I was *raised* on the *New York Times* crossword puzzle." He rejected her olive branch, and the contest never happened: that Sunday, fresh off a depressing reconnection with an ex, Love was in such a bad mood that when her bus arrived at the venue, she stormed into her room, slammed the door shut, and hurled the complimentary deli platter at the door. As far as I can tell, Love has never been an answer in a *Times* puzzle, and LOVE has never been clued via her, an unimaginable oversight, at least to this fan. One of the only references to her I know of: a theme answer in a 2006 Patrick Berry Sunday puzzle—I wonder if she solved it—titled "Kneecaps" because the long answers were phrases with the sound "nee" tacked on to the end, then punnily clued. 41-Across was [Love hate?], with the answer being CONTEMPT OF COURTNEY.

Which brings us back to the King's Court.

The law is language that makes things happen; poetry "makes nothing happen," per crossword solver and poet W. H. Auden. Does a crossword make anything happen? Would it be better if it didn't? Could the crossword, at least, be a Schrödinger's cat, a box in which work and leisure happen at once, in which language was simultaneously alive and dead, punned on and mummified? The puzzle then could be a parody of work; its knowledge could be a parody of erudition; tragedy might be taking the puzzle too seriously.

In 1935, the same year as Lord Hewart's crossword ruling, A. P. Herbert published *Uncommon Law,* a book of parodies of English common law. Herbert, born in Surrey in 1890, was called to the English bar but never practiced. Still, his legal prose was lucid enough to have one Lord Atkin, in his introduction to *Uncommon Law,* proclaim "there are several judgments the diction and close reasoning of which many judges would be glad to imitate." Lord Hewart himself contributed commentary, murmuring that Herbert "may have decided that it is more agreeable on the whole to suffer an introduction than to be committed for contempt of Court."

In Herbert's own preface, he notes that his fictional litigant, Albert Haddock, "has made some disturbing escapes into real life." In one parody, "Board of Inland Revenue v. Haddock," Haddock, to pay his income tax, makes out a check on a white cow (no purples available) and leads it to the office of the collector of taxes; there's no law against it. Someone sent Herbert a cutout of an article in the American *Memphis Press-Scimitar* titled "A Check Can Be Written on a Cow," citing the case as if it were real. In another, Haddock, on a bet, jumps off Hammersmith Bridge into the Thames, then gets arrested by police who aren't sure what law, exactly, he's broken. A serious work of American reportage, *The Lawyers,* contains in its index this citation: "p. 167 *Rex v. Haddock* C.C.A. miscellaneous law, *Criminal Law* (31) 1927," though the story appeared in a humor magazine. The law, it would seem, is not so simple as that.

Many of Haddock's escapades involve the "peculiar" distinction in English law between libel (written or printed) and slander (spoken); the former was treated much more severely by the law. Is it libel or slander if the defamatory language arrives via gramophone record ("The Lawyer's Dream")? If it is sufficiently ephemeral, as with skywriting ("End of a Nonsense")? If delivered by semaphore ("Slander at Sea")? In "Silvertop v. The Stepney Guardians" a man had trained a parrot to say three times after every meal, "Councillor Wart has not washed today." That, it was held, was libel.

In another Haddock tale, "A Cross Action," Sir Antony Dewlap, K.C., explains to Mr. Justice Snubb that the rascal Haddock—a man of "loathsome antecedents and inconsiderable income"—is at it again. The crime this time is libel; the channel "is no other than the innocent and familiar 'Crossword.'" Justice Snubb doesn't know what that is, Dewlap offers a horribly convoluted explanation punctuated a dozen times by the word "milord," Snubb still doesn't get it, so:

SIR ANTONY DEWLAP: . . . milord—milord, if I were to ask you to give me the name of a learned and sagacious High Court judge in five letters, beginning with "S," I think your Lordship would readily arrive at a solution? *(Laughter)*

MR. JUSTICE SNUBB *(benevolently)*: I should give you the name of
    my learned brother Swift. *(Laughter)*
SIR ANTONY: Your Lordship is too modest. *(Laughter)*
    That, however, milord, is the principle of these puzzles.

Dewlap says the crossword mostly concerns dead things, or things
never quite alive: "mythical animals and Biblical characters . . . classical writers, obscure musical instruments." But Haddock has written
crosswords whose definitions disparage living persons of distinction:

Across

2. Bibulous bishop.
4. Titled lady, banting at Nice.
5. Peer. Powders his face.
6. The favourite indulgence of No. 2 (above).
7. No. 4's next husband—if he's not careful.

Down

4. Political. A time-server. Or so they say.
5. An English humorist. Or so he says.
7. That clever young dramatic critic with the toupee.

Well, lots of bishops could be bibulous, you might say, but since
these clues correspond to answers of a particular length, with such and
such letter in the second position, "these limitations divest the clues
of much of their innocent vagueness and impersonality." The crossword, in other words, is trying to be cute; being a crossword, it's not
hard to solve for who Haddock is sending up. Or down, as it were:
Bishop BOWL, the answer to 2-Across, has, it turns out, appeared in a
slew of recent Haddock crosswords, redescribed variously as [A prosy
humbug], [An intolerably hearty and overpaid clergyman], and [The
world's worst golfer]. It gets worse: "In the last two puzzles, milord, this
unhappy victim of the defendant's spite had not even the satisfaction
of a principal (and horizontal) place in the puzzle, but was degraded to

the position of a word in four letters, reading downward, an indignity intolerable, milord, to a man of his years and sensibility."

In the case of the defaming crossword clue—libel either way—Haddock's angle is obvious: he wrote the clues, but it's the solver who writes the answer, the person's name, in the grid. Haddock isn't liable. In his cutesy, mischievous way, Haddock is revealing another difference between the art of crosswords and literature: in *Ulysses* or *Tender Buttons,* it's the language that's beautiful, but in games—as philosopher C. Thi Nguyen has argued—what's beautiful is you, the player.

In *Uncommon Law,* Justice Snubb adjourns for lunch, and then Sir Antony says Haddock and the plaintiffs have settled; "the legal question, then, remains in doubt." Part of the case's joke, of course, is that expanding the puzzle's frame of reference beyond the dead or the esoteric *does* make something happen: it implicates the world as it currently lives and breathes; it names names that might thrill to their inclusion in the black-and-white grid (Eliot, in the *Times* of London; any of the celebrities hat-tipped in *USA Today;* the contemporary Black artists in Juliana Pache's *Black Crossword,* whose slogan is "If you know, you know"; the young poets cited in *New Yorker* puzzles). These figures might also, on finding their portrait cockeyed, complain (Bishop Bowl; Bob Dole, on a Tuesday in November). A Maleska puzzle could rightfully be called obscure because it dragged from the darkest corners of the library the mustiest dead letters, recalling Stephen Dedalus's memory, in *Ulysses,* of insectoid Parisian students in the stacks who seemed "fed and feeding brains about me: under glow-lamps, impaled, with faintly beating feelers." Knowledge, in this dimly lit vision, is static, arachnid, consumed by the nearly lifeless. Dedalus had been a history teacher, had seen the children taunt one another darkly when one got a name, a date, or a place of battle incorrect.

Shortz, and those who came after, let the light in: the neon of brand names, the pop star supernovas, the fireflies of colloquialism or coinage, caught and then released, the language remaining alive. There's an irony in the fact that, like a postmodern novelist, one of Shortz's trademarks is trademarked products (OREO and IKEA and SERTA and all the rest): rather than making the puzzle feel more ephemeral or of its time, trademarks, as the scholar Joseph Slaughter writes of their use in literature, "have the potential to fulfill the romantic fantasy of immortality through authorship. The life of a trademark is perpetual; as long as it remains active, it never dies." Nothing lacks more context than a trademark; Shortz's trademark was extracting crosswords from the supposedly contextless, indisputable canon of old Latin pulpits and Greek colonnades, and allowing the puzzle to make its context new—a game his inheritors have taken up a notch. As far as I know, the *Times* has never been sued because it misclued OREO; when, as in a Joel Fagliano and Christina Iverson *Times* Sunday, a theme answer invokes a brand name like LITTLE SEIZERS* clued as [We've rebranded! Now we sell tiny tongs!], well, that's parody.

That line from Auden also requires more context: "In context," writes poet Don Share, but "only part of that context, since I can't legally quote the entire poem . . . the poem actually says 'For poetry makes nothing happen: it survives . . . it survives . . . A way of happening, a mouth.'" A crossword doesn't make anything happen, but it's a way of gathering a world, a hundred little tender buttons, a small bid on the knowledge one hopes survives—not intact, but redescribed by those who come after. The crossword is an intellectual exercise, but like the "mouth" in Auden's poem, it happens in the body: hunched over a desk with a pen or thumbing a smartphone screen, deciding if the answer, today, is BAT or CAT.

---

* What is a poem if not a little seizer.

CHAPTER 8

Time Frames

[This isn't what it looks like!], 15 letters*
—CAITLIN REID, *The New York Times*, 2022

n 1983, the artist David Hockney made *The Crossword Puzzle, Minneapolis,* a photo collage of the married couple Martin Friedman (head of the Walker Art Center in Minneapolis, where Hockney was staying) and Mildred Friedman (the Walker's curator of design). The couple was solving a morning crossword together as Hockney, sipping tea, watched and clicked his Polaroid. Until these collages, Hockney had seen photography as a lifeless medium, compared to drawing or painting. To him, these latter media had a fuller relationship to—and could better frame—time. To look at a painting, as artist and writer Jenny Odell explains, was to "inhabit the physical, bodily time of its being painted," but to look at a photograph was to adopt "the point of view of a paralyzed cyclops—for a split second . . . [b]ut that's not what it's like to live in the world, or to convey the experience of living in the world." Hockney's post-Cubist experiment could convey the caffeinated narrative of a morning solve between lovers:†

---

† SOLVER and LOVERS, after all, are anagrams.

· OPTICAL ILLUSION

The way they did [the crossword] together, it was like an intellectual contest of some kind. . . . I think probably the first picture was
taken when [Mildred] was almost ready to write the word, and then
as she got more excited thinking the word is correct and moves
down. [That sequence] starts with the top of her head and ends
with the tip of her pen. And I realized you could make portraits
more and more complex . . . using the passing of time.

When we look at a painting, or read, or solve a crossword, our eyes
dart around, making rapid movements called saccades; Hockney's
photos are out of sequence, unsnapped from a grid's perfection, to
mimic how looking is always nonlinear. The Friedmans' crossword
does affirm the passage of time: some shots of the grid appear to have
more letters filled in than others. And as viewers, we're invited to read
the collage as a set of clues, off-kilter crossword cells open for interpretation, if not solution; an image of Hockney's hand sits in the lower
left, hovering near a pen.

Then there's the French conceptual artist Sophie Calle's work entitled *Take Care of Yourself.* Calle ("the Marcel Duchamp of emotional

dirty laundry") had just been dumped by email; the man who'd ended their affair concluded his letter with "Take care of yourself." Calle asked 107 women to analyze the missive according to their professional idioms. A copy editor lacerates the ex's grammar and syntax. A forensic psychiatrist determines he was a "twisted manipulator." And a crossword writer *(cruciverbiste)* breaks up the breakup letter into letters, scrambling the text and context of the original (putting the email's words into the grid out of narrative order; these are in red in the piece) but also fashioning the context anew (adding crossing words in black to make the grid, if not the relationship, work). In Calle's piece, the filled grid is presented absent the clues: the ex—like Woolf's Mr. Ramsay, reduced to his letter, "X"—has said everything he has to say; any further interpretation will be supplied by us, the viewers. Where in Hockney's piece the crossword could stand for the passage of time, settling into a few minutes of domestic play, in Calle's it could stand for an unsettling closure.

Calle had asked her collaborators to "analyze this letter"; on XWord Info, the site that bills itself as "*the* essential resource for crossword constructors and enthusiasts," one can find a past *Times* crossword and click a button labeled "Analyze this puzzle." Like a fitness app, quantitative evaluation will issue forth; like the dimensions and material elements on a gallery placard, fittingly called a "tombstone"— photo collage, 83.8 x 116.8 cm. (33 x 46 in.), for the Hockney—this grid analysis can feel a little cold. You will learn, for instance, that the Thursday, June 28, 2012, *Times* crossword has the standard 15 rows and 15 columns; 76 words; 32 black squares; 23 of 26 letters (lacking J, X, and Z); an average word length of 5.08; letters whose tile value in the game Scrabble would be, on average, 1.55 (as a proxy for entries that look more like QUIZZICAL than RELENTLESSNESS); 5 entries that appear *only* in this puzzle (RINSINGS, SNITCH ON, TISDALE, VANILLA ICE, and TIME FRAME); and a "Freshness Factor" of 41.8, a percentile calculated using the number of other times each word in the puzzle appears under Shortz's editorship at the *Times*. You can, catching your breath, see this data visualized:

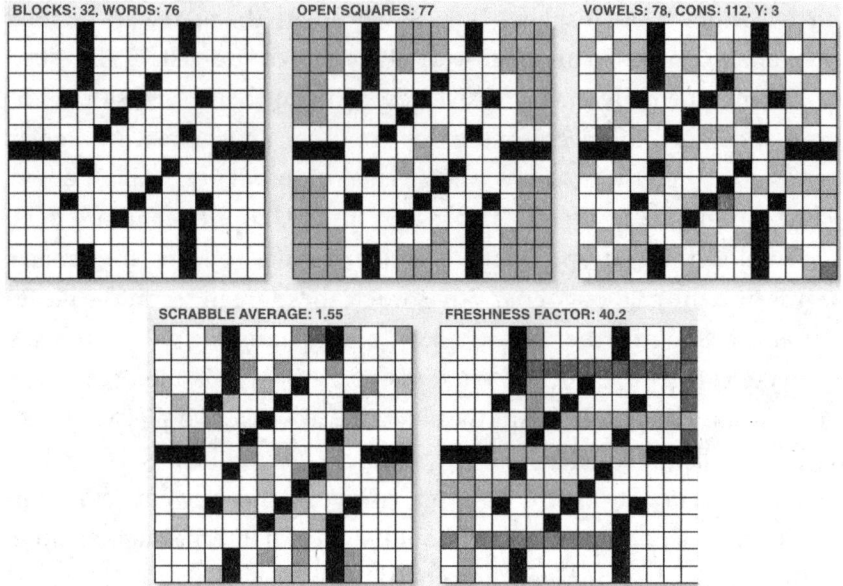

One aesthetic game crossword constructors play is to optimize for these measures. Often this arms race benefits the solver: striving to debut a word that's never been in a *Times* puzzle can mean keeping the crossword current, introducing solvers to neologisms, proper nouns, or slang heard or seen everywhere except the grid. (*Times* debuts in 2023 include BEACH READ by Kate Hawkins, VIBE CHECK by Sam Ezersky, STREET PROPHETS by Kameron Austin Collins, BIG IF TRUE by Ada Nicolle, CORNEL WEST by Ryan McCarty, and CAN I SEE SOME ID by Robyn Weintraub.) And introducing high Scrabble value letters (J, Q, X, Z) can be pleasurable when the grid subsequently buzzes and gurgles with JACUZZI or QUIXOTIC or JUKEBOX, less so when you get LIQ [Water, e.g.: Abbr.] crossing QID [Four times a day, in prescriptions]—which could easily have been LIB / BID, LID / DID, LIE / EID, and so on, all of which admit of more varied clue possibilities. (Opting for an X or Z where a stalwart T or L makes for more interesting fill is a faux pas called, by a newer generation of cruciverbistes, Scrabblefucking.)

There's similar competition to produce wide-open grids, Rothkolike expanses of white with minimal drippings of black. The game here is to feature as few words as possible, as few black squares as possible, or impressive "stacks" of adjacent 15-letter entries. Pursuing these records is not unlike the logologists' quest for bigger and better word squares—the primary difference being word squares are meant merely to be viewed. When a crossword writer vies for one of these feats of construction, the result can be beautiful to behold, but unpleasant to solve. (Even then, the eyes of the beholder are often trained: few every-day solvers pay attention to word or black square counts.) As of this writing, the records for fewest words (50) and fewest black squares (17) are both held by constructor Joe Krozel, known for his roguish, boundary-pushing grids.

Stacks of 15-letter answers, on the other hand, are noticeable imme-diately. On seeing Kevin G. Der's Friday, February 12, 2010, *Times* puz-zle, the first crossword to feature two "quad stacks"—groups of four 15-letter answers one atop another—the constructor Ben Bass effused: "Look at this thing. It's not a crossword puzzle, it's a challah twist. It's a tablecloth. It's a standing wave. It's an EKG chart." Not to be outdone, a quintuple stack was published—the only such puzzle to date—on Saturday, December 29, 2012, by none other than Joe Krozel.

These are baubles, perhaps: beautiful to squint at, but as if behind glass. Such heady feats are commonly the province of difficult "theme-less" puzzles: Saturdays in the *Times,* Mondays in *The New Yorker*. But Hockney and Calle had thematized the puzzle—its shape, its arrange-ment of words—and some of the more beautiful crosswords do the same. The crossword, like a visual poem, can enact its subject matter. The June 28, 2012, crossword "analyzed" above has a theme Hockney might have enjoyed: its central answer, TIME FRAME, is a hint to the entries on the edges of the grid. The words around the puzzle's perime-ter (its frame) are all types of time, clued in that context: HARD is [You might give this to someone you don't like], as in "Hard time"; QUAL-ITY is [Focused face-to-face contact] as in "Quality time"; SNACK is [When to have a nosh]; and so on. The puzzle was made by one of the crossword grid's greatest artists: Elizabeth Gorski.

Gorski was born in 1955 in Perth Amboy, New Jersey, to Polish parents who came to America after World War II. Her mother was a refugee, interned in the Dachau concentration camp, then sheltered in Poona, India, and Karachi, Pakistan, eventually making her way to Nottingham, England, where she met Gorski's father. He was in the Polish army under British command, stationed in Alexandria, Egypt. A cryptologist, he taught his daughter to write secret codes, and lavished her with books tattooed with hieroglyphics and rebuses, early lessons in the dazzling visuality and semantic breadth of language. He'd tap out

Morse code to young Gorski on the kitchen table and she'd reply, and her mother would scream at them, "Please stop!"

After immigrating, both of Gorski's parents found work in the manufacturing sector, at a time when New Jersey was clanking with postwar steel mills, gasworks, and soap factories, when Trenton's through-truss bridge proudly shouted TRENTON MAKES THE WORLD TAKES—the city's motto—at its own neon reflection in the Delaware River, and when sandstone was barged into Brooklyn along the Gowanus Canal like trays of champagne offered to the vieux riche. Gorski's mother found work as a dressmaker. Gorski's father worked nights at a paper mill; he'd make her lunch, open-faced ham sandwiches or placki ziemniaczane (Polish latkes), when she came home between morning and afternoon periods at school. They ate together and watched a new show that was now a favorite of Gorski's, and NBC's biggest ever hit in its daytime slot, before it moved to weeknights: Merv Griffin's *Jeopardy!* At home, Gorski was Elzbieta, her parents chattering in Polish or laughing in their hardscrabble Eastern European way whenever Mets manager Casey Stengel was ejected by the umps, repeating in accented English: "Yer outta there!"—standing up for your players, *that* was loyalty. She was Elizabeth at roll call in New Jersey's public schools. She was Liz to her friends, the other Polish or Hungarian kids unleashing a stream of Slavic affricate, plosive, and palatal like snowballs at the playground.

Gorski and the other Eastern European kids were precocious: they picked up English quickly, won local spelling bees, impressed their teachers. The word for "bee" in Polish is "pszczoła," she told me, grinning, as though all those consonants were a weighted vest, and English a breezy jog on shedding it.

At nine, she started viola lessons, "open[ing] up a beautiful new world of symbols." She took up the violin too, then blues guitar. After high school, she crossed the Hudson River into New York, where she's been ever since. She accelerated through Barnard College in three years, a trail of musical activities like sheet music flapping in the wind behind her: singing in the Barnard-Columbia chorus, playing violin with the Riverside Orchestra and New Amsterdam Symphony, a summer as archival intern at the New York Philharmonic. She'd take ear training courses at Juilliard and additional violin and viola lessons at the Manhattan School of Music, and still plays in the Broadway Bach ensemble and in string quartets on the Upper West Side. When her childhood love of hieroglyphics spun into an interest in calligraphy, she'd find herself admiring how the strokes of a capital S resembled a G clef in reverse.

Though she remained a loyal *Jeopardy!* fan, crosswords didn't come into the picture until Gorski's early thirties. She was working as a paralegal at Sullivan & Cromwell, where solving ability was a badge of honor, and where puzzles and legal memos rubbed elbows in many a leather briefcase. The first puzzle she completed start-to-finish was a Sunday-sized *New York* magazine offering from renowned constructor Maura Jacobson ("the Queen of Puns"), who was among the first contestants on *Jeopardy!* when the show was only a month old (she won three times, taking home $3,150), and who produced over 1,400 puzzles for *New York* across her three-decade career. Jacobson had a weekly Sunday puzzle in that magazine, and seeing her steady byline "reinforced a tiny spark of possibility" for Gorski. "This woman had her own weekly gig in a slick, gorgeous magazine. Maybe I could make a crossword someday. I wanted to be like her."

Gorski became a regular contributor to the *Times* in 1995. From the start, her wordplay was tuned to both the artistic and the personal. In an homage to her parents' place of birth, her first 21-by-21 Sunday puzzle in 1997 spotlighted a quote by the POLISH BORN (72-Across) WISLAWA SZYMBORSKA (80-Across), who'd won the Nobel Prize in LITERATURE (50-Across) the year prior:

> *WHEN I PRONOUNCE THE WORD*
> *SILENCE I DESTROY IT*

The title of Gorski's puzzle is "Paradox"; the title of Szymborska's poem, in which these lines originally appear, is "The Three Oddest Words":

When I pronounce the word Future,
the first syllable already belongs to the past.

When I pronounce the word Silence,
I destroy it.

When I pronounce the word Nothing,
I make something no non-being can hold.

The soft wisdom of Szymborska's words is made odder by the edicts of the crossword, appearing in all caps as if screamed, swapping the silences of the poem's white space—the emptiness of the page enveloping a sparse 6 lines—for the clatter of the grid's crossings. Crossword writers prize the 15- or 21-letter phrase (WHEN I PRONOUNCE THE WORD) because, in spanning the length of a grid, they suggest completeness, even predestination. Gorski's grid is like Calle's, translating existing sentences as if playing someone else's score: the new line break creates a new meaning—"When I pronounce the word / Silence I destroy it"—as if pronouncing the word, *any* word, runs the risk of destruction. The tinkling piano of Szymborska's minimalism cedes to the orchestral swell of the crossword, the piano joined through Gorski's conducting by the other words in the grid: linguistic tubas (HOBNOB, WADDLE), harps (DAZED, RANKLES), and flutes (OLIO, TENDERED). *When I construct a crossword, I destroy language, then reconstruct it . . .*

Gorski made a couple more Sundays featuring long, jerkily enjambed quotes, including one from her parents' beloved Casey Stengel, the Mets manager ("The secret of managing / is to keep the guys who / hate you away from the / guys who are undecided") and one from comedian Steven Wright ("When the man who made / the first drawing / board got it wrong / what did he go back to?") Then, in October 2002, she published the first puzzle in what was to become her signature style. Through the middle of the grid was a braid composed entirely of the letter O, aping a DNA molecule's double helix:

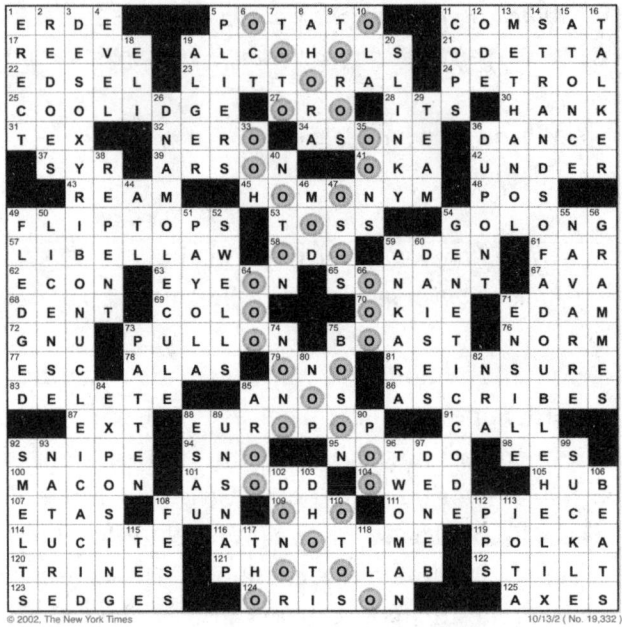

10/13/2 (No. 19,332)

In "The Aesthetics of Crossword Puzzles," philosopher and speed-solver Robbie Kubala divides "grid art," as Gorski's trademark has been called, into three categories. In one case, the grid's appearance is pleasing or even suggestive of a puzzle's theme, but not crucial to uncovering it. In Joe Krozel's wily Thursday, June 19, 2008, *Times* puzzle, for instance—Shortz's favorite of that year—the black squares spell out LIES. But solvers only required the clue at 56-Across, [Number of clues in this puzzle that contain factual inaccuracies], to hunt for the TEN lies or errors spread around the grid.

In a second case, grid art contains information relevant to solving the puzzle. This might be apparent pre-solve, as in Jeff Chen's Sunday, November 27, 2011, *Times* puzzle titled "Yin/Yang," whose black square placement and gray shading are clear signals for the solver to think in opposites, as found in the symmetrically placed phrases SUMMER BREEZE and OLD MAN WINTER. More artful is when the *aha!* moment arrives mid-solve: in Gorski's double helix puzzle, on filling in HOMONYM, EUROPOP, or PHOTO LAB, whose O's appear in

```
 O T T O   S P R A N G   C A D
 N E O N   H O A G I E   I R R
 E R R S   E N F A N T   G T E
 S E E P   L E A S E S   A U S
 E S S E     E S A U     R R S
 C A T C H A G L I M P S E O F
       I C U         E T T O
 L E A G U E     E R E C T O R
 O U G H T S     R E P R E S S
 G R A T E S     I L L I E S C U
         A A A     T M A C
 S E E I N G E Y E   C O N C
 T O L L G A T E S   O K I E
 R E S I L I E N T   D E N S
       T E N   E R I S
```

6/19/8 (No. 21,408)

```
 D E M O   S H I N E   H O M E R   R A M A
 O L A V   A B N E R   E N O L A   O F I T
 R I D E   H O T A N D H E A V Y   U R G E
 K H A N   A M E L I A   S T E G O S A U R
 S U M M E R B R E E Z E   S U D S I E R
   I T A     E N D S   N E E D L E
 F I L T H   H A R I   A A H S   S A O
 U N I T   M O R O S E   Y O U D   U F O S
 M S G   C O N S U L S   D O N N A   T R E
 A T H   A T E   G A P   R I Y A L   H A T
 N A T   R H Y T H M   S E N A T E   E L P
 C T A   L E M O N   P E A   T E N   D E I
 H E S   A R O N I   E N M A S S E   A X E
 U S A F   S O N G   U S E N E T   T R A C
   F O B   N E H I   E R I N   A S K M E
 S H E R Y L   S T D S     S H U
 C O A S T A L   O L D M A N W I N T E R
 O N T H E N O S E   A R C H I E   A W R Y
 O S H A   C A U G H T A C O L D   M I R A
 T H E M   I N I G O   B O Y L E   I R O N
 S U R E   A S T O N   S O S A S   S L R S
```

11/27/11 (No. 22,664)

circled cells, the solver may cotton to the fact that the double helix is all O's.

Kubala's final case is a form Gorski innovated, in which the solver takes up the pen hovering in Hockney's collage and "trace[s] a shape only *after* the puzzle is completed." A 2008 Gorski puzzle called "Spy

Glass" is at first a straightforward tribute to the actors who've played James Bond on screen: GEORGE LAZENBY (1969), ROGER MOORE (1973–85), TIMOTHY DALTON (1987–89), PIERCE BROSNAN (1995–2002), SEAN CONNERY (1962–67, 1971), and DANIEL CRAIG (2006–present). As with noticing WHEN I PRONOUNCE THE WORD is 21 letters long, there's pleasure in observing that these actors' names might form a symmetrical set: DANIEL CRAIG and SEAN CONNERY are both 11 letters long; PIERCE BROSNAN, GEORGE LAZENBY, and TIMOTHY DALTON are all 13; and ROGER MOORE can be paired with Bond's creator, IAN FLEMING, both 10. But a note above the puzzle's grid announces its visual coup: "When this puzzle is done, the seven circles will contain the letters from A to G. Starting with A, connect them alphabetically with one continuous line, and you'll get an image of a 39-Across." 39-Across, at the spy glass's meniscus, is MARTINI.

The visual crossword, writes Adrienne Raphel in *Thinking Inside the Box,* is "a cross between a Mondrian and latte art." The gap in this assessment isn't only a question of high and low; it's also a comparison of the enduring (Mondrian's iconic grid painting *Broadway Boogie Woogie,* now in MoMA's permanent collection) against the ephemeral (the latte art forgotten once the microfoam has dissolved; the newspaper discarded once the crossword has been solved). And the spectrum implies a labor politics: art worker (Mondrian) versus artful worker (a minimum-wage barista generating a commodity).

Scholars of aesthetics are most interested in how *you* are artful as you work a puzzle; how, as do other games, per Robbie Kubala, "crosswords merit aesthetic experiences of our own agency: [. . .] the experience of struggling for and hitting upon the right solution." But there is something beautiful about the puzzle itself, even outside the experience of playing it—the collage of words from manifold registers suddenly in the same frame, the cleverness of an inventive theme, the elegance of a devious clue. In Sophie Calle's installation, the crossword is more art object than puzzle—the answers are already there, no clues are given. Still, the viewer is invited to appreciate the collision of the ex's words with the surrounding fill, or to make meaning of how exactly the breakup missive has been scrambled and disarmed, or simply to muse on what's different about a crossword that's framed, behind glass.

And why not frame a crossword? After Calle's example, then, imagine a kind of Elizabeth Gorski retrospective, a tour of her most interesting puzzles, plus the contemporaries she's inspired. In the spirit of Calle's experimentalism, what follows is modeled on the wall text at a gallery exhibition, borrowing the art world's idioms but making that language, as any good crossword does, newly strange.

Architecture and Text

"If crossword puzzling were architecture," says the writer Nikki Gloudeman, "Elizabeth Gorski would be I. M. Pei." In Gorski's hands these grids, like Pei's designs, gesture at the grandiose: *Monumental Achievement* (2014) asks the solver to connect a series of circled letters to spell PYRAMID, and in so doing trace one out. (66-Across: THE LOUVRE; 89-Across: GLASS DESIGN BY I M PEI). Gorski's puzzles from this era induce a vertigo of multiple meaning: in *Architectural Drawing* (2019), Gorski includes rebuses that pun on 67-Across, the 1971 neonoir thriller THE FRENCH CONNECTION. A French connecting word would be "et" ("and"), and nine ETs hide in entries like AR[ET]HA, [ET]HEREAL, and [E T]ICK[ET]. The *coup de place*: draw a line connecting the French connections and produce an image of a French connection—the wrought-iron lattice of 118-Across, the EIFFEL TOWER.

Representational Crossings

Where does Gorski get her ideas? "Matisse the teacher said, 'Copy nature.' It's good advice for puzzle-makers," Gorski the artist has said. Others copy Matisse: David J. Kahn's *Picture This* (2008) pays homage

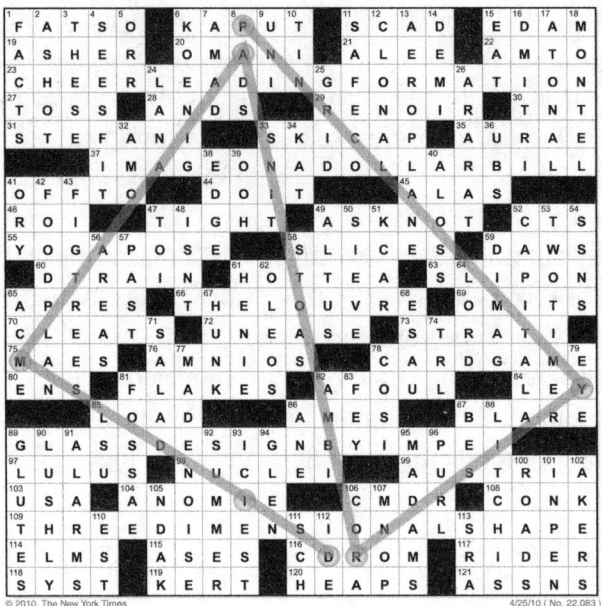

Elizabeth Gorski, *Monumental Achievement* (2014),
Crossword, ink on paper, *The New York Times*, 21 x 21

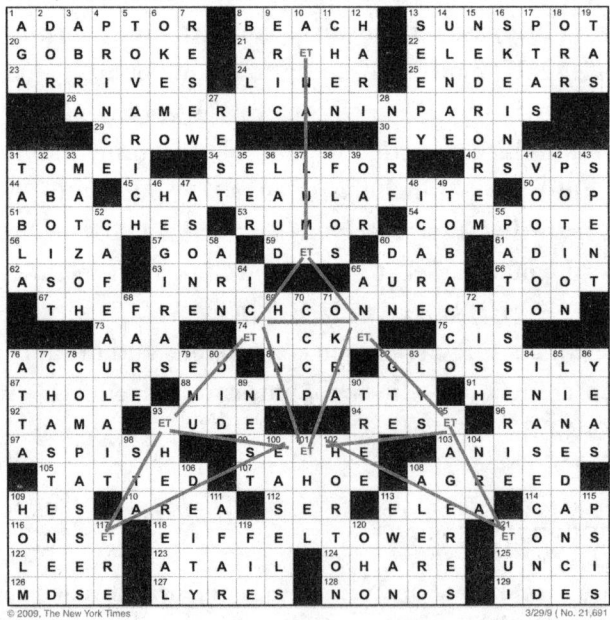

Elizabeth Gorski, *Architectural Drawing* (2009),
Crossword, ink on paper, *The New York Times*, 21 x 21

to *Le Bateau,* a Matisse gouache paper-cut featuring a blue sailboat and its watery copy, reflected in the water. Executed in very simple lines and shapes, the boat and its double look so similar that the work, also at MoMA, was in 1961 infamously hung upside down—an error undiscovered by curators, museum staff, and some 100,000 visitors for forty-seven days. Still others copy Gorski: the surrealophile Andrew Zhou tipped his bowler to Gorski and Kevin G. Der "for having contributed the finest puzzles of this sort" on the publication of his *The Art of Puzzle-Making* (2018), a tribute to René MAGRITTE's 1929 *La Trahison des Images* (68-Across: TREACHERY OF IMAGES). The solver is instructed to draw a line connecting the circled letters, which spell "Ceci n'est pas une pipe," and sketch Magritte's epochal briar. In the grid, Magritte's surrealist précis is also an answer (and stages a question): IT'S JUST / A REPRESENTATION / IS IT NOT? So too with the crossword, which puns self-referentially: a French connection of French connections; in copying Matisse's copies or Magritte's pipe, the puzzle becomes a representation of representations.

The appropriateness of "Mondrian and latte art" rests on the pedestrian fact that Gorski could, had she the time, experience both on the same Manhattan afternoon. Having taken in a Mondrian at MoMA, she might, newly caffeinated, walk the two miles of hexagonal asphalt along Central Park East to the site of her best-known representation: the Guggenheim. An exuberant panegyric to the institution's half-century anniversary, Gorski's *Ahead of the Curve* (2009) opts for an asymmetrical black square arrangement to depict FRANK LLOYD WRIGHT's iconic spiral ramp. This puzzle sees Gorski shifting from the use of pen-or-pencil solver-drawn lines to employing the puzzle's black squares as a ready-made vocabulary of pixelated images. Gorski includes nine artists in (and some arguably of) the grid, whose work the Guggenheim holds: 1-Across: *Before the Mirror,* MANET; 68-Across: *Green Violinist,* CHAGALL; and 34-Down, *Tableau 2:* MONDRIAN. Reacting to Gorski's tribute, museum staff reported guests stalking the spiral with spiral crossword in hand (a representation of a representation) and employees too busy with anniversary duties to solve "over a cup of espresso in [our] Cafe 3." Staff demurred on the question of

David J. Kahn, *Picture This* (2008), Crossword, ink on paper, *The New York Times*, 21 x 21

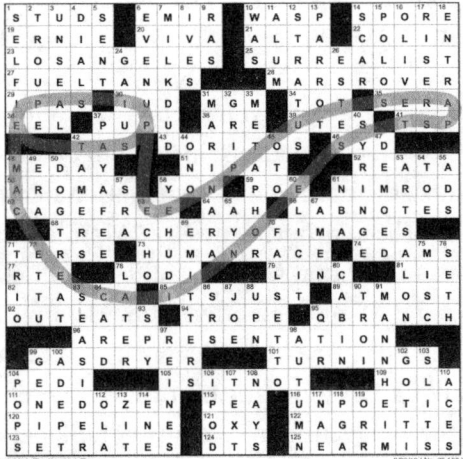

Andrew Zhou, *The Art of Puzzle-Making* (2018), Crossword, ink on paper, *The New York Times*, 21 x 21

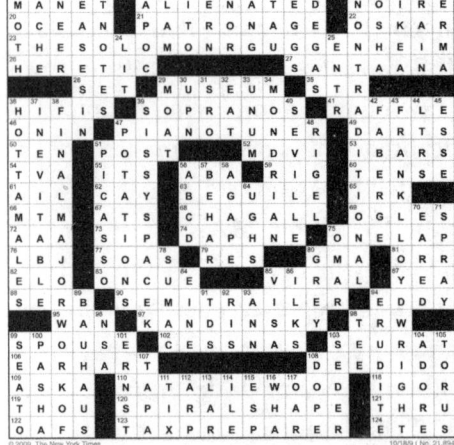

Elizabeth Gorski, *Ahead of the Curve* (2009), Crossword, ink on paper, *The New York Times*, 21 x 21

"Is it art" / "Is it not?" A crossword puzzle isn't art, "it's play—though, would [Anish] Kapoor call it mental sculpture?"

The Most Puzzling of Ideas

These grids show Gorski, one of few women constructors in her generation, puzzling through the idea of the vernacular. *On Wheels* (2014), a kind of crossword accompaniment to Mondrian's *Broadway Boogie Woogie,* was "inspired by and dedicated to Alternate Side Parking—the NYC tradition that drives semi-clothed New Yorkers to their cars at strange hours in search of a parking space. . . . [While waiting] they drink coffee, talk on the phone and solve crosswords." In describing the work, Gorski puns to position the puzzle as a nexus of erudition and camp: "I'm sure that these folks will swing into high gear . . . in no time flat: [realizing] names of car models sit atop circles that contain the letter O . . . the solver is asked to inflate each circle with an O and imagine a tire." The scene of everyday life that inspired Gorski's grid art is also the scene in which she imagines that art best consumed.

"Everyday life," writes the feminist theorist Rita Felski in *Doing Time,* "is the most self-evident, yet the most puzzling of ideas." To Felski, against the masculinized notion of linear progress are the cyclical routines of feminized work: social reproduction, the spiral of life. One solves the crossword every day; Gorski conceptualizes a crossword while baking cakes—*Untitled, Themed* (2016)—inflating pumpkin-shaped balloons with canisters of helium, or lingering at the supermarket over a bin of fruit called "Avocado Pears." The crossword constructor organizes these everyday routines into a mental sculpture, elevating them against the mundane backdrop of equilateral cells. The grid and the spiral: a reproduction of social reproduction.

Elizabeth Gorski, *On Wheels* (2014), Crossword, ink on paper, *The New York Times*, 21 x 21

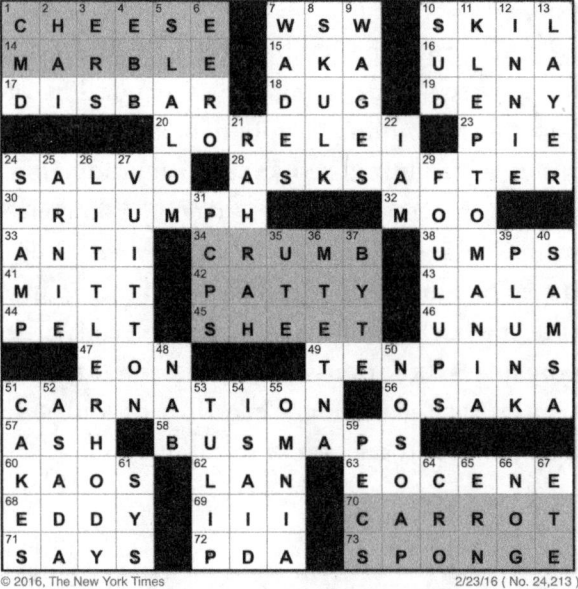

Elizabeth Gorski, *Untitled, Themed* (2016), Crossword, ink on paper, *The New York Times*, 15 x 15

Follow Directions

Some get the newspaper and discard everything except the crossword: tearing the puzzle from its native section, or folding the news underneath the grid, as though blocking out the rest of the world. Exemplifying the materiality of the predigital era, these four grids ask the solver to tear and fold the puzzle itself, producing a new object: a paper airplane *(Come Fly with Me)*, a six-sided die with shaded letter O's for pips *(On a Roll)*, and a fortune teller, also called a cootie catcher *(I Fold)*. In a spoof of a *Mad Magazine* fold-in, Kwong and Choset's *Abridged Edition* (2010) asks the solver to FOLD PAGES SO A AND B ARE LINED / UP IN THE TOP AND BOTTOM ROWS. On doing so, existing answers become things that are folded: LAM fits over RUN DRY to make LAUNDRY, ORIGIN pairs with AMI to make ORIGAMI. Paper airplane, titillating magazine, cootie catcher, die: these three-dimensional juvenilia evince an era of the crossword's history when it was seen as a time-wasting and infectious—cootie-catching—sin. By asking solvers to follow directions to transform the puzzle's objecthood, these works paradoxically subvert the call, common to Jazz Age auditoria, libraries, and workplaces, to follow directions and put the puzzle away.

Life, Every Day

This series of 312 crosswords is the result of Malaika Handa, a software engineer at Google, and Quiara Vasquez calculating that, following the standard conventions of crossword construction (no two-letter words; rotational symmetry; no full rows or columns of black squares; the white areas must all connect), the number of valid, distinct 7-by-7 grids equals 312. 312 is 6 times 52: Handa realized if she published 6 puzzles a week, it would take exactly a year to use every 7-by-7 grid.

Rather than commit to creating 312 puzzles, Handa, in the fashion of Sophie Calle's collective experiments, circulated a Google form and enlisted more than 180 crossword-makers, novices and experts both, to fill and clue the grids. Arranged here from the most open (fewest black squares) to the most closed, the grids, produced during the COVID-19 pandemic, exhibit a sense of impending doom, the black squares encroaching on the blankness of an empty space. The grid with no black squares provided by Paolo Pasco leans into this subversion, breaking conventions by taking convention to its logical end: each Across answer is BUFFALO (as in the lexical ambiguity exemplar, "Buffalo buffalo Buffalo buffalo buffalo buffalo Buffalo buffalo," which can be read "Buffalonian bison that other Buffalonian bison bully also bully Buffalonian bison"). The nonsense Down answers are fitted with earnest, gestural clues: AAAAAAA is [Report card for a stellar student] and OOOOOOO is [Really tall snowman, visually].

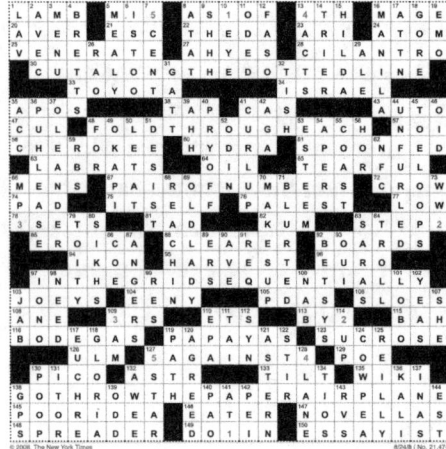

Kevin G. Der, *Come Fly with Me* (2008), Crossword and paper airplane, ink on paper with scissors, *The New York Times*, 23 x 23

Ben Pall, *On a Roll* (2010), Crossword and die, ink on paper with scissors, *The New York Times*, 21 x 21

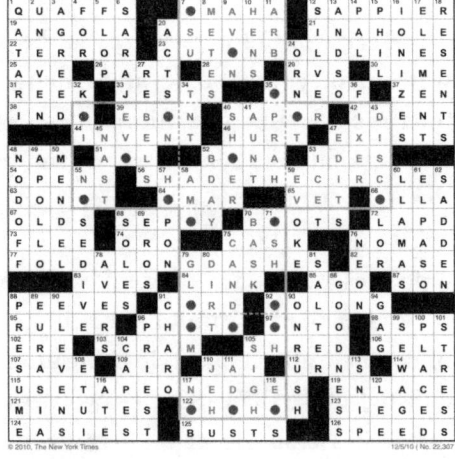

David Kwong and Kevan Choset, *Abridged Edition* (2010), Crossword and fold-in, ink on paper, *The New York Times*, 23 x 23

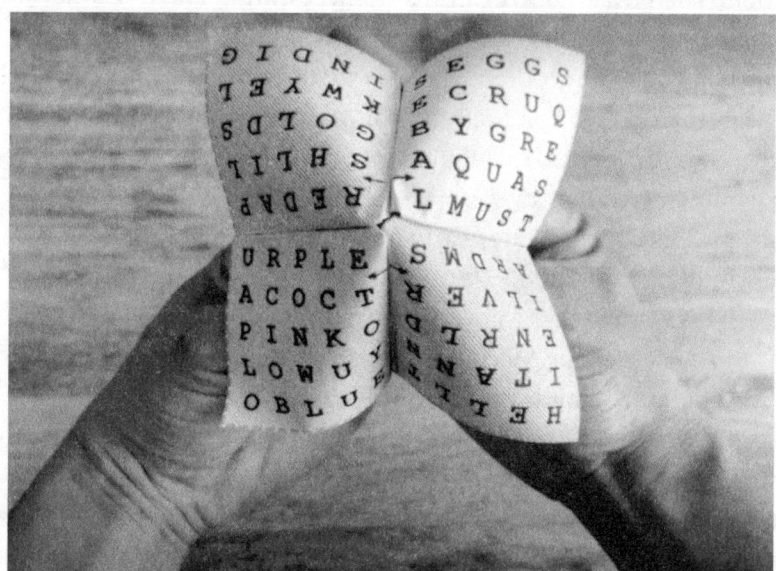

Malaika Handa, *I Fold* (2021), Crossword and fortune teller, colored ink on paper with scissors, Girlsbosswords.com, 9 x 9

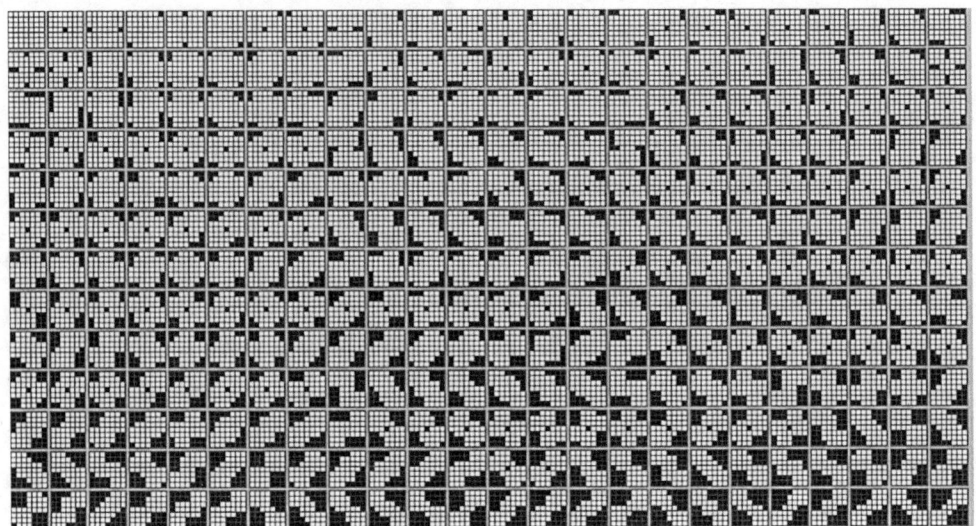

Malaika Handa et al. (2021), Crosswords, digital grids, 7xwords.com, 7 x 7

Joseph Pulitzer's *New York World* headquarters was a geological cross-section. There was Pulitzer in his dome, glinting like a just-surfaced diamond; copy editors, photoengravers, reporters in the sunlit top floors below the dome, their desks set up to best domesticate the light; then production staff in well-lit "composing rooms," rifling through vitrines for drawerfuls of uppercase and lowercase linotype letters; finally down into the cavernous lower floors and cellars, where enormous presses churned out nearly fifty thousand eight-page papers an hour. Pulitzer had been early to invest in a high-speed rotary color press in 1893, crowing the next year in his own paper about the seventy-ton "Most Marvellous Mechanical Production of the Age," which was more or less the length, width, and height of two elephants, locking tusks in a brawl. Pulitzer was just then tussling with William Randolph Hearst, who'd begun his journalistic career by purchasing the *San Francisco Examiner* and proceeded to ape the sensationalist Pulitzer playbook. Hearst's 1896 opening salvo was the *New York Journal*'s five-cent color supplement, *The American Humorist,* which he called "eight pages of iridescent polychromous effulgence that makes the rainbow look like a piece of lead pipe." After Hearst poached *World* cartoonist Richard F. Outcault, and with him his popular strip *The Yellow Kid,* the barons badmouthed each other in a string of grandiloquent ad hominems; Outcault's strip, and its role in this war of the sensationalists, is the origin of the term "yellow journalism."

Ernie Bushmiller Jr. grew up reading neonate comic strips like Outcault's. Bushmiller was born in 1905 in the 23rd Ward of New York City: the South Bronx. His father (Ernest Sr., a German immigrant) and mother (Elizabeth, an Irish one) had met on the streets of New York, and raised Ernie and his two sisters in a series of gas-lit, cold-water apartments in flinty industrial districts of the borough: Port Morris, Melrose. Bushmiller's street had some three hundred kids—"they all turned out to be cops, firemen, plumbers"—but he was the sort who prized rainy days, when he could stay inside and draw.

In 1919, Bushmiller convinced his parents to let him quit Theodore Roosevelt High School after just six months to fill a vacant copy boy post at Pulitzer's vertical factory. (He flipped a coin; had it gone the other way he'd've signed on as a cabin boy with the Cunard steamship line.) Whatever their reluctance, his parents could use Bushmiller's help with the bills, and even the *World*'s meager nine dollars a week was something. Bushmiller's father, a bartender who also peddled life insurance, had been a vaudeville chalk-talker in his youth, wringing laughs and doodling onstage at Tony Pastor's on 14th Street, a haunt for vaudevillians. If he couldn't make it as a creative, maybe his son could.

Each weekday morning, Bushmiller paid his nickel fare and rode the Lexington Avenue IRT to Brooklyn Bridge–City Hall for nearly an hour. In the Babel of the *World*'s city room, on a pew-like hard wooden bench, he and a congregation of copy boys would sit and wait like pious birdwatchers until a writer squawked over the din "Copee-ee-e!," at which point the next available boy would hop to attention, then gather and relay the typewritten sheets to the relevant editor. While at the *World,* Bushmiller would encounter the call of cultural luminaries (many of them Algonquin Round Table regulars) like Alexander Woollcott (cardinal, vibrato), Franklin Pierce Adams (a squeaky linnet), and Heywood Broun (husband of Ruth Hale, thunderous as an owl).

When he could get away from the bench, Bushmiller spent as much time as possible shadowing the art department, watching the cartoonists at work. (He wasn't the only copy boy who dreamt of comics; Harry Haenigsen, who'd go on to create the popular strip *Penny*, arrived at the *World* around the same time as Bushmiller. "He was kind of an older office boy," Bushmiller remembered. "He had long pants and I had short pants.") In 1920, Bushmiller was made art department assistant, at first running the cartoonists' personal errands and sweeping their cigar butts, but soon tasked with actual artwork: brushing in solid blacks, lettering word balloons, and laying out the weekly crossword puzzle.

This was a thankless assignment—Margaret Farrar had yet to appear onstage to unkink Arthur Wynne's chaotic process—but Bushmiller put his own visual spin on things. Not only were his grids accurate, they were interesting. For one Sunday grid, he deployed a "ye olde" woodcut finish, for another a halftone ink wash followed by a calligraphic nib. He made the gridlines fatter one week, spindlier the next. He'd usually ink the black squares in solid black, but sometimes drew them striped, other times speckled, like a modish dresser varying his outfits. "I became [the *World*'s] expert crossword puzzle line drawer," he said, a job that "did nothing for my sense of perspective but . . . gave me a lasting familiarity with the T-square."

The crossword paid the bills, but Bushmiller wanted to draw comics. In 1924, only five years into his career and not yet twenty years old, he sold his first continuing strip: *Mac the Manager,* about "the daily doings of a hungry boxing promoter and his thick-witted meal ticket." It premiered not in the natty back pages of Pulitzer's *World* but in ex-strongman Bernarr "Body Love" Macfadden's uptown scandal sheet: the *New York Evening Graphic,* aka the "pornoGraphic," launched that year. Macfadden is the Cartesian origin point of the manosphere, a nineteenth-century Joe Rogan who advocated fasting and ice baths (he started the Coney Island Polar Bear Club, which each winter plunges into the numbing Atlantic), vowed to live to 150, and pumped the English language with protein until it bulged with veiny illegibility: he established "healthatoriums," self-styled as a "kinisitherapist," began a religion called "Cosmotarianism." He added the jutting deltoid of an A to "Mcfadden" because it was "picturesque"; he spot-reduced the fatty D off "Bernard" since "Bernarr" sounded leonine. To the extent Macfadden was the naked and oiled-up id of newspapermen, he was literally irrepressible: in 1929 *Time* magazine noted "[n]ot all readers of that gum-chewers' sheetlet [the *Graphic*] are gum-chewers. Some of them smuggle the pink-faced tabloid into Park Avenue homes, there to read it in polite seclusion." Not unlike when the *Times*'s publisher, Arthur Hays Sulzberger, received Lester Markel's plea to start a crossword puzzle after Pearl Harbor: Sulzberger, apparently a secret crossword addict, had been buying the rival *New York Herald Tribune* and devouring its puzzle in stealth.

It was not to be: though Bushmiller's *Mac the Manager* fit the mold of the *Graphic*'s other musclehead strips *(Ozzie and His Gym; Little Samson)*, he lasted only three months in Macfadden's back pages. But the *World* saw what he was capable of. For Bushmiller and puzzles, 1924 would prove to be a banner year. He landed a plum assignment on the Sunday *World*'s new Red Magic supplement, ostensibly edited by Harry Houdini and printed in blood-red ink. It promised "EDUCATION as well as ENTERTAINMENT" and featured visual puzzles, anagrams, cryptograms, even exposés of stage illusions that got Houdini in hot water with his colleagues. At a November 1924 launch party for Red Magic presided over by the real Harry Houdini, Bushmiller rubbed elbows with John O'Hara Cosgrave (the Sunday *World* editor and Margaret Farrar's boss), Herbert Bayard Swope (the *World*'s executive editor), and F. Gregory Hartswick (crossword editor along with Farrar and Prosper Buranelli). Photographs of Hartswick's office look like the studio of the Russian avant-garde artist Kazimir Malevich, whose 1915 *Black Square* is considered an inauguration of the twentieth century's aesthetic obsession with the grid. Also in 1924, the *World* added a daily crossword, and then Farrar, Hartswick, and Buranelli asked Bushmiller to do the squares, numbering, and letter-

ing for Simon & Schuster's *The Cross Word Puzzle Book*. Business was booming.

Bushmiller slipped ideas of his own into Red Magic. He created a stable of recurring characters: Enigmatic Edgar, Anagram Ann, Cryptic Clarence. His pen, per cartoonists Mark Newgarden and Paul Karasik, had "ripened into a pleasing workmanlike cartoon style that would be more at home on the newspaper's comics page than ever before."

Capitalizing on the puzzle craze sweeping the nation, in early 1925, Bushmiller scored a successful pitch for his second recurring strip: *Cross Word Cal.*

◼◻

Cross Word Cal sewed the puzzle into the fabric of daily life. Literally so: one strip depicts Bushmiller's hero exclaiming "Dog-gone these moths!—There's my spring overcoat ruined" before realizing the coat's pattern and the puzzle's match. He cuts out a grid, pastes it on the moth-eaten coat, and hits the town, outerwear now paired with debonair boater hat, cane, city strut, puff of cigar smoke: a tableau vivant of the Jazz Age bon vivant.

Nobody in a *Cross Word Cal* strip does what they're supposed to. When Cal is up late working a puzzle, his wife chucks a rolling pin at his head ("Now will ya come to bed?"); he sees stars, only to realize ("Hooray that's it—") STARS is the answer he needs. Cal is variously seen exhausting the workingman (refusing to depart a barber's chair until he finishes a puzzle, having already wearied a battalion of six floor-ridden haircutters) and capitalizing on puzzle mania to work smarter (Cal the cabbie laments a downturn in the taxi industry; a passerby calls him "old-fashioned" and recommends he get a Checker cab; gluing cut-out crosswords to his vehicle has the desired results). In one strip, a cop pulls him over ominously, only to ask "Wot's 'Pleasantly diversified' in nine letters."

In 1925, Bushmiller secured yet another big break. He was tapped to ink a second strip whose hero, like Cross Word Cal, flouted the expectations of the age. In May, *World* comics staffer Larry Whittington abruptly dropped his fledgling flapper strip *Fritzi Ritz,* having been poached by Hearst in a ritzier deal to draw a comic called *Mazie the Model.* At nineteen, Bushmiller was asked to fill Whittington's shoes and drafting table, becoming the youngest artist ever to author a nationally syndicated comic strip. He learned Fritzi's lines: cloche-hatted, lipsticked, stilettoed, silver-tongued. To brush up on his figure drawing skills, he'd enrolled in night classes at the National Academy of Design on Manhattan's Upper West Side, whose alumni included Frank Lloyd Wright and the painter Winslow Homer, and was embarrassed enough at the syllabus of heirloom rigor that he kept his three years of scumbling still lifes and sketching nudes a secret from coworkers and family alike. "All I ever learned to draw there," he'd later grumble, "was a plaster bust of Dante."

Cross Word Cal showed readers what puzzleitis looked like on the inside; *Fritzi Ritz* depicted its outward style. The grid and the flapper were already intertwined during the craze of the 1920s. "The cross-word hat now rules the millinery world," wrote the *San Francisco Chronicle* in 1925. "And the smartest thing of the moment for masquerades is a cross-word costume." In "Cross-Word Mamma, You Puzzle Me," a Frank Crumit novelty ditty, the crossword stands for the flapper's newly unleashed sexuality, the unlatched corsets and binned customs of the Victorian age. Donning slippers with cross-word buckles or checked satin "cross-word pumps," the flapper has got the man on the back foot:

> *You call me Honey and that means "Bee,"*
> *Looks like I'll be stung no doubt.*
> *Your zigzag ways are keeping you out late.*
> *I walk in squares so I can get you straight.*
> *Crossword Mamma you puzzle me*
>
> *But Papa's gonna figure you out.*

With the flapper doing as she pleased came predictable male displeasure: "Our cynical bachelor friend," goes one image from the age, "declares that the 'cross-word puzzle frock' is but a preliminary to the 'chess problem frock,' giving the wearer the right to 'mate' in one move!" Even haute Parisian fashion wasn't immune to the crossword's beauty: in the winter of 1924, as warmer angora wool replaced silk at the hosier, a French shopkeeper saw two American women working a crossword and got an idea. A few days later "he displayed in his windows a stocking of checker-board design with the squares in black and white." ("Cross-Word Stockings—Calculated to Fascinate the Most Diffident Admirer," went an ad.) American women in Paris loved it; naturally, French women found it "hideous." It wasn't until some years later, when *mots croisés* arrived in France, that the grid was accepted as elegant. An advertisement for a masquerade costume featured a woman festooned with a crossword peplum dress, a crossword-emblazoned capelet, and a cubic headpiece with grids on every side.

Even as the raucousness of the Jazz Age subsided, Fritzi, Bushmiller, and the crossword continued to thrive. There were hurdles: Bushmiller and his strip survived the stock market crash of 1929, the failing

World's sale to the Scripps-Howard chain, and the paper's collapse in 1931, when nearly three thousand employees lost their jobs overnight. *Fritzi Ritz* was among the strips picked to carry on under the auspices of Scripps's United Feature Syndicate. When on the strength of *Fritzi* Bushmiller received an offer to "create gags" for Paramount's forthcoming feature *Movie Crazy,* he and his wife, Abby (recently married; she was also a Bronx native, the daughter of an El train conductor), spent a year in Los Angeles. They took the train rather than flying, on Bushmiller's refusal ("If I'm up in an airplane and they run out of gas, where are they gonna go to get gas?"); they were houseguests in actor/director/comedian Harold Lloyd's forty-four-room Greenacres mansion in Beverly Hills; they ate weekly dinners at the Brown Derby with Groucho Marx.

Then, in 1933, Bushmiller introduced Fritzi's mischievous eight-year-old niece: Nancy. Nancy and her giggly aplomb soon took center stage, with Fritzi receding and Sluggo the ragamuffin shambling into the foreground. The comic was renamed *Nancy* in 1938. World War II paper shortages meant space and column size erosion for strips, a constraint that turned out to accommodate Bushmiller's increasingly austere, get-to-the-point visual style. *Nancy* would go on to be one of the most successful and beloved strips of the twentieth century, running in some seven hundred newspapers at its height in the 1970s. Part of its successes owed to Bushmiller, as Mark Newgarden and Paul Karasik write in *How to Read Nancy,* having "the hand of an architect, the mind of a silent film comedian, and the soul of an accountant." Which sounds like the profile of a crossword constructor: the sculpting of a handsome grid, the crafting of a punny theme, the fact-checking of an obscure and possibly inaccurate clue. Ever in search of "the perfect gag," Bushmiller inked his "snappers"—the last panel punch lines—first, then reverse engineered the setups. "I know a guy who works upside down," he joked, "so I don't worry much about drawing backwards." To Newgarden and Karasik, "it was the only logical way to work for this ex–crossword puzzle designer." Bushmiller's last panel, then: at his drafting desk in Connecticut, an accomplished cartoonist, ruling fence slats or brushing in night skies. Which implies the setup in the first square: an art assistant of fifteen, hunched over a table at Joseph Pulitzer's *New York World*, making sure the crossword grid was perfect.

◼

In 2016, Elizabeth Gorski became that rare thing: a full-time puzzle-maker. Nearly a century after *Cross Word Cal* and *Fritzi Ritz*, the puzzle was still very much a man's world, and Gorski wanted to strike out on her own, make the rules herself. Once, Shortz had changed Julie DELPY in one of her *Times* grids to DELTA without asking, excising the award-winning director, actress, and musician because he found the entry "unappealing." Once, in another paper, Gorski had clued AMAL as [Barrister/activist Clooney], but the male editor unceremoniously substituted [Mrs. George Clooney]. "The industry is sometimes locked in the Mad Men era," Gorski says.

Gorski proved a savvy businesswoman. She was commissioned to create crosswords for the Sandra Bullock vehicle *All About Steve* (2009), a story about an awkward, logorrheic, lovelorn crossword writer (Bullock), who falls in love with the titular Steve, then falls into a mine shaft. (The film, trying perhaps for the antic passion of *Cross Word Cal* but trafficking instead in the slapstick essentialism of *Fritzi Ritz,* was universally panned, though Gorski and Bullock did okay; Fortis Films, the production company Bullock founded, turned a profit, and in 2010 Bullock accepted her Razzie Award for Worst Actress, for *All About Steve*, the day before accepting her Oscar for Best Actress, for *The Blind Side*.) In 2011, when subscription services like Substack and Patreon were but a pixel glimmer in the internet's eye, Gorski launched Crossword Nation, a paid subscription that digitally delivers "small-batch" puzzles every week. "This is the future of puzzle distribution," Gorski says, "and it's radically different from the traditional model." As of this writing, Crossword Nation has put out over six hundred puzzles: easy-ish Tuesday affairs; colorful, since the software Gorski uses, Crossword Compiler, supports highlighting cells in shades other than white or black; and, per Gorski's website, "hand-craft[ed]."

This last descriptor isn't quite right: though she started constructing with pencil, paper, and dictionary in the 1990s, Gorski, like nearly all modern constructors, employs software that "eliminates the repetitive drudge work [such as] making grid templates, numbering, etc.," which once would've been performed by an eagle-eyed Ernie Bushmiller. If anything, Gorski is tech-savvier than most her age, having built four websites, actively pruned her digital wordlists, and even sent suggestions, many of them implemented, to Crossword Compiler developer Antony Lewis.

But it's true that Gorski's puzzles have a handcrafted mood to them. Part of this is her focus on those pyrotechnic visuals, and on writing and rewriting clues over the course of days, not hours: "It helps to let a puzzle breathe," she says. "Think of a bottle of wine." Gorski often fills a grid while watching the New York Giants on her HDTV ("Talk about ballet!"), noting quarterbacks tend to have clipped, crossword-useful names (Drew BREES, CAM Newton, ELI Manning, Tony ROMO). When she manicures her wordlist, it's a matter of "adding interesting words (BESTIE) and removing terrible words (UNHAT). . . . I don't waste time assigning number values to words—that's where I draw the line with software." As we've seen, nearly all modern constructors rank words differentially—e.g., 100 for Scrabbly, slangy, poppy fare like RIZZ or SQUID GAME or EXSQUEEZE ME, 10 for "less clean" fill, usually crosswordese like ANOA or MOA or ULEE. But everything in a Gorski grid has its place—it's all language culled from life; she'll find a workable clue. Crosswordese in a Gorski grid has a wabi-sabi quality to it, a tiny crack in a ceramic bowl that somehow makes the object more beautiful. Like Hockney's skewed grids, we get the sense someone—an artist— spent time on the work, rendering it perfectly imperfect.

The fantasy of the "clean grid" is an aesthetic native to and ubiquitous in the twentieth century, writes art critic Rosalind Krauss. Her seminal 1979 essay "Grids" echoes Szymborska's poem. Szymborska: "When I pronounce the word Silence, / I destroy it." Krauss: "[T]he grid announces . . . modern art's will to silence, its hostility to literature, to narrative, to discourse." The grid is "antinatural," "geometricized," more aesthetic decree than study of the world, less like a story than a myth. "The grid's mythic power," writes Krauss, "is that it makes us able to think we are dealing with materialism (or sometimes science, or logic) while at the same time it provides us with a release into belief (or illusion or fiction)."

But this rigid transcendence can feel like a man's world too. Gorski has a fellow traveler of the grid in artist Laurie Anderson: both classically trained violinists, both Barnard women, both interested in using the grid to quilt a kind of story. When Anderson was at Columbia for her MFA in the early 1970s, the orthodoxy ("implicitly masculinist," notes one critic) made enormous, heaving steel monoliths: architectural monuments to endurance and vastness. Anderson went the other way, working mostly with newspaper, the paragon of handheld ephemerality—of story, not myth. She'd cut multiple papers into strips and weave them together, as in *New York Times, Horizontal/China Times, Vertical.* Then, in 2020, she spiraled back to this technique, producing *Crossed Crosswords (New York Times Horizontal/New York Times Vertical)* for a retrospective at the Hirshhorn Museum, part of D.C.'s Smithsonian. It's the ultimate in Mondrian and latte art—beautiful, but immune to solving. The utilitarian squares of the crossword grid are woven into cells that, unreadable, can only gesture at the crossword.

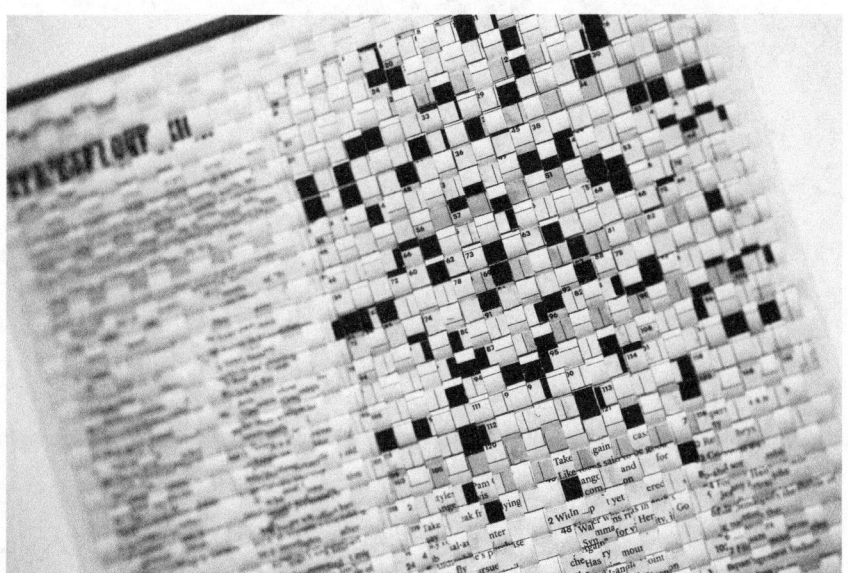

Part of Gorski's frustration with the discourse around "clean grids" is that one man's crosswordese might be another woman's everyday life. "The old 'crosswordese' debate is just that—it's old. . . . I use an ETUI every day," she has written, "and yet there are people who insist it's a fake word." Each day, Gorski opens her etui, a small ornamental case holding her needles, thimbles, and pin cushions. She practices her viola arpeggios. She inks a copperplate G on sheets of graph paper over and over until it's almost but not quite perfect. She writes a crossword, every day, tapestries that tell a story with every clue: from the Middle English *clew,* which means a ball of thread.

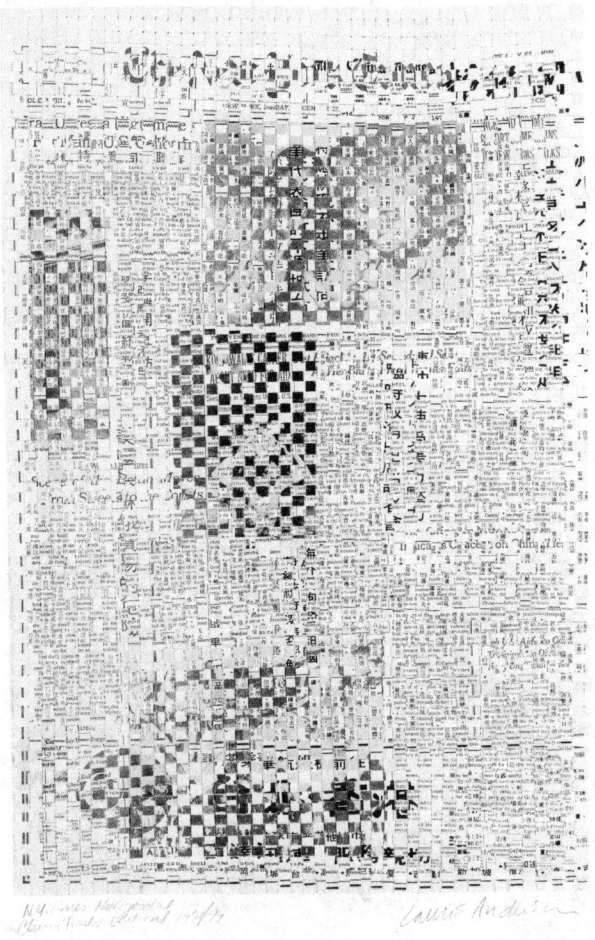

CHAPTER 9

Are You the Frivolity Theatre?

[See one's way out?], 10 letters*
—KATE CHIN PARK AND BRIAN THOMAS, *a wee little puzzle,* 2022

I went to Stuyvesant High School in Manhattan, a glittery ten-story expanse teeming with mathletes and AP credit hunter-gatherers, future significant figures and grade-point-averages featuring four significant figures, and enough donor Nobelists and financiers who'd trudged its mustard corridors and broken escalators to make its computer labs the envy of magnet schools nationwide. With all the academic pressure, sometimes hormonal overtures slipped out of focus. As a result, the school had an annual tradition called Crush-lists, in which departing seniors posted, on a wall in the second-floor atrium, a visual styling of everyone they'd crushed on in those four years; people really went ham, their creative right-brained and horny subcortical impulses finally let loose; we'd stand in the atrium and gawk, admiring handiwork, scanning for our names; weeks left in our high school careers, we'd consummate what college applications and BC Calc had forestalled. Naturally, my Crushlist was a crossword.

I remember realizing the grid could be the shape of a heart. I remember sheepishly asking my dad where the color ink cartridges were, so the black squares could be printed red. I remember the dumb luck, a crossword constructor's cosmic gift, that the lengths of the names of the girls I had crushes on formed a symmetrical set—two 6-letter names; two 7s; my high school sweetheart, 5 letters long, set in the grid's middle.

But what I remember best is publicly defacing the puzzle. In addition to a giant oaktag grid, on which I'd hung a Sharpie, I'd printed out dozens of copies of the puzzle. By day's end, satisfied that enough people had solved it on paper, my goonish friends and I began entering insipid juvenilia into the cells of the grid, like delinquent vaudevillian chalk talkers. Each giggly four-letter-word felt like a minor reclamatory graffito. Someone would place a nonsensical phrase—I remember SEX BOYS fitting nicely, which tells you everything you need to know—then someone else would have an idea, grab the Sharpie, and cross it with a joke of their own. I'm not claiming this crass improvisation as high art, but it did feel, at the time, like subversion. If the precociousness of our math-science, college-readiness high school led to an explosion of eleventh-hour sexual confession, then the precociousness of the crossword—its puns, its clever question-mark clues, its collection of nouns and verbs from the erudite adult world—could be undone by a bunch of teens, noses out of books, minds in the gutter. And if the crossword, both making and solving it, was traditionally a private pursuit, meant to be solved and forgotten, then my friends and I were getting new mileage out of the grid, as a prop in a group performance.

At the height of the crossword craze in the 1920s, the puzzle was at work disrupting the expectations of group life. Ephemera from the time lament the grid's chokehold on the family: in the novelty song "Since Ma's Gone Crazy over Crossword Puzzles" (1924), "She starts to cook and then she'll look, / For some funny word, / And when we eat, instead of meat, / She passes us the dictionary."

Those afflicted with crossworditis were depicted as brainiac sad sacks ("Since the 'cross word' puzzle bit him he can never get a hat to fit him," reads the caption in a comic from around 1925—you can hear the offstage tuba). But just as often, they were women whose domestic duties had slipped their alphabetic minds ("Why Lizzie was late with the lunch!," reads a postcard from 1930, as a crossword sits atop unwashed floor tiles, checkered black-and-white). Like Jazz Age flappers, these women are shown flipping social scripts, flouting gender expectations by harnessing the communal syntax of the crossword ("Hey, what's a six-letter word for . . .") to smuggle in a winking openness about sex: "She wants a word with thirteen letters, meaning 'to flirt.' / But Pa wants something clean he can use for a shirt." As writer and crossword constructor Anna Shechtman notes, the crossword "allows verbal and physical taboos to be breached, as members of the opposite sex say four-letter words to each other, cuddling around the newspaper page." The crossword is again acting as a prop, in this case facilitating that cuddling, just as my last-minute high school flirting was facilitated not by frankness but the courtship dance of Crushlists. In the same spirit, in the 1925 film *The Freshman,* Harold Lloyd's character begins solving a crossword with a young woman on a train. They lean closer to each other; the intertitles read: "I think I know the word for number 19 vertical—'*a name for the one you love.*'" "Sweetheart," he says. "Darling," she says. They say "dearest," "precious," "honeybunch." It doesn't look like flirting, it looks like thinking, but when a woman behind them hears the words without seeing the grid, she clasps each of them on the shoulder: "Isn't it wonderful to be in love?" Embarrassed, the two look at the camera; Lloyd freaks out, runs out of the train car, and knocks over a waiter in the process.

Outside the household, public institutions were also playing host to these puzzling performances. "Crosswords began to appear in the most unlikely areas of public life," writes Alan Connor in *The Crossword Century.* "Puzzle competitions between Yale and Harvard were to be expected, perhaps less so those between New York's fire brigade and police department before packed houses at Wanamaker's Auditorium." This is back when you'd solve without tabbing over to Incognito Mode to google a proper noun. If you were stuck on a clue, and your reference tomes came up empty, you telephoned a friend; if your friend was stumped too, you called zoos and theaters—not to book visits but to strip them of their trivia. In the caption of a chiding postcard from the time, a man in a phone booth says into the receiver: "Are you the Frivolity Theatre? Can you tell me what it is a ballet girl wears—beginning with N?"

Like the flapper's sexuality, these performances were not always welcomed with open arms by the powers-that-were. In 1925, the London Zoo bemoaned a stampede of "requests for aid in solving 'crossword' puzzles'": "What is a word in three letters meaning a female swan? What is a female kangaroo, or a fragile creature in six letters ending in TO?" The *Nottingham Evening Post* sniffed that the zoo "has enough to do with the care of its own animals, and cannot act as consultant to the world at large." Ernie Bushmiller poked fun at this novel social mode in a May 1925 *Cross Word Cal* comic strip. Zoo placards are swapped for crossword-clue descriptors of the animals, dripping

"CROSSWORDS."

"Are you the Frivolity Theatre?
Can you tell me what it is a ballet girl
wears — beginning with N?"

CROSS WORD CAL   By E. Bushmiller

with Latinate esotericism: THREE-LETTER DROMAEUS for the grid
stalwart "emu"; 7 LETTER ANTHROPOID, presumably "primate";
4 LETTER BOSINDICUS for "zebu," and so on.

If what you're supposed to do at the zoo is look at the animals,
nearly everyone has something else in mind; hatted heads in books or
newspapers, they're there for the crossword. In all these performances,

crossword puzzlers refuse to hew to expectations, to be just one thing: you think the math-science high school is full of sexless calculators, but here they are, playing an intellectual game for raunchy laughs. In *The Freshman*, the puzzle allows the couple to flirt and solve a crossword at the same time, but once the older woman thinks *all* they're doing is flirting, the romance is gone. Life needs to be punned upon, always doubled: in Bushmiller's chaotic zoo scene, a man scans a book called DICTIONARY AND GUIDE TO THE ZOO, as though paper definition and real-world experience had, as in a mad scientist's lab, hybridized.

Like a swath of checkered Op Art, the crossword, when trotted out in public, could dramatize these questions of order and chaos, familiarity and defamiliarization, expectations and fresh experiments in living. Armed with a new daily tradition, solvers could slip the diktats of old traditions they didn't like. It was as if the orderliness of a postwar world were transposed down into the black-and-white grid, and in that vacuum pandemonium rushed in. Sometimes literal pandemonium: postcards from the era show solvers in Model Ts entering T's into grids, oblivious to a traffic jam they've caused; filling in grids on a capsized vessel, ignoring the nearby drowned; and glued to puzzles across from caged, howling monkeys, below a caption that reads "Everybody's doing it!" Everywhere societal strictures counseled one way of civic being, the crossword not only refused, it invented a new order itself.

That new order needed a cure, as we've seen ("crossword
itis" was "an inflammation . . . perhaps of the cortex of the brain—the seat of the intellect"); all the neurologist could offer was truth serums, lobotomies, and, in Elsie Janis's Broadway revue *Puzzles of 1925*, more crosswords. The show features a group of solvers with "cluing fever" in a crossword puzzle "sanitorium," where, like one square of a Dantean hell, the walls themselves are crosswords, as if those afflicted with crosswordditis required a maximalist exposure therapy of the grid.

Janis's revue is another early instance of the crossword as a prop. It's more accessory than motif, directing the gaze of the crazed patients; in

between their lines, they look down, filling in the lines of the puzzle. When a *social worker*, of all people, confesses onstage to inventing the crossword, the other patients—almost all of them men—kill her where she stands. Then the emcee darkly quips: "She came in vertical; she's going out horizontal."

Janis was a subversive performer in her own right, a triple threat (singing, acting, dancing; theme, fill, clues) who'd paid her own way to entertain British troops overseas in France and Belgium, fearing her itinerary would be smothered by the Red Cross or the YMCA, the usual underwriters of wartime entertainment. She was an early cross-dresser, male impersonator, and, at the front, was dubbed a "dough-girl," a riff on the term "doughboys," the nickname for American infantrymen in World War I. (Her epitaph at Forest Lawn Cemetery in Glendale, California, reads simply, "Sweetheart of the A.E.F.," the American Expeditionary Forces, the name for the U.S. troops sent to defend foreign soil.)

As someone interested in the disruption of norms, Janis was naturally intrigued by the puzzle's disruptive power. In a collection of her writings called *If I Know What I Mean,* she sets down her New Year's "revolutions" for 1926: "Revolt No. 6: Against modern dancing for myself except with people I'm in love with." "Revolt No. 7: Against discussion about Europe with people who have never been any nearer to it than Hoboken." Revolt No. 8 mixes puzzles and performance:

REVOLT NO. 8:

Against cross-word puzzles . . . after two hectic months early this year of writhing among words and struggling with synonyms I have decided that I must either give up my career or can the cross-words—I am physically unfit to do both.

In the midst of a puzzle I suddenly thought of my performance and dashed to the theatre to do my stuff. In the midst of my performance I suddenly thought of a word and wanted to dash back to the hotel to do my puzzle. One night I nearly announced to the audience that I would give them an imitation of a well-known actress whose name suggests an undertaker in nine letters. Of course you have guessed it—Barrymore. Now you know why I must stop.

It's tempting to read this as two of Janis's obsessions simply jockeying for her attention. But crosswords and performance interfere with each other precisely because crosswords are a species of performance art. Whether one is solving a puzzle by cracking the theme, or delivering a line in an over-the-top inflection, part of what's beautiful is that sensation of, well, *acting*—of being, to borrow terminology from the philosophy of games, an agent confronting constraints and selecting one pathway over another.

And the audience takes pleasure in these choices. When we watch three speed-solvers tackle a puzzle by breaking into different sections of the grid, or hear three actors interpret the same piece of dialogue in distinct ways, we're encountering movement sculpted by the rules of a game. In this light, the desire to share one's wordnerdery in public is a cousin of the instinct to perform. All the words a stage, and all of us merely players, whether we're calling up a theater for help with a cross-word clue, or scribbling frivolous jokes in the cells of a grid.

❒■❒

A minute into the fifth installment of Zach Sherwin's *The Crossword Show*, he says, "I have to say, it is so nice when the *crowd*, as requested, does *shower the host* with applause. But you didn't come here to be nice. You came here to be entertained, with wordplay." Behind him, a PowerPoint slide reveals that CROWD SHOWERS HOST and THE CROSSWORD SHOW are anagrams. There is more applause; there are no groans. "This is what we consider fun at *The Crossword Show*," Zach warns. "Please get on board as quickly as you possibly can."

Zach's show, which I first saw at the Caveat Theater in 2021 ("We LOVE smart, joyfully-nerdy comedy," says their website) in New York's Lower East Side, is less a show about crosswords than one in which crosswords show off. The puzzle is an excuse for tripping every wire in the word nerd's neural circuitry. Rapping, goofy dad jokes, pandemic-inspired epics, paranoid research rabbit holes hung on orthographic coincidence—all of it flashes in Zach's show like tarot cards touting vastly different narratives, but cut, ultimately, from one deck. Solving a crossword, you encounter some eighty words whose connection to one another at first feels—is, to a degree—random, until their presence in the grid starts to feel fated, eerily familiar, like the tarot reader's prediction; watching Zach's show, with a crossword at its labyrinthine center, each mode of wordplay began to feel like a parallel route to some fundamental truth about language.

After introducing himself, Zach brings on a panel of "guest solv-ers": comedians who will solve the crossword live, with the audience as backup if necessary. The comedians the first night I go are Aparna Nancherla and Mehran Khaghani; behind them, a new PowerPoint slide crosses their names "cleverly . . . in a crosswordish fashion" at a meager A. "How did he do that??" shrieks Mehran in faux-surprise. "And that's the end of the show!" jokes Zach.

Mehran—a "Crossword Show" newbie who'd slept three hours

the night before ("You're gonna see some top-shelf stupid")—and Aparna—a four-time guest who, during the COVID-19 pandemic, erased social media from her phone and replaced it with "compulsively" doing the *New York Times* crossword ("doomsolving," offers our host)—jostle into place as complementary archetypes. Mehran is the zany: overwhelmed by every clue, scoffing when the crossword resembles a test. He brandishes, when the linguistic going gets tough, a geisha fan. Aparna is the stalwart: old hand, star student, riffing calmly on clues she easily dispatches. And Zach, displaying what he once described as his "Jewish camp counselor energy," follows their jokes to the grid's precipice, then tugs them back; they have a script to stick to.

Before the solving is underway, Zach introduces the puzzle's constructor. Tonight's crossword, titled "Showdown," was written by Paolo Pasco, who constructs for the *Times* and *The New Yorker*, edits games for the professional social networking site LinkedIn, and maintains his own blog called *Grids These Days*. (After Mehran gets the pun, a few beats late, he turns to the audience to deadpan, "I'm just so fucked.") Paolo developed the theme and built the grid. But Zach, a veteran of the show *Epic Rap Battles of History*, has written the clues himself, in the form of a rap he calls a "Clue Tune." Here are the first four Downs:

1. They may accompany slapped thighs
2. Land in which 12-Across originally appetized
3. Messy tresses like a nest where a rat hides
4. Insurer that was too vast-sized to capsize

To Zach, rapping is puzzle-solving—if some clues are a tad clunky, it's because they set up a rhyme in the next line. And the restriction of rap lyrics mixed with crossword-clue grammar—they have Pusha T prosody and Shortzian syntax—is the source of the fun for Zach. "I'm very much of the 'constraint is freedom' school," he says. Rather than, as at an improv show, asking for a word from the crowd, Zach has asked Paolo for dozens, and riffs on every one.

Take 1-Across, [Root veggie with an orange hue]—YAM. "To most of the rest of the world," Zach begins, "the root veggie known as a yam does *not* have an orange hue. But here in America, we use Wiktionary's third definition: 'A sweet potato; a tuber from the species *Ipomoea batatas.*'" There's a slide with a picture of a tuber, then a slide with a photo of a band named Tuber. "Do you think they all agreed on that name?" asks Aparna. "They all have big tuber energy," winks Mehran. On the next slide, their Wikipedia page, we learn the band is from Greece—Crete, originally, but now based in Serres ("Sellouts," sneers Aparna); Zach points out Serres is a palindrome, spelled the same forward and back. We learn, via posters for various Freak Valley Festivals (a German psychedelic rock extravaganza) that Tuber has appeared alongside other bands whose names, if you're primed for wordplay, are plausible nicknames for yams (Orange Goblin, Orange Sunshine) and, in 2013, were on the roster with a band named Moonless. Then the Freak Valley Festival site, Riffipedia ("The Stoner Rock Wiki") reveals that Moonless were intended for the 2013 festival but ultimately canceled; the band that replaced them was called YAMA.

Like the show's id and superego, Mehran and Aparna spring into reaction. "Noooooooooo!" yells Aparna, feigning disgust. "Too clever! No!" Mehran, meanwhile, plays at being spooked: "That's too fucking weird. This is weird." Then Zach drives in the last of the linked, manufactured daggers—at the 2013 festival, YAMA performed on May 31, following an act named Brutus, which yields another palindrome: '13, YAMA, MAY 31. Mehran says the whole thing "felt like I was being touched inappropriately by a ghost." With a snap, the geisha fan unfolds.

Mehran's got his finger on it: the thrill of interconnection; the chilly, invisible imprint of that interconnectedness's design; the tutting disgust and pantomimed judgment aimed at the person pointing out these connections; the cuteness of a slant rhyme; the desire to plunge down these rabbit holes in the first place—watching Zach's antics (and Aparna and Mehran confront them) was like seeing a brain scan of the crossword constructor's mind, lobes red then green then blue like the endless rainbow handkerchief yanked from inside a clown's sleeve. The three of them were staging how the crossword stages the endlessly different things we can do with words. A good crossword

clue might be a performance in itself, a pun in muscular prosody—
[Crew's control?] for OAR. It might stretch further still: [Ones who
aren't super dupers] for BAD LIARS or [They might be put on a
stretcher] for YOGA PANTS. A clue can also wag an all-knowing finger at you: yams, usually, are white, true—but we're using the third
definition. Writing a clue might be the result of a sudden unacknowl-
edged association, or an occasion to spread out browser tabs like the
letters on a Ouija board, hunting for both bewilderment and illumination, moving the cursor until a message is received.

A good comedian, like a good joke, defies your expectations. Zach is
relatively new to crosswords. He doesn't come from a family of obsessive solvers. At Brandeis University in Massachusetts, he felt direction-
less, preferring sketch comedy to his classes. He and his sketch group,
the Late Night Players, stuck around the Boston area post-graduation,
pinballing between college performances. In 2007, after five years of
gigging, the group "died a natural and reasonably amicable death."

Zach lit out for Los Angeles in 2010, and began honing his skill in
the art of comedy rap. He joined two friends, Peter Shukoff and Lloyd
Ahlquist, on their new show, *Epic Rap Battles of History*. They were
old improv buddies, but the show wasn't working well live, so they
cobbled together $250 for costume rentals, built a homemade green
screen, and took to the then-untapped digital Wild West of YouTube.
The very first episode, "John Lennon v. Bill Reilly," has, as of this writing, more than forty million views. Since then, Zach has had a writer's
credit on dozens of episodes, and portrayed Albert Einstein (*I'm as
dope as two rappers, you better be scared / 'Cause that means Albert E.
equals emcee squared*), Sherlock Holmes (who spits at Batman, *I once
met a rich fellow who smelled of guano and pain . . . / I deduce this deuce
stain as Bruce Wayne*), and Ebenezer Scrooge (*How dare you disturb
me when I'm napping in my chair / You're a crappy rap spitting appari-
tion, I ain't scared*), among others.

Despite the success of *Rap Battles*, there came a time when Zach wanted to leave comedy behind. He felt full of ambition, uncertain where to plug it in. Then, in summer 2017, crossword constructor Will Nediger messaged him on Twitter. They spoke a similar language, with the accent marks swapped: Will liked Zach's wordplay-laden jokes, and Zach liked Will's clever, joke-forward crosswords. (Twitter has, of course, birthed the written-down one-liner, and representative Zach tweets include "'All QUIET on the Western Front' is one of the nominees for Best SOUND?!" and "If Hemingway had called it 'The Old Man and the Ocean' the initials would have been TOMATO." Meanwhile, a typical Will clue might be [Event that might include poetry, but not pros?] for the answer AMATEUR NIGHT. Parker Higgins, while brainstorming a crossword theme, immortalized the overlap between silly jokes and letter-based curiosities with a have-you-ever-noticed tweet: "If you take the 'c' and 'x' off the ends of 'cardboard box,' you're left with a perfectly repeating ardbo-ardbo.")

Will suggested they collaborate, and Zach was game. A friend of Zach's had just fled the corporate world to produce comedy albums, and suggested he make a vinyl onto which a crossword was pressed—grid on the A side, clues on the B. The last track could weave the answers together in a single song. Zach heard the idea and thought, *That's not a merch item, that's a show.* A longtime admirer of "punch line" rappers—a style epitomized by the Lil Wayne line "Real G's move in silence like lasagna"—he realized the clues could be written as a rap. There was precedent. The rapper MF DOOM, who Zach lionizes and whose most memorable album is the anagrammatically titled *Mm.. Food,* has been described as "the cryptic crossword of intricate rap" and a "lyrical cruciverbalist." His command of esoterica meant a peacocking reference to *Jeopardy!* was par for the course:

> *I'd like to take "Means to the End" for two milli'*
> *"Doo-doo-doo-doo-doo!" That's a audio daily double*
> *Rappers need to fall off just to save me the trouble*

The crossword, like rap, relies on a kind of sampling: repeating the sounds of mass culture in a new context. This collaged recontextualization is often pleasurable in itself: just as a clue picks one petal of meaning from a word's ring of polysemy, "a hard-ass beat could come from anything," writes Ta-Nehisi Coates in a profile of MF DOOM: "the opening piano riff from Otis Redding's 'Hard to Handle,' the horns from Inspector Gadget's theme song, a hook from 'Schoolhouse Rock.'" The cultural range in DOOM's lyrics is formally backed by the cultural range of the backing track. The wordplay is simultaneously comedic (go ahead, say "Mm . . . Food" out loud), playfully autofictional (he might have anagrammed anything, but chose his stage name), and generative (as with a crossword theme, once one has written, say, "Rapp Snitch Knishes," ideas for new food-based tracks—"Fig Leaf Bi-Carbonate," "Kookies," "Potholderz"—are easier to cook up).

In the same way, a crossword show could sample the tools of stand-up comedy: misdirection, callback, observational precision about communal experience. Comedian and constructor Ada Nicolle told me she views cluing a grid as eighty "writing prompts" for jokes. Two of the puzzle's primary modes—puns and knowledge of trivia—pair so well, perhaps, because jokes are often *about* shared knowledge, per the philosopher Ted Cohen. Jokes, on Cohen's view, "highlight our connection: our common knowledge, understanding, and attitudes." C. Thi Nguyen, the philosopher of games, sees Cohen's work on humor as a theory of intimacy:

> The basic structure of a joke forces the teller to *presume* the existence of a shared background. The teller must take a risk, a leap of faith. And when it works—when the audience laughs—then that laughter emphasizes the connection between them. The laughter is a vulnerability redeemed. . . . Jokes, then, are intimacy pumps.

Crosswords are intimacy pumps too; every clue is a setup. And every cultural reference is then a leap of faith, a bid that a morsel of knowledge is as delicious to you as it is to me. This bid is immediate, unlike other media: you can sit through the concert or movie, but either you solve the puzzle, or you don't; either you laugh at the joke, or you're silent; either the vulnerability is redeemed, or it isn't.

Likewise, every joke creates insiders and outsiders: jokes construct a world some are left out of, just as surely as much is left out of a given crossword grid. The proliferation of new puzzle venues might be a way of getting more people in on very particular jokes, or of giving new comedians a shot. This is partly the genius of MF DOOM, *Epic Rap Battles of History,* and nerdcore rap generally: virtuosic skill aside, the goofiness is a kind of vulnerability, an admission of just how nerdy the rapper is, and so laughter is validation from a fellow traveler.

When we don't laugh—at a punny crossword clue, a joke, a line of nerdcore—it's often due to unfamiliarity with the source material. Just as we sometimes need the crossing letters to fully "get" a clue, not getting a joke can be a matter of unfamiliar knowledge, delivery, or both:

> **According to Freud, what comes between fear and sex?**
>   *Fünf*

This joke requires the listener to know that Freud's language was German, that Freud wrote about things like fear and sex, and how to count up to six in German (in which four is "vier," which sounds like "fear"; five is "fünf"; and six is "sechs," which sounds like sex). But it's also delivery dependent: it works better when spoken, the inverse of how crossword clues often rely on the veil of spelling: [Give a number?] for SEDATE, which hides the pronunciation of "numb-er," or [Apple cores?: Abbr.] for CPUS, which hides that Apple is a proper noun. Freud himself was familiar with the contextual twists and turns of wordplay; the first example in his *Jokes and Their Relation to the Unconscious* comes from Heine:

> And, as true as God shall grant me all good things, Doctor, I sat beside Salomon Rothschild and he treated me quite as his equal— quite famillionairely.

Freud treats the joke like puzzle construction. *Famillionairely* appears at first "to be a wrongly constructed word, something unintelligible, incomprehensible, puzzling," but illumination succeeds our bewilderment as clue resolves into answer: "The comic effect is produced by the solution." We're familiar with famillionaires, and how they might behave; part of the magic of jokes and puns, in and out of crosswords, is seeing our subconscious solve the setup in a way that marks the answer as simultaneously surprising and familiar. Speed-solvers will tell you nearly every entry in a crossword is something you've seen before—it's the clue that's unfamiliar, masking what you already know, a joke waiting for you to get it. Part of the magic of Zach's show, then, is seeing him indulge his pattern-seeking in a way that feels less like paranoia and more like uncovering connections already there: a shared language, callbacks that lay in a collective unconscious, the childlike play of the dad joke, the vulnerability of a nerdy reference. As Thomas Pynchon puts it, "There was that high magic to low puns," "puns prob[ing] ancient fetid shafts and tunnels of truth," as though there were an eldritch recovery in the goofy pun, a reconstruction of a bygone dialect. Or, per Zach's friend Gary Gulman, also a brilliant comedian: "A lot of my comedy relies on saying words you forgot you knew."

□■□

The second time David Kwong met Will Shortz he had concealed in his jeans pockets and up the sleeves of his button-down the following items: knife, deck of cards, kiwi, Sharpie, some invisible string. It was New Year's Day, 2010. Kwong and Shortz were playing table tennis at the club Shortz had opened the year before, in a nondescript blocky building a few tree-lined minutes from the Pleasantville train station. Shortz has for decades been coached by the club's comanager, whose smiley demeanor and reduplicative name—Robert Roberts, a pro from Barbados—echo the Chinese brand of the club's eighteen "Double Happiness" tables. So, Shortz is good. In three games, Kwong won just two points. Could they maybe, Kwong wondered, switch to something *he* was a pro at: magic.

Shortz summoned a crowd. Kwong made four jacks appear from his bare hands, then turned them with a twist of a palm into aces.

He handed over the kiwi for audience inspection, and they all agreed it was a kiwi. He had Shortz sign a dollar bill, which he turned into a thousand Korean won, a net loss for the puzzlemaster given the exchange rate. Then ten spectators in turn picked a card. Kwong cut and waterfall-shuffled until each of the spectators' cards were revealed. He asked Shortz to slice the kiwi with that knife, from the first act. The dollar bill with Shortz's signature was inside. Shortz would have to wipe seeds off his hands before resuming play. The invisible string was probably used in the kiwi trick, but I prefer it as a metaphor.

When Kwong was seven years old, he saw a magician perform in a pumpkin patch in upstate New York. What prompted Kwong to pursue magic wasn't that *he* was fooled by the magician's trick—the mutation, in a closed fist, of one red sponge ball into two, like a demonstration of mitosis—it was that his biochemist father was fooled too. Kwong's father is a professor at the University of Rochester, "an omniscient figure" to his son. Magicians "conjure states of baffled conviction"; Adam Phillips writes of Houdini that "[audiences] always had to be shown that he could do something, but not how he could do it. He was, in other words, rather like a scientist or a priest, except that he invited scrutiny but never tendered explanations of any sort." Mystification and performances of omniscience are displaced across generations: Kwong is the son of a scientist; Zach Sherwin's mother is a Kabbalah-loving rabbi.

Kwong would devour *The Klutz Book of Magic,* Bill Tarr's *Now You See It, Now You Don't!,* and soon the "bible of card sleights," *The Royal Road to Card Magic.* He also played Scrabble constantly with his word-loving mother. As a teenager, already a member of the National Scrabble Association, he saw Shortz give a talk at the Wellfleet Library, on Cape Cod. He earned a warm dedication in the book of *Games* magazine puzzles he'd brought for Shortz to sign (*For David—A puzzle "champ"!*) because he successfully anagrammed, during one of Shortz's audience participation puzzles, LACKIES + P into SPECIAL K—which could've been Kwong's emcee name, had he gone the way of MF DOOM. Instead he stuck with magic, studying its history at Harvard, exploring the role of race and orientalism in vaudeville, enamored of performers like Herrmann the Great, Carter the Great, and Chung Ling Soo. Then, in 2006, he'd publish his first crossword in *The New York Times,* a collaboration with Kevan Choset. The puzzle was an implicit homage to both Houdini and the cerebral brand of magic Kwong practiced: 39-Across, clued as [How you have to think to solve this puzzle], was OUTSIDE THE BOX. In certain answers, the letters T, H, I, N, and K had escaped, and were literally outside the box of the crossword, so that the H of OVERFLOWETH flowed over the gridlines.

After college, Kwong moved to Hollywood, and juggled magic gigs with development roles at HBO and DreamWorks. He was inspired by entertainment's double lives, filmmaker/magicians whose interests were sawed in half by that slash, then made whole again by the trick of success: Orson Welles sawed Marlene Dietrich in half in his *Mercury Wonder Show for Service Men* during World War II, performed on-screen tricks in *Follow the Boys* (1944), *Magic Trick* (1953), and *Casino Royale* (1967), and was working on *Orson Welles' Magic Show* for television at the time of his death. J. J. Abrams, who directed *Star Trek* (2009) and cocreated *Lost* (2004–10), was also a magician as a kid. Abrams keeps an original sign from Tannen's Magic, a renowned Manhattan magic shop, at the offices of Bad Robot, his production company, and still has a "mystery box" from Tannen's—full of a unique assortment of the store's merchandise, including instruction manuals for hard-to-perform card tricks—that he has yet to open. In 2009, Kwong moved to New Orleans to be the lead magic consultant on the film *Now You See Me,* where he taught Dave Franco, Isla Fisher, Jesse Eisenberg, and Woody Harrelson sleight of hand. He was beginning to be seen in the film world. But above all, he wanted to impress his fellow magicians.

In 2010, Kwong was struggling to come up with a trick splashy enough to perform at the Magic Castle in Los Angeles, a Gothic Renaissance château in Hollywood boasting a Parlour of Prestidigitation, a piano-playing ghost named Irma, and the sculpture of an owl to whom one must say "Open sesame!" in order to get inside. Kwong wanted something bold for the Castle's private magicians' club. He especially wanted to do something no one else could, and it dawned on him that his skills as a crossword constructor were, in the magic world, unique. An idea for an illusion arrived: spontaneous crossword constructing, improvising a *Times*-caliber grid before your very eyes.

The crossword constructor can labor over her grid for days or even months, placing and erasing black squares until the words are just right. Kwong would have to perform his trick in minutes. To do so, he took the constructor's heuristics—the "letter-based arithmetic" of grid-filling, as Georges Perec called it—a step further. The logic of "letter-based arithmetic" includes the following rules of thumb:

1. Build "stairsteps": the black squares in the middle of a crossword often proceed diagonally, and they do so more often from the lower left to the upper right than the other way around—more forward slash (/) than back (\). This allows tricky consonants like J to do double duty starting both Across and Down words; otherwise, the J would begin one word, but end another, and very few words end in J.

2. Pick ending letters carefully. If you put a black square underneath an I or U or J or Q, you are vastly reducing the number of words that fit that position. I've often heard the lower-right corner of a puzzle described by solvers as an "afterthought"—a word in the last row might be something bland like REASSESSED, whose letters all work well at the end of the words going down.

3. Try alternating consonants and vowels: placing MAGIC over ARENA, say, where every digraph going down could begin a valid English word. But be careful, English's tendency for consonant blends at the beginning of words—all those words starting STR-, SPL-, or THR-, for example—often invalidates this advice, and is the reason for the vowel-heaviness of crosswordese.

4. As with ending letters, know where in a word letters are likeliest to appear. For instance, know which consonants rarely appear as a word's second letter (and thus why crosswordese like AFTA, UBID, EDAM, and AGEE recurs); this sort of arithmetic will be familiar to dedicated players of Wordle.

Kwong practiced with index cards laid out on his kitchen table, representing not just letters but, as he got better at constructing on the fly, stacks of words as well. He got so good that he began drilling himself on mnemonics for entire swaths of a grid, tapping into the memory specialist's hacks of surrealist visualization:

> I drew pictures on the cards to help me remember word combinations. If the word ANTARCTICA necessitated surrounding words SOMBRERO, COUSIN, and BARLEY, I would sketch a picture of my cousin Daniel, holding a sombrero full of barley, standing on a glacier. For months I was never without flashcards, often drilling myself while stuck in Los Angeles traffic.

The night of the show, surrounded by his peers, Kwong did some card tricks to open. In the last trick, he failed to produce the Jack of Hearts, and promised he'd return to it. Then he swiveled to an enormous, 15-by-15 dry-erase whiteboard and a side table dotted with various premade shapes of black squares, like a Tetris game before color TV—single squares, bars of three, L and T shapes.

"Name a U.S. state," Kwong said.

"Massachusetts," someone yelled, which has an odd number of letters, so it went into the center row, with a single black square on either side. Kwong started filling in the rest of the grid, placing more black squares, soliciting occasional words from the audience. When the last white square was filled, the audience cheered. He stepped back. There was one last thing. He circled 12 letters along the grid's diagonal, which spelled JACK OF HEARTS, and the Magic Castle went wild.

◻◼◻

Elsie Janis, David Kwong, and Zach Sherwin built entire shows in which frivolity makes for great theater: constructing a puzzle, as if magically; solving one, then musing on its solution; all but living in one, as on Janis's manic set. These performances center the crossword itself, but they also sample its linguistic games—as with Zach's associative tapestries spun up from a single word, or the card spelled diagonally in Kwong's trick.

But even when the puzzle is merely a prop, it signals what a performer desires. I wanted to tell dirty jokes with other stressed high schoolers, the couple on the train in *The Freshman* wanted to flirt, the Jazz Age flappers wanted a respite from society's uglier demands. On *The Office*, Stanley performs unengaged disgruntlement, answering his coworkers' questions without looking up from his puzzle book— he's too smart to be bothered, maybe even to be at this job. On an episode of *30 Rock*, Tracy has filled every cell of a crossword with a smiley face, performing his dopey serenity—he's too dim to solve a puzzle, but still seeks affirmation for his imagined intellect. And in Season 20, Episode 6 of *The Simpsons*, Lisa and Bart start a lemonade stand that quickly closes because they lack a vending permit. The line at the licensing bureau is at a standstill; the clerk won't look up until he's finished his crossword, another Stanley performing workplace shirking via the puzzle. He's a buffoon, though ("Let's see, 10-Across, Franklin Roosevelt's middle name—EXCITEMENT! Oh wait, that don't fit"), so Lisa marches up to the window and solves the puzzle for him.

Brainiac obsessive that she is, Lisa's hooked. It's fitting the episode opens with her starting a lemonade stand, a perfect image of the child performing adulthood, sugared whimsy that's also a business. Lisa wants desperately to be a grown-up. When she informs Marge and Grampa Abe of her new hobby, her grampa tells her crosswords are an old man's game: "I've been doing 'em since 1958! Back then we called 'em Alphabet Hotels, 'cuz every letter gets its own little room." The cross-generational bonding will be cut short, though, when Abe says he still does the *Springfield Shopper* puzzle every day; everyone knows the only real game in town is the *Times*, says Lisa, edited by Will Shortz. "Will and shorts," sighs Abe. "Two things I'm no longer allowed to change by myself." Call it a granddad joke—punny, but sad.

The puzzle is a way for Lisa to connect, however fickly, with the generations above her—with Superintendent Chalmers, who encourages her to compete in a puzzle tournament, and with mopey Gil Gunderson, who defeats her in the final round. It's also a way for her to perform her precociousness. There aren't many kids in Springfield interested in puzzles—but in the real world, the next generation of cruciverbalists has found all sorts of ways to perform their love of crosswords—and thus their own wide-ranging interests, not to mention their precociousness—in public.

There are the platforms already mentioned—Discord, for discussions of all things crossword, and Twitch, which has turned solving into a spectator sport. For years, there was a vibrant crossword community on Twitter. There are TikTokers whose posts are puzzle-centric. One account called "nytmini" humorously narrates as he solves the *Times* mini: "[Emotion felt by Adam and Eve after eating from the Tree of Knowledge] . . . GUILT? No. SHAME? Cuz they realized they were naked." Another account called "coffeeandcrosswords," run by Katie Grogg, explains puzzle conventions via musical theater: "A clue that's PLURAL means the answer will be PLURAL too. / And TENSES must remain the SAME between answer and clue!" And the singer Janani K. Jha, not unlike my teenage self, sings about a crush who loves puzzles:

> *What's a 9-letter word for how you feel?*
> *There's a U and I together*
> *But it's missing a few letters*
> *Is it MISGUIDED? Or DISGUISED as something real?*
> *It can't be UNREQUITED, 'cause my feelings are too big.*
> *There's so much I want to tell you, but I don't know if it will fit.*

The link between musical theater's lyrical dexterity and the puzzler's wordplay has a long history—its center of gravity being Stephen Sondheim, who helped popularize the British cryptic in America—but its latest, and one of its youngest, incarnations came in 2022, when a group of Yale students wrote a musical called *Word Nerd*.

Word Nerd is the story of Bob Otto, part Alex Trebek and part Will Shortz, and the host of a crossword game show. Otto's producers hatch a shady, ratings-boosting scheme that he wants no part of. The ruthless producers, of course, think crossword-solvers are too nerdy to make good TV or compelling performance; they want potential contestants to peek at the grids before taping. For research, the students watched the documentary *Wordplay* and studied videos of Kwong on YouTube. One student, Nico Kidd, was the crossword dramaturge, and learned to construct for the show. Kidd, who like many his age got deeper into crosswords during the pandemic, began to recognize and admire the "voice" of constructors—the talkiness of a Robyn Weintraub puzzle, the sly, youthful humor of Paolo Pasco. Bob Otto, a palindrome twice over, is always going back and forth on whether crosswords are art, science, or frivolity theater:

> *I've sometimes heard it said that building crosswords is an art,*
> *A claim with which I'm eager to engage.*
> *Since even if a puzzle comes from deep within your heart,*
> *You're still just filling boxes on a page.*
>
> *But you'll also hear the counterclaim, delivered with defiance:*
> *That, since it can be formalized with ease,*
> *The work of cruciverbalists is actually a science,*
> *Though I think you'll find that Feynman disagrees.*

Will Wegner, the show's co–book writer, learned that the American Crossword Puzzle Tournament was held in Stamford, Connecticut, less than an hour by car or train from New Haven. It was the weekend he'd be back from spring break. He sent an email to the generic ACPT address, explaining that he and the show's production team would love to attend the tournament for a day, but that, as college kids, the $145 price tag for spectator tickets was steep. Could they, perhaps, come for free, just to observe? Or maybe, Wegner half-joked, they could sing to pay their way?

Shortz responded to the email directly. Wegner says that after only a handful of messages Shortz had scrapped the ACPT's Sunday morning talent show so the students could perform. They did *Word Nerd* in front of what they knew would be their most sympathetic audience ever: nearly five hundred word nerds, many of them musical theater buffs to boot. The dig at *Wheel of Fortune* ("glorified hangman. The coward's crossword") got big laughs. The glowering at nonword games, and *Word Nerd*'s competitor shows, went over great *("The CREW MEMBERS laugh. They all hate SUPER SUDOKU")*. After the performance, Shortz said he couldn't wait to read the libretto to savor every clever rhyme. One ACPT-goer enjoyed the show so much, he tried to see it at Yale a month later, but tickets had sold out. The students told me they'd love to see the show on a bigger stage, that they milled about the Marriott lobby half-hoping some crossword millionaire with a budding interest in musical theater would take them aside and promise to make their dreams come true, but that's probably its own show.

Word Nerd was a performance—like all musical theater, a lovingly exaggerated facsimile of life. But it wasn't just the tenets of crossword construction the students got right. In Wegner's back-and-forth with Shortz, the latter used a turn of phrase that matched almost word for word part of Bob Otto's lyrics. Their art was imitating life, now life was imitating art, back and forth like a palindrome. The game of creating a character is like writing a perfect clue, anticipating, like a punch line, an audience's thrill at finding the solution, at feeling the answer was familiar all along. Shortz, who takes crosswords more seriously than maybe anyone, had used in one of his emails the line "In answer to your query . . ."; Bob Otto sings, in "Just a Game":

> *. . . in answering your query*
> *I'm inclined to share my theory*
> *That it's best to take it seriously*
> *Only when you must,*
> *Because you'll trust*
> *It's just*
> *A game.*

Conclusion: Zooming Out

[Pool noodles], 8 letters*
—ERIK AGARD, *Glutton for Pun*, 2018

F | or nearly four decades, my father taught middle school math in a public school in Brownsville, Brooklyn, then drove west along Eastern Parkway to a yeshiva in flat but relatively leafless Flatbush, fished a yarmulke from the glove compartment, and marched into Torah Temimah to teach some math again. He has described his success as an educator as a balance between honed and crystalline clarity (pet explanations for multiplying polynomials; mnemonics like SOHCAHTOA he sees as disrespectful, you should be able to *derive*) and kind but martial leadership (don't talk in Mr. Last's class if you know what's good for you). It was out of a natural sense of father-son rebellion, and for reasons of, let's say, cultural mutualism, that when I began to teach a bunch of mostly Jewish retirees how to make crossword puzzles, I chose anarchy.

For more than a decade, I have taught "Get a Clue! Crossword Construction" in an education program ("Sundays at JASA") offered by the nonprofit Jewish Association Serving the Aging. The program was hosted for many years at John Jay College in Hell's Kitchen, over-looking the Hudson; students, who had to be fifty-five and over to join, could choose among courses on opera, current events, Shake-speare, and bridge. At the pre-semester open houses, the opera teacher upstaged me. Whenever my time slot overlapped with bridge class, my students took deep breaths, and I won't pretend I didn't lose some to the siren song of cards.

I would stand in front of an enormous screen onto which was pro-jected an unfilled black-and-white grid and seventy- and eighty-year-olds would sit at desks made for college kids and together we would make a crossword. My father taught young Jews about triangles and the unit circle; I'd teach older Jews about squares. One semester, a twenty-five-year-old appeared in my class; nobody knows how. I didn't know if I should report it or pretend not to notice. She waited out the semester and never came back.

By 2020, the JASA class had had some sixteen puzzles published in the *Times*. When we made themed puzzles, the themes were sourced from the students, all of them shouting wordplay basically in unison. In one, Sue Friedwald—there were usually three or four Susans—noticed PARALLEL PARKING was a grid-spanning 15 letters, and she wondered if, as crossword themes often suggest, we could interpret the phrase literally: hiding car brands in longer phrases and stacking the phrases to make the cars parallel, so the AUDI in CLAUDIUS was parked atop the FORD in UP FOR DISCUSSION. The clues were a mix of references new and old. I loaded up the music video for Cold-play's "Viva La Vida" to explain who CHRIS MARTIN, the lead singer, was; his name hid SMART, the German auto manufacturer. Someone suggested we clue 29-Down, TEACH, as [Head of a classroom, in slang], and we did; I suggested the class begin calling me "Teach," and they didn't.

Then the COVID-19 pandemic happened, and the class moved to Zoom. There were advantages: less mobile seniors could attend, those not in New York City could too. The class size ballooned. The crosstalk became too much, even for me. Landlines rang in more than one Zoom window, and the green outline indicating who was talking jumped from senior to senior, like a cursor on a crossword grid, a divisive episode of *Hollywood Squares*. I had to start asking students to mute, after I taught them how to log into Zoom. I was becoming a crotchety grandson, I was becoming my father. One of the punniest students had to stop attending because he was going deaf, and the closed captioning feature wasn't working properly, and I felt like I was letting down my future self. They said time had ceased to exist, but how could that be true for my students? Every week, we talked about etymologies (the past) and puns (a possible future). Every week, you could hear ambulances out my window, or a van parallel parking.

The summer before he entered high school, David Steinberg became curious about *Times* crosswords before Will Shortz's editorship. Steinberg, born in 1996, had his first puzzle in the *Times* at fourteen, just after finishing eighth grade at Lakeside School in Seattle, the second-youngest constructor to be published during Shortz's tenure. At the time, the website XWord Info maintained a database of every puzzle since Shortz took over in 1993, but nothing before that. As a freshman at Palos Verdes Peninsula High—he and his family moved to California, where his mother worked as a psychologist for UC Irvine—he set upon a project: digitizing the pre-Shortzian puzzles, all the way back to 1942.

That would be over fifteen thousand puzzles. After doing a few—downloading the PDFs of grids and solutions from research libraries; typing up clues, answers, author, title, and publication date into a single file; proofreading; then uploading to XWord Info—Steinberg realized it would take him "the rest of my life" to finish. All this on top of editing crosswords for *The Orange County Register,* a job he began at fifteen, the youngest-ever editor of a newspaper puzzle. He was spending so much time at the computer that his parents kept asking him to please take their dog, Skipper, for walks. After attending his first ACPT—his parents flew from California to Connecticut as chaperones—Steinberg came home and established a website— preshortzianpuzzleproject.com—and put out a call for volunteers.

Soon, he was supervising over thirty "litzers," Steinberg's neologism for his merry band of digitizers. The project expanded to include a kind of oral history: Steinberg and others began interviewing constructors from the pre-Shortzian era, who'd worked with Margaret Farrar, Will Weng, or Eugene Maleska. Constructors waxed Proustian about the smell of eraser crumbs and pencil nubs. They described the trials and tribulations of sourcing, in the old days, newer clues: Ed Julius wanted to use TIGE in a puzzle, and telephoned several Buster Brown shoe stores to confirm that Tige was Buster Brown's dog. Jane S. Flowerree had AMUSS in a submission, certain she'd heard it, at least in the South ("My hair is all amuss!"), but couldn't find a dictionary entry to appease Eugene Maleska; years later, merely googling the word turned up dozens of citations, dating back to when she'd submitted the clue. Jeffrey Wechsler recalled, around 1970, at the age of twenty, wandering into the *New York Times* offices wearing sneakers, asking where might he find the desk of puzzle editor Will Weng, and presenting Weng with a sample of his work then and there.

The project overturned certain long-held constructor records. Artie Bennett, around sixty when interviewed by Steinberg's team, had a hunch he'd been the youngest-ever *Times* constructor, publishing his first puzzle at thirteen with Will Weng. His mother had Xeroxed a hundred or so sheets of gridded paper for Bennett to noodle on. He and his sister found a complete, ten-volume set of the *Oxford Universal English Dictionary on Historical Principles* in the incinerator room of their grandma's apartment building in Brooklyn: "Some yahoo had apparently discarded it. My Old World grandmother didn't understand why I refused to share my bounty. All she asked for was one measly volume: A–Bro, Bro–Dec, Dec–Fit . . ." When Bennett's first puzzle ran, dailies still lacked bylines. He used the $15 for a trove of baseball cards, jawbreakers, and comic books. But he didn't tell his friends, worried they'd think him a liar: "Yeah, Artie, and you just pinch-hit for Joe Pepitone and knocked in the winning run for the Yankees last night too!" He put the $75 from his second Sunday puzzle—that one had his name on it—toward his first car, an Oldsmobile Cutlass. He put ORGASM in a puzzle, but Weng said they couldn't use that word. As if forever imprinted by the forbidding, he went on to write a series of perfectly bodily children's books, including *Belches, Burps, and Farts—Oh My!* and *The Butt Book*.

Digital completionism led to sociological intrigue. Working backward, Steinberg and the litzers were blowing dust off old snapshots of language. They looked up archaicism after archaicism, those little dots handholding between syllables like ghosts holding on to life, dictionary whispers of [DATED] or [VARIANT] tarring the time capsule vocabulary. Steinberg underlined the following clue/entry pairs:

Bowls for babies	PORRINGERS
Of the back: Zool.	TERGAL
Caves: Poetic	GROTS
Pours out a potation	LIBATES
Nigerian native	ARO
Monkshood	ATIS
Saddletree strap	LATIGO
Ultimate end	TELOS
Rotten: Comb. Form	SAPRO
Eternity: Heb.	OLAM
Damned or detestable	ACCURST
Scottish dirk	SKEAN

It's a trivia Rorschach; yes, I recognize some of them too. Wherever you come down on the words' relative obscurity, it's incredible how big a difference an editor makes: the last six are from 1992, the year before Shortz took over. And the young solver's curiosity about ill-fitting, hand-me-down language is an old trope, as a tongue-in-cheek warning on an early edition of 1924's *The Cross Word Puzzle Book* indicates:

A little boy was recently heard addressing his sister in this fashion: "You *Zeugma*, you *Ixia*!" His mother asked him where he learned these terms. "In the answer sheet to the *Cross Word Puzzle Book,*" he replied. Keep this book away from the babes. . . . It is meant only for people from eight to eighty-eight.

Steinberg grew up in the crossword's angular spotlight, like an extremely niche child actor. If the crossword puzzle could bottle the preoccupations of its editors—zoomed out, decade by decade, from 1913 to 2013—it could also be a time capsule for a person growing up preoccupied with crosswords. At the 2014 ACPT, Steinberg shared data from the Pre-Shortzian Puzzle Project demonstrating that the gender imbalance in *Times* constructors had worsened over time: under Weng (1969–77) and Maleska (1977–93), women constructed 35 percent of all puzzles, and up to then in the Shortz era, women accounted for less than 20 percent. Steinberg, a teenage boy who liked computers, suggested puzzle construction's digitization was to blame—that, as puzzles became "less of a literary exercise and . . . more of a mathematical exercise," women were "left behind." The next year, now a freshman at Stanford, Steinberg had a *Times* themeless puzzle published, built around the entries PLAYBOY MANSION and TOPLESS DANCERS, which, as he wrote in notes accompanying the puzzle on XWord Info, "seems kind of weird now that there are girls living in close proximity . . . oh well, YOLO! I still think that symmetrical pair is pretty awesome, even though I'm obviously much more mature now that I'm in college ;)"

Steinberg was rightfully taken to task by solvers and constructors, many of them women, who saw sexism and leering in his entries. The very project he was running—the oral history much more than the data, perhaps—was proof that editors had much more power than he let on: that they by turn forbade and encouraged certain words, certain jokes, and by their examples certain ways of being. He was in the process of deciding what kind of editor *he* would be—a kid deciding, like a parent, what he'd forbid and what he'd encourage. Though many thought him bound for Silicon Valley—where, one imagines, that gender essentialism would have been all too nurtured—Steinberg, like Shortz, decided to make puzzles his job. In December 2018, he was named editor of the Universal Crossword, a daily and Sunday internationally syndicated puzzle published by Andrews McMeel Universal. He kept up with the changing winds of puzzle politics led by his peers. In 2020, while brainstorming a theme, the constructor Rebecca Falcon had the idea to call for a "Women's March"—in this case, a month of puzzles with as many woman crossword bylines as possible. After coordinating with various publications, and helping source new voices, Falcon estimated more than one hundred women-made crosswords were published. The *Times* signed on for the first week. Ben Tausig, at indie crossword outlet AVCX, featured women guest editors. Steinberg devoted thirty plus puzzles to women bylines. Among the constructors were new powerhouses like Rachel Fabi and Sally Hoelscher, longtime cruciverbalists like Stella Zawistowski, and, making her *Universal* debut, Karen Steinberg, David's mother. "Yup, that's my mom!" the younger Steinberg tweeted. "I've been mentoring her!"

He was returning the favor. In 2012, Steinberg wrote to Bernice Gordon, a legendary constructor whose pre-1993 work he kept coming across while litzing. He was sixteen and she was ninety-nine—born on January 11, 1914, three weeks to the day after Arthur Wynne's Word-Cross ran in the *New York World*. She'd published some 150 puzzles in the *Times,* but never a collaboration. The idea delighted her. Gordon was a jokester. "I do not really have a [construction] style," she told Steinberg, "but I have a great sense of humor and try to put it in my puzzles. For instance, in the case of the word BOOB, it was a cartoon character and not part of the body." TOPLESS DANCERS, PLAYBOY MANSION, whatever; Gordon would make the boys blush—"I wrote [Will Shortz] and said I was having a love affair with a 16-year-old boy . . . he wrote and said it was sensational, go right ahead."

They collaborated entirely online. They traded theme possibilities. Steinberg didn't know what a handsome Harry was (the plant, also called a Virginia meadow-beauty). Gordon hadn't heard of Uggs (the boots). They settled on a celebration of their AGE DIFFERENCE: [83, for the creators of this puzzle . . . or a hint to the ends of 17-, 25-, 51- and 60-Across]. Some theme answers added AGE—[Looting of a legislature?] for DIET PILLAGE—while others, getting younger, took

it away—[What an exploding microwave can make?] for INSTANT
MESS. I don't know if Gordon saw Steinberg's data, or if they discussed women in crosswords or constructing software. Gordon had
heard it all before, recalling her mother saying, "My child, if you spend
as much money on cookbooks as you do on dictionaries, your family
would be better off." But crosswords were about change, not essential-
ist stasis. Those little shifts in meaning from seeing a word cockeyed.
The commitment to changing what one put in a grid, as editor or constructor. The effort to do things differently, no matter one's age. For
nearly half a century, Bernice Gordon worked on crosswords in the
wee hours of the night—by hand, on graph paper, surrounded by reference books. Then, at ninety, she switched to a computer.

The JASA students and I got the hang of Zoom. Sometimes I'd log
on and hear a conversation in progress about some new morsel of
slang. Maybe you can see me, tentatively explaining the phrase "cuff-
ing season" to twenty versions of my grandparents, only to have one
student shake her head and say, "It's just not something my friends and
I talk about." Maybe you can imagine a student whose camera angle
has never shown more than half her face, only half-moon spectacles
and séance light, suggest a clue for SLAP: "What about like *This song
slaps,* like is really excellent?" Maybe you solved our double rebus puzzle in the *Times,* themed around Freudian IMPULSE CONTROL, in
which the same rebus squares represented EGO going Across and ID
going Down, as in OFFIC[E GO]SSIP crossing MAMA SA[ID]. That
was the semester we discussed the origins of the phrase "dad joke,"
whether bad puns were a kind of fatherly restriction on the full range
of comedic speech, a way of saying meaning could go only so far—a
forbidding, not an encouragement, and a discussion at least three of
my students knitted through. I talked about psychoanalysis and New
York real estate; I was an old man. Someone suggested we clue MAUI
via the marijuana strain "Maui Wowie" and I heard some pretty great
stories; they were teenagers.

My collaborations with the JASA class, Steinberg's with the litzers and Bernice Gordon, are the tip of the iceberg—crossword puzzles, traditionally an isolated pursuit, are more collaborative than ever. Themes are developed not in the stacks but in group chats or over Zoom. Data from Alex Boisvert show that the number of bylines with more than one constructor are rapidly increasing. I often come back to the Tabula Rasa Project, the idea that the same grid will be clued twenty different ways by twenty different people, that you'll learn not just trivia and correct spelling from someone's crosswords, but a little bit of what they're like.

One of my students, Kathy Antrim, became a solver in the Margaret Farrar era. She deliberately slowed down when "they began using proper nouns"—referring to Shortz's takeover, no doubt, though proper nouns have always been a part of crosswords; it's a matter of *which* proper nouns, *whose* knowledge base. Then, during the pandemic, she started solving again. The new puzzles still didn't feel satisfying. Partly out of a desire familiar to the figures in this book—to see one's life reflected in the crossword, to ask solvers to enter our knowledge as affirmation of its worthiness, to laugh at our jokes—she started tinkering with her own grids. "I've been in the class several years," she says, "and when each class ends, I don't feel I've learned enough, that there's more—and there always is."

Acknowledgments

I sought an apt anagram for the word ACKNOWLEDGMENTS and unearthed only these surly Hemingwayesque three-word-stories: SCAN, MELTDOWN, KEG (a reasonable description of my editing process, over time) and TWO MANGLED NECKS (a nice image of writer and reader bowed over the same text, like ghostly swans). But the great pleasure of writing this book has been how thoroughly my understanding of crosswords has been rearranged—anagrammed— and how my language for this language game has been reconstructed in committee. For that I have the crossword community to thank; this is above all a book about their ardor, a result of hundreds of structured interviews and informal conversations. I'm immensely grateful for their time, humor, and intensity: Erik Agard, Paritosh Agarwal, Eric Albert, Deb Amlen, Scott AnderBois, Enrique Henestroza Anguiano, Milo Beckman, Tracy Bennett, Kevan Choset, Kameron Austin Collins, Ricky Cruz, Lee Diaz, Sam Ezersky, Rachel Fabi, Joel Fagliano, Mangesh Ghogre, Matt Ginsberg, Elizabeth Gorski, Matthew Gritzmacher, Malaika Handa, Parker Higgins, May Huang, Brooke Husic, Christina Iverson, Adalena Kavanagh, Andy Kravis, David Kwong, Wyna Liu, Kyle Mahowald, Everdeen Mason, Liz Maynes-Aminzade, Tom McCoy, Will Nediger, Ada Nicolle, Paolo Pasco, Brendan Emmett Quigley, Amanda Rafkin, Adrienne Raphel, Hadas Reich, Nancy Serrano-Wu, Anna Shechtman, Zach Sherwin, Sid Sivakumar, Matthew Stock, John Temple, Nicholas Tomlin, Ross Trudeau, Finn

Vigeland, Stella Zawistowski, Ben Zimmer, and the Yale *Word Nerd* word nerds (Nico Kidd, Simon Rabinowitz, Charlie Romano, and Will Wegner).

Likewise, I hope this book benefits from my being an active crossword constructor. I have deep gratitude for the editors at *The New York Times, The New Yorker,* the *Brown Alumni Magazine, Atlas Obscura,* and *Hyperallergic,* all of whom allowed me to regularly ventriloquize their voices, and in so doing let me find my own. Special thanks, of course, are owed to Will Shortz, who welcomed me into his home, his profession, and his way of thinking; who trusted me to redo grids and kicked my ass at table tennis; and around whom the communitarian ethos of CrossWorld is built. Thanks as well to the JASA Crossword Class, who showed me you never age out of cleverness or an abiding love of words; on the contrary, the love only grows with time.

To the extent I am, and thus this book is, intellectually involved in seemingly disparate discourses, I have an omnivorous coterie of brilliant friends and interlocutors to whom I am indebted. For their expertise, wisdom, and directness, I'm grateful to those who read chapter drafts and provided invaluable feedback: Megan Amram, Jonathan Cohen, Kameron Austin Collins, Kate Dwyer, Parker Higgins, Brooke Husic, Roddy Howland Jackson, Robbie Kubala, André Lazar, Kyle Mahowald, Ben Naddaff-Hafrey, Adrienne Raphel, Haley Rose Smith, Benjamin Aldes Wurgaft, and Ben Zimmer.

Thanks to the editors and publications in which excerpts or early versions of this material first appeared: Adam Sternbergh at *The New York Times,* which carried a version of chapter 4, on the crossword's role in moments of crisis; Leo Carey at *The New Yorker,* which published a version of chapter 6, on Mangesh Ghogre's immigration narrative; Snigdha Sur at *The Juggernaut,* which ran the section of chapter 5 on South Asian words in crosswords; Jennifer LaForce at *The Henry Ford Magazine,* where I wrote about the *Times*'s diversity efforts; and Lauren Williams at *The Atlantic,* where the first piece I ever wrote on crosswords (and what would become chapter 5, on the politics of crosswords) found a home.

Always a good sign when a first meeting revolves around the subjects of drumming and Red Hook haunts: thanks to my editor Denise Oswald, who is not only wiser but cooler than me, for her thoughtfulness and sharp instincts. I'm forever grateful to my agent, Kate Garrick, for her encouragement and guidance, and to Lisa Lucas, for kicking this whole thing off. Deep gratitude as well for the labor of the Pantheon/Penguin Random House team: Kathleen Fridella, Lisa D'Agostino, Mark Abrams, Cassandra Pappas, Juliane Pautrot, Bianca Ducasse, Fred Chase, Chuck Thompson, Samantha Mocle, Lisa Kleinholz, and Shanna Milkey.

I wrote this while working full-time in refugee and asylum seeker advocacy, a vocation that can, for me, feel hard to turn away from. Still, the brief moments of total focus on this manuscript were as necessary as they were welcome; thanks especially to Cathy Lutz, in whose Stonington, Connecticut, home I was able to pass three productive autumn weeks and finish the manuscript's first draft. Between the Lutzes and the Winklers, it's hard to imagine marrying into a warmer, smarter, more pun-positive family.

My love of language in all its forms comes from my parents: my father, Neal, multiglot and parodic songster, and my mother, Rachel, whose storytelling ability is something to behold. My wife, Hannah, to whom this book is dedicated, is the person who taught me how to be an artist again, and that whatever my poetic excesses, the best words are sometimes the clearest. And so: I love you.

Notes

Chapter 1 HELLO, WORLD

4   In 1989, there were: Kelly, "The Rise of the Stay-at-Home Dad."

4   about as many suburbanite: Deming, *Work at Home: Data from the CPS.*

4   Eric sought advice: Bilger, "Meet the Marquis de Sade of the Puzzle World."

4   Photo captions from: "The National Puzzlers' League," wiki.puzzlers.org.

5   "Few people could": Albert, "Crosswords by Computer," 11.

5   One constructor ordered: Interview with Jeffrey Wechsler, "The Pre-Shortzian Puzzle Project," preshortzianpuzzleproject.com.

5   Mary Virginia Orna: Interview with Mary Virginia Orna, "The Pre-Shortzian Puzzle Project," preshortzianpuzzleproject.com.

7   "I wanted to make": Albert, "Crosswords by Computer," 12.

7   "mathematics uncontaminated by utility": Gardner, *The Scientific Book of Mathematical Puzzles & Diversions.*

7   When Loyd died: Liu, "Sam Loyd: Classic Puzzles and Riddles."

8   "Suppose that you go": Berkeley, *Giant Brains,* 181.

8   "going to South America": Berkeley, *Giant Brains,* 181.

8   He made an impression: Goodman, "The Mentor," brownalumnimagazine.com.

8   The game was: Adams, "Here's Where It All Began . . . ," rickadams.org.

10   He was saved: Bailey, "The Last Days of Professor Donovan."

10   In it, a pawnbroker: Conan Doyle, "The Red-Headed League."

10   The best-known specimen: "Sator Square," britannica.com.

11   Patients were instructed: Wilkinson, "The Ancient Palindrome That Explains Christopher Nolan's Tenet."

11   "back when newspapers": Albert, "The Best 9x9 Square Yet," 195.

12   "All words not identified": Borgmann, "More Quality Word Squares," 16.

12   "The pattern of the thing": Raphel, "The Crossword Mentality," 6.

13   The solution space: Albert, "The Best 9x9 Square Yet," 196.

13   If it discovered: Albert, "The Best 9x9 Square Yet," 196.

14   Disappointed, he went: Albert, "The Best 9x9 Square Yet," 197.

14   "My friends with": Albert, "The Best 9x9 Square Yet," 198.

14   "to the great hardware museum": Albert, "The Best 9x9 Square Yet," 199.

15   "I went on and checked": Albert, "The Best 9x9 Square Yet," 199.

15   "All the eternal questions": O'Gieblyn, *God, Human, Animal, Machine.*

16   "It's known that": Clarke, "The Ten-Square."

16   "logology by computer": Frank, "Logology by Computer."

17   "It must be emphasized": "The Sator Square," earlychurchhistory.org.

17   "Why use a word": Ginsberg et al., "Search Lessons Learned from Crossword Puzzles," 211.

18   "I was going to get": Albert, "Crosswords by Computer," 12.

18   "spirits sank to my sneakers": Albert, "Crosswords by Computer," 12.

18   "The program": Albert, "Crosswords by Computer," 12.

19   But another criterion: Albert, "Crosswords by Computer," 13.

20   "Word-ranking": Albert, "Crosswords by Computer," 12.

20 After his word square odyssey: Hovanec, "A Man, a Plan, a Computer: Eric Albert," 7.
20 "Whenever some wise guy": Albert, "Crosswords by Computer," 12.
22 "a tedious, meticulous, maniacal task": Perec, *Les mots croisés.*
22 "with obstinacy and tenacity": Perec, *Les mots croisés.*
23 "DUNKIN' DONUTS": Creadon, "Wordplay."
23 To fit these answers: Sunday, November 16, 2008, xwordinfo.com.
24 Their nondoubled letters: Sunday, March 20, 2016, xwordinfo.com.
24 "A computer looks": Bilger, "Meet the Marquis de Sade of the Puzzle World."
25 I remember solving: Thursday, March 8, 2007, xwordinfo.com.
25 "[My] favorite thing": Thursday, March 30, 2023, xwordinfo.com.
26 "talking with my cat": Hovanec, "A Man, a Plan, a Computer: Eric Albert," 7.
26 "Cindy Fox was a waitress": Sher, *Wishcraft: How to Get What You Really Want.*
27 *"I got the first three wrong"*: Albert, "Colloquy," *Word Ways.*
27 Here he is again: Albert, "Colloquy," *Word Ways.*
27 "was originally coined": Albert, "Colloquy," *Word Ways.*
28 Eric strove for: Albert, "Making Your Vibrator Really Hum," ericalbert.com.
28 "Crosswords have always": Eckler, "Pop Culture in NY Times Crosswords."
29 "Why are crossword": Albert, "So Damn Dull," 2.
29 "death, disease, war": Feigenbaum, "Crosswords at a Crossroad," 44.
29 "I'm friends with": Albert, "So Damn Dull," 2.
29 "The things that make us sweat": Albert, "So Damn Dull," 2.
29 "most people in the business": Albert, "So Damn Dull," 2.
30 Also, *Eric* is: "Eric," puzzlers.org/members.
31 He's lucky to be alive: Counsell et al., "Primary Intracerebral Haemorrhage."
31 *Quoiquoiquoiquoiquoiquoiquoiq!*: Funk, "Beyond Quinquennially," 118.
31 "He lifts the lifewand": Joyce, *Finnegans Wake.*
32 "Do crossword puzzles": Clavurier, "Les mots cachés de la psychanalyse."

Chapter 2 CROSSWORDS FOR FUN AND PROFIT

35 "In my younger": Natan Last, facebook.com.
35 [Film character known for her buns]: Sunday, January 31, 2010, xwordinfo.com.
35 When, that June: Monday, June 28, 2010, xwordinfo.com.
35 Ellen Ripstein, a celebrated: "History," crosswordtournament.com.
36 Gamache was legendary: Saturday, January 5, 2008, xwordinfo.com.
37 profiled on NPR: "Puzzle-Making Students Search for the Right Words," *Weekend Edition Sunday.*
37 in the *Times*: Horne, "Monday: Brown Week."

37   *The Chronicle of Higher Education:* Troop, "A Happily Puzzling Week for Students at Brown."

38   He liked all the 1990s: *Highly Evolved,* genius.com.

38   None of these enormous: Burrows and Wallace, *Gotham.*

38   "physical ratification": Burrows and Wallace, *Gotham.*

39   That was at the behest: Domosh, "A Method for Interpreting Landscape."

39   who'd bought the *World:* Raphel, "The Crossword Mentality," 22.

39   He could look down: Domosh, "A Method for Interpreting Landscape."

39   "Is God in?": Burrows and Wallace, *Gotham.*

40   He called his creation: Raphel, "The Crossword Mentality."

40   Instead, his great innovation: Raphel, "The Crossword Mentality."

40   "first mobile game": Amlen, "How the Crossword Became an American Pastime."

40   "The only thing": Raphel, *Thinking Inside the Box.*

40   Two weeks in: Arnot, *Four-Letter Words.*

41   Maybe too well: Hovanec, "A Crossword Hall-of-Famer: Margaret Farrar," 5.

41   "a nearly endless supply": Bogost, Ferrari, and Schweizer, *Newsgames,* 85.

41   Meanwhile, everyone else: Raphel, "The Crossword Mentality."

41   In January 1925: "The Press: Barometer," time.com.

42   "Said one Rudolph": "The Press: Barometer," time.com.

42   After all, *Time:* Jelly-Schapiro, *Names of New York.*

42   The inaugural competition's: Raphel, "The Crossword Mentality," 261.

42   "Judging from the number": Raphel, "The Crossword Mentality," 40.

43   She was born: Ware, *Notable American Women,* 201.

43   "the work of cranks": Hovanec, "A Crossword Hall-of-Famer: Margaret Farrar," 5.

43   The *World* had hired: Lague, "Franklin Pierce Adams," leadersedge.com.

43   His column: Raphel, *Thinking Inside the Box.*

43   F.P.A. quickly produced: Wiles, "Baseball's Sad Lexicon Immortalized a Historic Infield."

44   Someone would: Sunday, July 14, 1963, xwordinfo.com.

44   FPA, as it happens: xwordinfo.com.

44   "the throes of acute": Hovanec, "A Crossword Hall-of-Famer: Margaret Farrar," 5.

45   Clues, unlike in: Hovanec, "A Crossword Hall-of-Famer: Margaret Farrar," 5–6.

45   "Cross-word puzzles for FUN": Tausig, *The Curious History of the Crossword,* 24.

45   She conferred with: Buranelli, Hartswick, and Petherbridge, *The Cross Word Puzzle Book.*

46   "there is a sermon": "World Building," old.skyscraper.org.

46   "fancy weeklies": Dauber, *American Comics.*

46   "all I did was": Feigenbaum, "Crosswords at a Crossroad," 23.

47   At the time: Raphel, *Thinking Inside the Box.*

47   "was just one of those": Connor, *The Crossword Century.*
47   "to work becoming": Gordon, *Comic Strips and Consumer Culture, 1890–1945.*
47   "bathed in money": Feigenbaum, "Crosswords at a Crossroad," 32.
48   Spotting a copy: "Richard Leo Simon Dies at 61," nytimes.com.
48   It was the dawn: Ruby, "Dig It Up Again," poetryfoundation.org.
48   "*may* be a great poem": Jackson, "Beastly Clues."
49   Later, once Boni: "Reminiscences of Bennett Alfred Cerf, 1968," columbia .edu.
49   "surely a formidable trio": Feigenbaum, "Crosswords at a Crossroad," 28.
49   "There are two friends": Willig, "15 Letters: Most Popular Game."
49   "lose their shirts": Raphel, *Thinking Inside the Box.*
49   "the worst idea since Prohibition": Willig, "15 Letters: Most Popular Game."
49   Sellers advised: Allen, *Only Yesterday: An Informal History of the 1920's.*
49   "then-munificent advance": Feigenbaum, "Crosswords at a Crossroad," 28.
50   "intimations of early bankruptcy": Feigenbaum, "Crosswords at a Crossroad," 29.
50   They set up: Feigenbaum, "Crosswords at a Crossroad," 29.
50   That year, three: Shortz, "My Top 10: Unusual Crossword Ephemera."
50   One hundred thirty-three of them: "Margaret Petherbridge Farrar," britannica.com.
50   For the house: Barry, "Unpublished Memoir of Simon & Schuster Co-founder Turns Up."
51   But by the end: Raphel, *Thinking Inside the Box.*
51   In this manner: Feigenbaum, "Crosswords at a Crossroad."
51   "To Aunt Wixie": Shortz, "My Top 10: Unusual Crossword Ephemera."
52   "STUMPED?": Sunday, August 5, 1990, nytimes.com, 34H.
52   The *Atlanta Journal:* Rothenberg, "Newspapers and Magazines Dial 900 for New Revenues."
52   On learning their: Rothenberg, "Newspapers and Magazines Dial 900 for New Revenues."
53   "immediate gratification generation": Hook, "Behind the Times."
53   "ür-FitBits": Raphel, *Thinking Inside the Box.*
53   "They were impressed": Hook, "Behind the Times."
53   "You naughty boy": Shechtman, "Escaping into the Crossword Puzzle."
54   "What is a word": Jackson, "Beastly Clues."
54   "something between a Palm Pilot": Raphel, "The Crossword Mentality."
54   Between the confusing: *Herbko Intern., Inc. v. Gemmy Industries,* casetext .com.
54   If the crossword: "An Interview with French Artist Camille Henrot," crash.fr.
55   "Why are they murdering us?": Quenqua, "No Puzzle in the Paper? I'm Blank!"
55   The crossword in: Quenqua, "No Puzzle in the Paper? I'm Blank!"

55   "We've had to focus": Quenqua, "No Puzzle in the Paper? I'm Blank!"

56   "It's *never* made": Feigenbaum, "Crosswords at a Crossroad."

56   "a blatant attempt": Feigenbaum, "Crosswords at a Crossroad."

56   "Premium Puzzles": Feigenbaum, "Crosswords at a Crossroad."

56   Initially a digital repository: "1 Million Subscriptions," nytco.com.

56   "the ideal project": O'Neill, "Old-Fashioned Beef Stew Recipe."

56   That same year: "1 Million Subscriptions," nytco.com.

56   The *Times* leads: Majid, "Mail Joins 100k Club."

57   That kind of success: Heller, "Introducing the Vulture 10x10 Daily Crossword."

57   The *New Yorker*: Remnick, "Introducing *The New Yorker* Crossword Puzzle."

57   In 2023, to compete: Weprin, "Apple Beefs Up Podcast and News Offerings."

57   "reimagined mainstays": puzzmo.com.

57   "challenging [the *Times*'s]": Totilo, "Hearst Launches Puzzmo, an Alternative to the New York Times' Gaming Dominance."

57   "for a low-seven-figure sum": Anslow, "A Time Before Wordle: Newspapers Used to *Hate* Word Puzzles."

57   "The *Times* remains": "Wordle Is Joining *The New York Times* Games," nytco.com.

58   That meant more people: Amlen, "The Decade in New York Times Crosswords and Games."

58   In 2020, the *Times*: "New General Manager for Games," nytco.com.

58   "*Times* crossword solvers": "The Quest for 'Queen Bee' w/Sam Ezersky," *The Keith Law Show.*

60   "Can't act, can't sing": "Can't Act; Slightly Bald; Can Dance a Little," quoteinvestigator.com.

60   "ASTAIRE isn't that exciting": Sunday, October 15, 2023, rexwordpuzzle .blogspot.com.

60   "graphically explaining": Everdeen Mason, twitter.com.

61   In 2023, if you include: Totilo, "Hearst Launches Puzzmo, an Alternative to the New York Times' Gaming Dominance."

61   In addition to classes: "Edward H. Julius, M.S., CPA," callutheran.edu.

61   "Crossword Construction for Fun": Interview with Ed Julius, "The Pre-Shortzian Puzzle Project," preshortzianpuzzleproject.com.

61   It also meant the union: NY Times Guild, twitter.com.

Chapter 3 **THE SCIENCE OF LETTERS**

63   Deb Amlen, humorist: Deb Amlen, facebook.com.

64   [Ride for 007]: Saturday, August 2, 2008, xwordinfo.com.

64   Machines can diagnose: "6 Things AI Can't Do Yet," incova.com, and "Self Driving Cars Begin to Emerge from a Cloud of Hype," scientificamerican .com.

65 "We think of machines": Roeder, *Seven Games: A Human History*.
65 "advanced technology has solved": Roeder, *Seven Games: A Human History*.
66 I'll introduce you: Raphel, *Thinking Inside the Box*.
66 Tinsley, a minister: Roeder, *Seven Games: A Human History*.
66 "The tournament": Lohr, "Computers Matching Wits with Humans," nytimes.com.
67 "I figured, well": "Matt Ginsberg," ai.stanford.edu.
67 The second time: Lohr, "Computers Matching Wits with Humans," nytimes.com.
67 One client: Morgan, "Humans Best Crossword-Puzzling Computer."
67 saving an estimated: Horne, "Explanatory Information Is Revealed."
68 One year, Muller's: Vardi, "The Highest-Earning Hedge Fund Managers and Traders."
68 The next, he released: Uitti, "Pete Muller Discusses, Premieres His Latest Track 'God and Democracy.'"
68 The answer to 11-Across: Sunday, February 3, 2008, xwordinfo.com.
68 Tyler Hinman, the champion: "History," crosswordtournament.com.
69 Mary Shelley's *Frankenstein*: Shelley, *Frankenstein; or, The Modern Prometheus*.
69 *Frankenstein* is also a drama: Shelley, *Frankenstein*.
70 "improved more rapidly": Shelley, *Frankenstein*.
70 Stuffed inside it: Ginsberg, "Dr.Fill: Crosswords and an Implemented Solver for Singly Weighted CSPs."
71 "first introduction to humanity": Shelley, *Frankenstein*.
73 And when either clue: "The 2017 Orca Awards," crosswordfiend.com.
73 It knows about anagrams: Ginsberg, "AI Seminar: Matt Ginsberg—What I Learned from Dr. Fill," youtube.com.
74 "good old-fashioned AI": Roeder, "An A.I. Finally Won an Elite Crossword Tournament."
74 ruly contexts like chess: Greenemeier, "20 Years After Deep Blue: How AI Has Advanced Since Conquering Chess."
74 "The hardest thing": "Matt Ginsberg Built a GPU-Powered Crossword Solver to Take on Top Word Nerds," spotify.com.
76 Veteran solvers sussed: "Boustrophedon," britannica.com.
76 "Did I want to beat": "2012 ACPT Vignettes, part 1," trickme.wordpress .com.
76 Ginsberg predicted: Lovecraft, "Computer Program Places 141st in National Tournament."
77 "a robot with two cameras": Dehaene, *Reading in the Brain*.
78 "We did not invent": Dehaene, *Reading in the Brain*.
78 The scientists Mark Changizi: Changizi et al., "The Structures of Letters and Symbols Throughout Human History."
78 The week of October 17: "Patrick Berry," xwordinfo.com.
79 "Our reading apparatus": Dehaene, *Reading in the Brain*.

79 "a fun thing": Ross Trudeau, twitter.com.
80 When he wasn't researching: Gardner, *The Universe in a Handkerchief.*
80 He obsessed over: Kornbluh, *The Order of Forms.*
80 "tension between *proliferating meaning*": Kornbluh, *The Order of Forms.*
82 In April 2021: crosswordtournament.com/2021.
82 It was manned: Justin Hosek, instagram.com.
82 Shortz, in an uncharacteristic: 2021 ACPT, Waveform Streams, youtube.com.
82 There was the year: 2021 ACPT, Waveform Streams, youtube.com.
83 Together the group: "The Language of Probabilities," engineering.berkeley
    .edu.
84 "Humans everywhere": 2021 ACPT, Waveform Streams, youtube.com.
84 "tot[ing] Dr.Fill": Raphel, *Thinking Inside the Box.*
84 Through machine learning: Roeder, "An A.I. Finally Won an Elite
    Crossword Tournament."
85 "we don't call": 2021 ACPT, Waveform Streams, youtube.com.
86 "the bitter lesson": "The Bitter Lesson," incompleteideas.net.
86 The hybrid Dr.Fill: crosswordtournament.com/2021.
87 Dan Klein, the Berkeley lab's head: "The Language of Probabilities,"
    engineering.berkeley.edu.
88 "An Elementary Treatise": "Did Lewis Carroll Send Queen Victoria a
    Mathematics Text?," snopes.com.

Chapter 4 A FAMILIAR FORM OF MADNESS

91 a nine-note jingle: Silva, "My One Consistent Source of Joy."
94 "Latest of the problems": "Topics of the Times," nytimes.com.
95 "Scarcely recovered from": "Topics of the Times," nytimes.com.
96 "act[ing] with a peculiar stimulus": Feigenbaum, "Crosswords at a
    Crossroad."
96 "prevalence of headache": "Cross-word Headache Booms Optical Trade,"
    nytimes.com.
96 "crossworditis": Feigenbaum, "Crosswords at a Crossroad," 34–36.
97 "fairly archaic": Polakovic, "How Did WWI Reshape the Modern World?,"
    today.usc.edu.
97 "develop your bust": Tausig, *The Curious History of The Crossword,* 13.
97 "still informed by Victorian": Barron, "A Scholarly Sort of Fun," 6.
98 "This loss to productive": Anslow, "A Time Before Wordle: Newspapers
    Used to *Hate* Word Puzzles."
98 "blotted out": Connor, *The Crossword Century.*
98 "puzzle 'fans' swarm": Raphel, "The Crossword Mentality."
98 banned the puzzle: Anslow, "A Time Before Wordle: Newspapers Used to
    Hate Word Puzzles."
98 "court attendants, policemen, lawyers": Anslow, "A Time Before Wordle:
    Newspapers Used to *Hate* Word Puzzles."
98 "police magistrates": Connor, "Crosswords: The Meow Meow of the 1920s."

98   "as officious as a surgeon general's": Raphel, "The Crossword Mentality."
99   By 1941, the *Times:* Raphel, "The Crossword Mentality."
99   "*Without* Comics, *Without* Puzzles": Dunlap, "Birth of the Crossword."
99   "I thought you would connect": Raphel, "The Crossword Mentality."
99   "on the cross word": Dunlap, "Birth of the Crossword."
100   "Shall we proceed?": Dunlap, "Birth of the Crossword."
100   The first *New York Times* crossword: "Charles Erlenkotter," xwordinfo.com.
100   "I don't think I have to sell": Feigenbaum, "Crosswords at a Crossroad."
100   But that puzzle: Dunlap, "Birth of the Crossword."
100   "Young people who want": Shechtman, "Escaping into the Crossword Puzzle."
101   The clue for SLEPT: Sunday, February 15, 1942, xwordinfo.com.
101   LIVE isn't [Exist]: Sunday, February 15, 1942, xwordinfo.com.
101   SIR doesn't reference: Conrad, "The Meaning Behind the Song: Little Sir Echo by Bing Crosby," oldtimemusic.com.
101   instead we get: Sunday, February 15, 1942, xwordinfo.com.
101   "Ask for me tomorrow": Culler, *On Puns.*
101   "Margaret Farrar practically enlisted": Interview with John Farmer, "The Pre-Shortzian Puzzle Project," preshortzianpuzzleproject.com.
101   "quagmire season": "Operation Barbarossa and Germany's Failure in the Soviet Union," iwm.org.uk.
102   same tonal cocktail: xwordinfo.com.
102   A million new subscribers: Roeder, *Seven Games: A Human History.*
102   Hours spent playing games: "Prospering in the Pandemic: The Top 100 Companies," ft.com.
102   spending on video games: Lazarus, "Video Games Are Thriving Amid COVID-19—And Experts Say That's a Good Thing."
102   "Americans are stocking up": Klein, "Americans Are Stocking Up on Dry Goods, Toilet Paper . . . and Puzzles."
102   "At the height of the pandemic": Roeder, *Seven Games: A Human History.*
102   "In normal life": Nguyen, "The Word on Wordle."
103   "puzzles and problem solving games": Biswas and Ganguly, "Pandemic Puzzle: What's the Craze About?"
103   "games are part of our human practices": Nguyen, *Games: Agency as Art.*
103   "painting lets us record": Nguyen, *Games: Agency as Art.*
103   "Just as novels": Nguyen, *Games: Agency as Art.*
103   "defamiliarize[s] the familiar": Raphel, "How Crosswords Put Your Brain into Hyperdrive."
104   [Ancients, for instance]: "Indie Puzzle Highlights: July 2020," blog .bewilderinglypuzzles.com.
104   "What do you need": Steinmetz, "The Crossword Revolution Is upon Us."
104   "create order out of chaos": "Why Do Millions of Us Drive Ourselves Crazy over a Crossword?," artofdoing.com.
105   "With its long history": Bizzarri, "Bringing Order to Chaos."
105   "This will be": Palmer, "More Puzzles to Pass the Time."

106   Wordplay can feel: Bizzarri, "Bringing Order to Chaos."

106   "value clarity": Nguyen, *Games: Agency as Art.*

106   "The value clarity of games": Nguyen, *Games: Agency as Art.*

106   That is, as he's said more strikingly: "C. Thi Nguyen on Games, Art, Values, and Agency," Sean Carroll's Mindscape, preposterousuniverse.com.

107   "homeless in time": Scheffler, *Equality and Tradition.*

107   "twin urges to revisit": Scheffler, *Equality and Tradition.*

108   "public, collective enterprises": Scheffler, *Equality and Tradition.*

108   "custodial chain": Scheffler, *Equality and Tradition.*

108   "It's a collaboration": Sosin, "A Collaboration Across Time."

109   "locally-foraged puzzles": brendanemmettquigley.com.

109   "Dark humor": "Do Me a Solid," brendanemmettquigley.com.

110   "From my seat": Shechtman, *The Riddles of the Sphinx.*

111   "There's a hell of a distance": Ratner-Rosenhagen, "The Vicious Fun of America's Most Famous Literary Circle."

111   "became famous for being famous": Ratner-Rosenhagen, "The Vicious Fun of America's Most Famous Literary Circle."

111   Cruciverb.com: cruciverb.com.

113   Why do they do this?: Zimmer, "'Mad Men'-ese."

113   "The ern upon the Azov sea": Hovanec, "A Crossword Hall-of-Famer: Margaret Farrar," 9.

113   At a macro scale: "*New York Times* Crossword Puzzle," noahveltman.com /crossword.

115   "a curated peek inside someone's brain": "Tabula Rasa Project," thedelicounter.blogspot.com.

116   "Bulb light invention thought": Interview with Alex Boisvert, crosswordcorner.blogspot.com.

117   The puzzle's theme: Thursday, October 3, 2019, xwordinfo.com.

Chapter 5   **EXCEPT FOR THE MARABAR CAVES**

118   On February 17, 2020: Monday, February 17, 2020, xwordinfo.com.

118   Hoelscher posted a photo: "Sally Hoelscher," facebook.com.

118   "passe[d] the crossword Bechdel test": Monday, February 17, 2020, crosswordfiend.com.

119   Hoelscher appeared: Monday, February 17, 2020, crosswordfiend.com.

119   Read tweets by Awkwafina: January 16, 2020, Olivia Wilde, twitter.com.

120   According to XWord Info: "EROTICA," xwordinfo.com/finder.

120   The *Times* puzzle weathered: Tuesday, January 1, 2019, xwordinfo.com.

120   [Exasperated comment from a feminist]: Wednesday, November 18, 2015, xwordinfo.com.

120   [Place with homies]: Wednesday, October 14, 2015, xwordinfo.com.

120   "an important issue for us": April 19, 2019, "Crossword Puzzle Collaboration Directory," facebook.com.

121   Rebecca Falcon could run: Friday, February 14, 2020, crosswordfiend.com.

121   Grid art could skew: "one-in-a-minion: a crosstina, kate, & meatdaddy joint," crosstina-aquafina.blogspot.com; "So It's Come to This: A Simpsons Quip Puzzle," crosswordnexus.com.

121   Swapping column inches: "one-in-a-minion: a crosstina, kate, & meatdaddy joint," crosstina-aquafina.blogspot.com.

121   *These Puzzles Fund Abortion*: abortionpuzzles.com.

121   *Queer Qrosswords*: queerqrosswords.com.

121   *Puzzles for Palestine*: puzzlesforpalestine.com.

121   "a weekly puzzle for libertarians": Soave, "Introducing the Reason Crossword, a Weekly Puzzle for Libertarians."

121   Young, politically minded: avxwords.com/about-us.

122   Ingrid, for building grids: ingrid.cx.

122   Spread the Wordlist: spreadthewordlist.com.

122   For many, the tide: Sunday, January 26, 2020, xwordinfo.com.

122   "brought something pretty radical": Last, "The Hidden Bigotry of Crosswords."

122   Because of Agard's: Carroll, "The Backstory: How This Jeopardy-Winning 'Word Nerd' Is Revolutionizing the Crossword Industry."

122   "It's a model": Last, "The Hidden Bigotry of Crosswords."

122   "a level of support": Last, "The Hidden Bigotry of Crosswords."

122   "could snap": Last, "The Hidden Bigotry of Crosswords."

123   "What is you doing, baby?": Bruner, "Jeopardy Player Wins Laughs by Answering with a Meme."

123   In a *USA Today* puzzle: Steinmetz, "The Crossword Revolution Is upon Us."

123   "liberatory potential": March 5, 2023, Erik Agard, twitter.com.

124   The first time INDIA: "INDIA," xwordinfo.com/finder.

124   "culturally refused a privilege": Said, *Culture and Imperialism*.

124   "Except for the Marabar caves": Forster, *A Passage to India*, 1.

124   To many, the harm: Martin, "Tear Gas Doesn't Deploy Itself," or Malone, "We Need to Abolish the 'Exonerative Tense' of Headlines," buzzfeednews.com.

125   "The bar": Steinmetz, "The Crossword Revolution Is upon Us."

125   But a new line of thinking: "NAAN," xwordinfo.com/finder.

126   "about viewing the crossword": Steinmetz, "The Crossword Revolution Is upon Us."

126   But one material effect: "75 Years of Crosswords," nytimes.com.

126   My original clue: Saturday, March 12, 2022, xwordinfo.com.

127   That's how we'd clued: "ANWAR," xwordinfo.com/finder.

127   And there were students: "ACLU Statement on Killing of Anwar Al-Aulaqi," aclu.org.

127   Whether or not al-Awlaki: "Anwar al-Awlaki," britannica.com.

127   In 2022, Lynn Lempel: Monday, January 10, 2022, xwordinfo.com.

128   "Clean coal is not": Walters, "NYT Crossword Puzzle Called Coal a Greener Energy Source and People Hated It."

128 "such a violent reaction": Frank, "Inside The New York Times' Crossword Correction on Coal."

128 "how easy it is": Walters, "NYT Crossword Puzzle Called Coal a Greener Energy Source and People Hated It."

128 As a bouquet: "MAU MAU," xwordinfo.com/finder.

129 "still finds the clue better": Frank, "Inside The New York Times' Crossword Correction on Coal."

129 "The clue for 47 Across": "Corrections: Jan. 12, 2022," nytimes.com.

129 "There's been more politics": Frank, "Inside The New York Times' Crossword Correction on Coal."

131 "the measure has been promulgated": "Censor Crossword Puzzles in Hungary to Curb Royalists," nytimes.com.

131 60-Across read: Sunday, December 18, 2022, xwordinfo.com.

131 It's also where Ronald Reagan: "Brandenburg Gate," britannica.com.

132 He also debuted: "Sid Sivakumar author page," xwordinfo.com.

133 Most puzzle critics: "Jeff Chen author page," xwordinfo.com.

133 "although I think": Saturday, March 11, 2017, xwordinfo.com.

133 When Agard had: Saturday, March 28, 2020, xwordinfo.com.

133 "Making a point of calling out": Friday, February 5, 2021, xwordinfo.com.

134 "I am tired of how": Saturday, February 6, 2021, xwordinfo.com.

134 "Why cater to a solver": Saturday, February 6, 2021, xwordinfo.com.

134 FLYING TIME: Tuesday, August 23, 2022, xwordinfo.com.

135 "creat[ing] grids that reflect": "Apply to the New York Times Diverse Crossword Constructor Fellowship," nytimes.com.

135 The Crossword Puzzle Collaboration Directory: February 16, 2020, "Crossword Puzzle Collaboration Directory," facebook.com.

136 On the very same day: Tuesday, August 23, 2022, crosswordfiend.com.

136 I recognized the name: Killelea, "In South Texas SpaceX Country, Big Starship Impacts Come with Big Questions About the Future."

Chapter 6 **THE MELTING POT OF THE CROSSWORD**

137 Root around in the alphanumeric soup: "Employment-Based Immigration: First Preference EB-1," uscis.gov.

137 His case, which spotlighted: Wang, "John Lennon's Deportation Fight Paved Way for Obama's Deferred Action Policy," npr.org.

137 Modern-day recipients: Rangarajan, "Melania Trump Got an 'Einstein Visa.'"

137 Of a half million: "FY22 Annual Statistical Report," uscis.gov.

138 In early 2021: Semotiuk, "Seven Ways to Get Your Green Card in the United States."

138 Yes; among the lone creators: Amlen, "60 Seconds with Mangesh Ghogre," nytimes.com.

138 The Times of India: Nayak, "Investment Banker's Crossword Features in Los Angeles Times."

138   It had, at the 2014: Shaikh, "I Want People to Think of Crosswords as Works of Art: Mangesh Ghogre."

138   In it, the string GANDHI: Wednesday, October 2, 2019, xwordinfo.com.

139   Each morning, a handful: Natarajan, *National Words*.

139   In a couple of years: "10 big dot.com flops," money.cnn.com, or "The Greatest Defunct Web Sites and Dotcom Disasters," cnet.com.

139   He wound up: "MPSTME Lineage," engineering-shirpur.nmims.edu.

140   Crossword lovers: Friday, June 25, 2004, "bull strong crossword," newspapers.com.

141   "crossword puzzles, Spider-Man comics": "The Biggest Ball of Twine in Minnesota," genius.com.

142   "Drug me with your sleeping pills": "Drug Me," genius.com.

142   Like much cultural work: Connor, *The Crossword Century*.

142   "Liverpool's two greatest gifts": Connor, *The Crossword Century*.

143   The crossword was becoming: Raphel, "The Crossword Mentality."

143   "The nation still stands": "Cross-Word Puzzles: An Enslaved America," newspapers.com; Connor, *The Crossword Century*.

144   "For someone like me": "Letter from Mangesh Ghogre," crosswordtournament.com/2012.

144   In 2012, nearly: crosswordtournament.com/2012.

145   "Something there is": Frost, "Mending Wall," poetryfoundation.org.

145   "There are crossword puzzles": Sondheim, "How to Do a *Real* Crossword Puzzle."

145   "People ask me": Auden, "I'll Be Seeing You Again, I Hope."

146   "the individuality of": Coan, "A New Country," newspapers.com, and Berray, "A Critical Literary Review of the Melting Pot and Salad Bowl Assimilation and Integration Theories."

146   "the [*Times*] puzzle today": Kurzman and Katz, "What 74 Years of Crossword History Says About the Language We Use."

147   At best, this is deliberate: Barron, "A Scholarly Sort of Fun," 3.

147   At worst, as we've seen: Thursday, February 16, 2012, xwordinfo.com.

147   Like Sid Sivakumar: "Sari," wikipedia.org.

147   "usual suspects": "Letter from Mangesh Ghogre," crosswordtournament .com/2012.

148   "list of names": Wojcik, "My Journey to Making a Crossword Puzzle That Looks Like Me."

148   Wojcik clued VIET: Friday, January 6, 2023, xwordinfo.com.

149   Its marquee answers: Tuesday, July 4, 2017, xwordinfo.com.

150   "He called himself": Phillips, *Houdini's Box*.

150   The writer Ocean Vuong: Allardice, "Ocean Vuong: 'I Was Addicted to Everything You Could Crush into a White Powder.'"

150   In Berlin in 1924: Boyd, *Vladimir Nabokov: The Russian Years*.

151   The American-style puzzles: Raphel, "The Crossword Mentality."

151   "Definition is always": Johnson, "Nabokov as a Man of Letters: The Alphabetic Motif in His Work."

151 He also wrote: Raphel, "The Crossword Mentality."
151 "a stroll in the land": Perec, *Les mots croisés.*
152 Though the EB-1A: "Employment-Based Immigration: First Preference EB-1," uscis.gov.
152 He's proud of: Tuesday, July 4, 2017, xwordinfo.com.
152 "Fill in the crossword grid": Raphel, "The Crossword Mentality."

Chapter 7 OLD POSSUM'S BOOK OF SCHRÖDINGER'S CATS

156 "crossword-puzzle school": Raphel, "The Crossword Mentality."
156 "The Great Crossword": "Lord Hewart's Comment on Puzzle," newspapers .com.
156 The "offer" was part: " 'The Spectator' Crossword No. 140," archive .spectator.uk.
158 The puzzle appeared: Tuesday, November 5, 1996, xwordinfo.com.
159 Because Schrödinger puzzles: xwordinfo.com/Quantum.
159 "For a while today": Creadon, "Wordplay."
160 "who, refusing to give": Brinnin, "Gertrude Stein in Paris."
160 "that being this day": Perloff, "Gertrude Stein's Differential Syntax."
160 "In this case a description": Jackson, "Beastly Clues."
160 "Cross-word puzzles are like": Jackson, "Beastly Clues."
160 This stuff: Perloff, "Gertrude Stein's Differential Syntax."
160 "radical reassembly": Jackson, "Beastly Clues."
160 "A sentence means": Perloff, "Gertrude Stein's Differential Syntax."
161 "Much more modern": Jackson, "Beastly Clues."
161 "A puzzle, a monster": Stein, *Tender Buttons.*
161 "*may* be a great poem": Jackson, "Beastly Clues."
161 "the same sort of gratification": Raphel, "The Crossword Mentality."
161 "The appeal to my": Jackson, "Beastly Clues."
162 "It was a cress": Stein, *Tender Buttons.*
162 "completely explainable": Raphel, "The Crossword Mentality."
162 "No doubt the notes": Raphel, "The Crossword Mentality."
163 "I'm doing my crossword": Wodehouse, *The Butler Did It.*
163 "Desperado, eh?": Wodehouse, *The Butler Did It.*
163 "two cups of coffee": "Will Shortz: Aging Gopher Maracas," npr.org.
163 "[His niece Jane]": Wodehouse, *The Butler Did It.*
164 "I've put in so many": Ellmann, *James Joyce,* and Raphel, "The Crossword Mentality."
164 "T. Eliot is toilet": Garner, "Yours Ever, Sam."
164 MARCEL PROUST: Raphel, "The Crossword Mentality."
165 *"Signa te Signa"*: Connor, *The Crossword Century.*
165 "I never saw a": Raphel, "The Crossword Mentality."
165 He also introduced: Burgess, "The Wild Men of Paris," architecturalrecord .com.

165   "in the act of blurbing": Jacket of *Are You a Bromide* by Gelett Burgess, loc.gov.

165   and contributed crosswords: Raphel, *Thinking Inside the Box.*

165   The crossword puzzle: "Corrections: June 8, 2015," nytimes.com.

166   Not long ago: Bongartz et al., "The Woman Behind the Crossword-Puzzle Craze."

166   Even the word: Ngai, *Our Aesthetic Categories.*

167   "maybe not a Rabit": Jackson, "Beastly Clues."

167   Not only as a staunch: *The Cambridge Companion to Nabokov.*

167   For trilingual Nabokov: Boyd, *Vladimir Nabokov: The Russian Years.*

167   In English: Cytowic et al., *Wednesday Is Indigo Blue.*

168   Nabokov was born: Boyd, *Vladimir Nabokov: The Russian Years.*

168   In Berlin, Nabokov's: Mills, *Nabokrossvords.*

168   In Nabokov's case: Boyd, *Vladimir Nabokov: The Russian Years.*

169   Many years earlier: Boyd, *Vladimir Nabokov: The Russian Years.*

169   "One letter which": Weintraub, "A Circus of the Senses," aeon.co.

170   "I love you unspeakably": Raphel, "The Crossword Mentality."

170   "average novel reader": Smith, *A Key to the* Ulysses *of James Joyce.*

170   And if *Ulysses:* Emre, "The Seductions of 'Ulysses.'"

171   "This surrender is love": Emre, "The Seductions of 'Ulysses.'"

171   "between words as procurers": Phillips, *Missing Out: In Praise of the Unlived Life.*

171   "O, touch me": Joyce, *Ulysses.*

172   "He reached Q": Woolf, *To the Lighthouse.*

172   In 1973, he retired: Barron, "Eugene T. Maleska, Crossword Editor, Dies at 77."

172   "the same knuckle-rapping rigor": Bilger, "Meet the Marquis de Sade of the Puzzle World."

173   As a constructor: Maleska, *Across and Down.*

173   Despite being a grump: "Correspondence Between Jim Modney and Eugene Maleska—1979–1985," preshortzianpuzzleproject.com.

173   "emerges as a smug": Solomon, "Crosstalk: Letters to America's Foremost Crossword Puzzle Authority."

173   "I may have a Polish": Barron, "Eugene T. Maleska, Crossword Editor, Dies at 77."

173   After law school: Crouch, "Will Shortz," law.virginia.edu.

173   Shortz and the other: Maynes-Aminzade, "Will Shortz's Life in Crosswords."

174   A divide was brewing: Raphel, "The Crossword Mentality."

174   "I'm afraid that once": Raphel, "The Crossword Mentality."

174   The group created: Raphel, "The Crossword Mentality."

175   Crosswords have odd-by-odd: Thursday, February 2, 1995, xwordinfo.com.

175   To get from one: Sunday, May 29, 2011, xwordinfo.com.

176   Solvers were to look: xwordcontest.com/2009/05.

177 "it came as a shock": Maynes-Aminzade, "Will Shortz's Life in Crosswords."

177 "Lots of hits": Maynes-Aminzade, "Will Shortz's Life in Crosswords."

178 It's a frustrating strategy: Saturday, November 14, 2015, xwordinfo.com.

178 the show, at its peak: Ho, "Social Media Savvy Shows."

178 A book of A poems: "Ben Lerner," novembermag.com.

179 On the 1995 Lollapalooza tour: *SPIN*, December 1995.

180 One of the only references: Sunday, July 9, 2006, xwordinfo.com.

180 "makes nothing happen": Share, "Poetry Makes Nothing Happen . . . or Does It?"

180 Herbert, born in Surrey: "Sir A. P. Herbert," britannica.com.

180 "there are several judgments": Herbert, *Uncommon Law*.

181 "p. 167 *Rex v. Haddock*": Herbert, *Uncommon Law*.

181 "Councillor Wart": Herbert, *Uncommon Law*.

181 "loathsome antecedents": Herbert, *Uncommon Law*.

182 "mythical animals": Herbert, *Uncommon Law*.

182 "these limitations divest": Herbert, *Uncommon Law*.

182 "in the last two puzzles": Herbert, *Uncommon Law*.

183 "the legal question": Herbert, *Uncommon Law*.

183 "If you know, you know": blackcrossword.com.

183 "fed and feeding": Emre, "The Seductions of 'Ulysses.'"

184 "have the potential": Slaughter, "World Literature as Property."

184 As far as I know: Sunday, September 24, 2023, xwordinfo.com.

184 "in context": Share, "Poetry Makes Nothing Happen . . . or Does It?"

Chapter 8 TIME FRAMES

185 In 1983, the artist: Hockney, "The Crossword Puzzle," artnet.com.

185 a photo collage: Fox, "Martin Friedman, Whose Vision Shaped Walker Art Center, Dies at 90."

185 "inhabit the physical": Odell, *How to Do Nothing*.

186 The way they did: "David Hockney on His Photocollage Process (1983)," youtube.com.

186 Then there's the French: Chrisafis, "He Loves Me Not."

187 And a crossword writer: Thaddeus-Johns, "Taking Care of Yourself," substack.com.

187 You will learn: Thursday, June 28, 2012, xwordinfo.com.

188 *Times* debuts in 2023: xwordinfo.com/Debuts.

189 As of this writing: "Fewest Words" and "Fewest Blocks," xwordinfo.com /BWStats.

189 "Look at this thing": Feigenbaum, "Crosswords at a Crossroad."

189 The words around: Thursday, June 28, 2012, xwordinfo.com.

191 They ate together: Jennings, "How Merv Griffin Came Up with That Weird Question/Answer Format for Jeopardy!"

192 When her childhood love: "Elizabeth Gorski," Instagram.com.

192   The first puzzle: Genzlinger, "Maura Jacobson, Creator of Witty Crosswords, Dies at 91."

192   "reinforced a tiny spark": Tausig, "The Crossword Puzzle: Where'd the Women Go?"

192   "WHEN I PRONOUNCE": Sunday, March 30, 1997, xwordinfo.com.

193   "When I pronounce the word Future": Szymborska, *Poems New and Collected.*

193   Gorski made a couple: "Elizabeth Gorski," xwordinfo.com.

194   "grid art": Kubala, "The Aesthetics of Crossword Puzzles."

194   But solvers only: Thursday, June 19, 2008, xwordinfo.com.

194   Jeff Chen's Sunday: Sunday, November 27, 2011, xwordinfo.com.

194   More artful is: "Elizabeth Gorski," xwordinfo.com, xwordinfo.com /GridArt, and xwordinfo.com/Visual.

195   "trace[s] a shape": Kubala, "The Aesthetics of Crossword Puzzles."

196   "When this puzzle": "Elizabeth Gorski," xwordinfo.com, xwordinfo.com /GridArt, and xwordinfo.com/Visual.

196   "a cross between": Raphel, *Thinking Inside the Box.*

196   The gap in this assessment: moma.org/collection.

196   "crosswords merit aesthetic": Kubala, "The Aesthetics of Crossword Puzzles."

197   "If crossword puzzling": Gloudeman, "Elizabeth Gorski."

197   The *coup de place*: "Elizabeth Gorski," xwordinfo.com.

197   "Matisse the teacher said": Horne, "Web Master."

197   Others copy Matisse: xwordinfo.com/Visual.

199   Executed in very simple: Cascone, "This Day in History: MoMA Hangs Matisse Upside Down."

199   "for having contributed": xwordinfo.com/Visual.

201   "it's play": "'Ahead of the Curve' Reaction," nytimes.com.

201   "I'm sure that": "Elizabeth Gorski," xwordinfo.com.

201   "Everyday life": Felski, *Doing Time.*

203   Exemplifying the materiality: Liu, "The Folded Puzzle," nytimes.com.

203   On doing so: xwordinfo.com/Visual.

206   Joseph Pulitzer's: "World Building," old.skyscraper.org.

206   rifling through vitrines: "Composing Room of the New York World," old.skyscraper.org.

206   enormous presses churned: "The World Building," nycurbanism.com.

206   "Most Marvellous Mechanical": Karasik and Newgarden, *How to Read Nancy.*

206   "eight pages of iridescent": Hoberman, "When the Yellow Press Got Color."

207   "they all turned out": Karasik and Newgarden, *How to Read Nancy.*

207   In 1919, Bushmiller: Karasik and Newgarden, *How to Read Nancy.*

207   Each weekday morning: Karasik and Newgarden, *How to Read Nancy.*

208   "He was kind of": Karasik and Newgarden, *How to Read Nancy.*

208   "I became [the *World*'s] expert": Karasik and Newgarden, *How to Read Nancy.*

208   "the daily doings": Karasik and Newgarden, *How to Read Nancy.*

208   Macfadden is the Cartesian: Wilkinson, "Look at Me."

209   pumped the English language: Adams, *Mr. America.*

209   He added: Watson, "The Strange Man Who Changed Fitness Forever."

209   "[n]ot all readers": "The Press: Turn to the Mirror," time.com.

209   Not unlike when: Raphel, *Thinking Inside the Box.*

209   Also in 1924: Karasik and Newgarden, *How to Read Nancy.*

210   Bushmiller slipped ideas: Karasik and Newgarden, *How to Read Nancy.*

211   Nobody in a: See "Cross Word Cal," dailycartoonist.com.

212   "All I ever learned": Karasik and Newgarden, *How to Read Nancy.*

212   "The cross-word hat": "Cross-word Clothes: 1925," mrsdaffodildigresses
      .wordpress.com.

212   *You call me Honey:* "Frank Crumit—Crossword Mamma You Puzzle Me,"
      youtube.com.

213   "Our cynical bachelor": "Cross-word Clothes: 1925," mrsdaffodildigresses
      .wordpress.com.

213   It wasn't until: Raphel, *Thinking Inside the Box.*

213   An advertisement for a masquerade costume: "Crossword Fancy Dress
      costume, c. 1920," meisterdrucke.de, and Raphel, *Thinking Inside the Box.*

214   "If I'm up in": Karasik and Newgarden, *How to Read Nancy.*

214   "I know a guy": Karasik and Newgarden, *How to Read Nancy.*

215   "unappealing": Amlen, "Lowdown," nytimes.com.

215   "The industry is sometimes": Ludolph, "Want to Know What the Future
      Holds?"

215   The film, trying perhaps: "Sandra Bullock Wins Both Best and Worst
      Actress."

215   "This is the future": "Interview with Elizabeth C. Gorski," crosswordcorner
      .blogspot.com.

215   "hand-craft[ed]": crosswordnation.com/our-mission.

216   "eliminates the repetitive": "Interview with Elizabeth C. Gorski,"
      crosswordcorner.blogspot.com.

216   "It helps to let": "Interview with Elizabeth C. Gorski," crosswordcorner
      .blogspot.com.

216   "adding interesting words": "Interview with Elizabeth C. Gorski,"
      crosswordcorner.blogspot.com.

217   "The grid's mythic power": Krauss, *The Originality of the Avant-Garde and
      Other Modernist Myths.*

217   She'd cut multiple papers: Jawoski, "Metrolingual art: Multilingualism and
      Heteroglossia."

217   Then, in 2020: Brodeur, "Multimedia Artist Laurie Anderson Comes Full
      Circle at the Hirshhorn," washingtonpost.com.

218   "The old 'crosswordese' debate": Hinman, "The War on Fill," tylerhinman
      .com.

Chapter 9 **ARE YOU THE FRIVOLITY THEATRE?**

220 "She starts to cook": "Since Ma's Gone Crazy over Crossword Puzzles," archive.org.
221 "Since the 'cross word' puzzle": "Comic Crossword Postcard from circa 1925," commons.wikimedia.org.
221 "Why Lizzie was late": "Why Lizzie Was Late with the Lunch," tuckdbpostcards.org.
221 "She wants a word": "Since Ma's Gone Crazy over Crossword Puzzles," archive.org.
221 "allows verbal and physical": Shechtman, "Escaping into the Crossword Puzzle."
222 "I think I know": Shechtman, *The Riddles of the Sphinx.*
222 "Crosswords began to appear": Connor, *The Crossword Century.*
222 "Are you the Frivolity Theatre?": "Puzzle Game Crossword Puzzle Man in Telephone Booth c.1910 Postcard," ebay.com.
222 "requests for aid": Jackson, "Beastly Clues."
222 "has enough to do": Jackson, "Beastly Clues."
224 Life needs to be: Raphel, *Thinking Inside the Box.*
224 "Everybody's doing it!": Jackson, "Beastly Clues."
224 "crosswordsitis": "A Serum for a New Disease," nytimes.com.
225 "She came in vertical": Shechtman, *Riddles of the Sphinx.*
225 "Sweetheart of the A.E.F.": Beard, "A Doughgirl with the Doughboys."
226 "Revolt No. 8": Janis, *If I Know What I Mean.*
227 "We LOVE smart": caveat.nyc.
230 Zach lit out: Kustanowitz, "Zach Sherwin's Live Jew-ish Crossword/Rap Shows."
230 They were old improv buddies: Francisco, "The Dudes Behind 'Epic Rap Battles of History' Eye an Uncertain Future."
230 The very first episode: "John Lennon v. Bill O'Reilly. Epic Rap Battles of History," youtube.com.
230 *I'm as dope as two rappers:* "Epic Rap Battles of History," youtube.com.
231 Twitter has, of course: Zach Sherwin, twitter.com.
231 Meanwhile, a typical Will clue: Will Nediger, xwordinfo.com.
231 "If you take the": Parker Higgins, twitter.com.
231 "Real G's move in silence": "6 Foot 7 Foot," genius.com.
231 "the cryptic crossword of intricate rap": Errett, "The Cryptic Crossword of Intricate Rap," substack.com.
231 *"I'd like to take":* Errett, "The Cryptic Crossword of Intricate Rap," substack .com.
232 "a hard-ass beat": Coates, "The Mask of Doom."
232 "The basic structure": Nguyen, "Twitter, the Intimacy Machine."
233 This joke requires: Cohen, *Jokes,* 17.
233 "to be a wrongly constructed": Freud, *Jokes and Their Relation to the Unconscious.*

234   "there was that high magic": Pynchon, *The Crying of Lot 49.*

234   The second time David Kwong: Kwong, *Spellbound.*

234   Shortz has for decades: "Westchester Table Tennis Center,"
        allabouttabletennis.com.

235   The invisible string: Kwong, *Spellbound.*

235   "[audiences] always had to": Phillips, *Houdini's Box.*

235   Instead he stuck with magic: Kwong, *Spellbound.*

236   In certain answers: Saturday, April 1, 2006, xwordinfo.com.

236   "mystery box": Kwong, *Spellbound.*

236   In 2010, Kwong: "Abracadabra! The Magic Castle," apartfrommyart.com.

238   "I drew pictures": Kwong, *Spellbound.*

239   On *The Office:* "Leslie David Baker Shares the Story Behind Stanley's
        Obsession with Crossword Puzzles," *The Office,* youtube.com.

239   On an episode: "Tracy Jordan's Crossword Puzzle," 9gag.com.

239   "Let's see, 10-Across": "Homer and Lisa Exchange Cross Words,"
        The Simpsons.

239   "Will and shorts": "Homer and Lisa Exchange Cross Words,"
        The Simpsons.

239   The puzzle is a way: "Homer and Lisa Exchange Cross Words,"
        The Simpsons.

240   There are the platforms: nytmini, tiktok.com.

240   "A clue that's PLURAL": coffeeandcrosswords, tiktok.com.

240   *"What's a 9-letter word for how you feel?":* Janani K. Jha, tiktok.com.

240   The link between: Hodgman, "Students Preview 'Word Nerd.'"

CONCLUSION: ZOOMING OUT

243   For more than a decade: jasa.org/saj.

244   By 2020, the JASA class: xwordinfo.com/JASAClass.

244   Someone suggested we clue: xwordinfo.com/JASAClass.

245   Steinberg, born in 1996: "David Steinberg," xwordinfo.com.

245   As a freshman: Zalman, "How Teenage Crossword Puzzle Maven David
        Steinberg Is Changing the Game."

245   "the rest of my life": "'Latest Report on the Pre-Shortzian Puzzle Project,'
        by David Steinberg," youtube.com.

245   After attending his first: Basheda, "Teen Crossword Whiz Helps New York
        Times."

246   Soon, he was supervising: "Pre-Shortzian Constructor Interviews,"
        preshortzianpuzzleproject.com.

246   The project overturned: "Pre-Shortzian Constructor Interviews,"
        preshortzianpuzzleproject.com.

247   "Bowls for babies": Fleming, "Spare Moments of Litzing."

247   "A little boy was recently": Buranelli, Hartswick, and Petherbridge,
        The Cross Word Puzzle Book.

248 "less of a literary": Shechtman, "Puzzle Trouble: Women and Crosswords in the Age of Autofill."

248 "seems kind of weird now": Friday, October 9, 2015, xwordinfo.com.

249 "Yup, that's my mom!": Last, "The Hidden Bigotry of Crosswords."

249 In 2012, Steinberg wrote: Smith, "Puzzling Collaboration Has Phila. Connection," inquirer.com.

249 He was sixteen: Fox, "Bernice Gordon, Crossword Creator for The Times, Dies at 101."

249 "I do not really have": "Pre-Shortzian Constructor Interviews," preshortzianpuzzleproject.com.

249 "I wrote [Will Shortz]": Smith, "Puzzling Collaboration Has Phila. Connection," inquirer.com.

249 Some theme answers: Wednesday, June 26, 2013, xwordinfo.com.

250 Then, at ninety: Fox, "Bernice Gordon, Crossword Creator for The Times, Dies at 101."

250 Maybe you solved: xwordinfo.com/JASAClass.

251 Data from Alex Boisvert: alexboisvert.com.

Bibliography

"75 Years of Crosswords." *New York Times,* 14 Feb. 2017, https://www.nytimes
.com/interactive/2017/02/14/crosswords/new-york-times-crossword-timeline
.html.

"ACLU Statement on Killing of Anwar Al-Aulaqi." American Civil Liberties
Union, https://www.aclu.org/press-releases/aclu-statement-killing-anwar
-al-aulaqi. Accessed 8 Jan. 2024.

Adams, Mark. *Mr. America: How Muscular Millionaire Bernarr Macfadden
Transformed the Nation Through Sex, Salad, and the Ultimate Starvation
Diet.* Reprint edition, Harper Paperbacks, 2010.

Albert, Eric. "The Best 9X9 Square Yet." *Word Ways,* vol. 24, no. 4, Aug. 1991,
https://digitalcommons.butler.edu/wordways/vol24/iss4/2.

———. "Crosswords by Computer—or 1,000 Nine-Letter Words a Day for Fun
and Profit." *Games* magazine, Feb. 1992.

———. "Puzzling Thoughts: So Damn Dull." *CROSSW_RD,* Oct. 1993.

Allardice, Lisa. "Ocean Vuong: 'I Was Addicted to Everything You Could Crush
into a White Powder.'" *The Guardian,* 2 Apr. 2022, https://www.theguardian
.com/books/2022/apr/02/ocean-vuong-i-was-addicted-to-everything-you
-could-crush-into-a-white-powder.

Allen, Frederick Lewis. *Only Yesterday: An Informal History of the 1920s.* First
Perennial Classics edition, Harper Perennial Modern Classics, 2010.

"Alternative Solutions to Cross-Words: Lord Hewart's Comment on Puzzle
Scheme with 'Lottery Written All Over It.'" *Manchester Guardian,* 8 Nov.
1935, p. 15.

Amlen, Deb. "The Decade in New York Times Crosswords and Games." *New
York Times,* 27 Dec. 2019, https://www.nytimes.com/2019/12/27/crosswords
/decade-crossword-puzzles.html.

———. "How the Crossword Became an American Pastime." *Smithsonian
Magazine,* https://www.smithsonianmag.com/arts-culture/crossword
-became-american-pastime-180973558/. Accessed 7 Jan. 2024.

———. "Lowdown." *Wordplay Blog*, 1412128855, https://archive.nytimes.com /wordplay.blogs.nytimes.com/2014/09/30/lowdown/.

———. "NYT Crossword: Who Made My Crossword?" *New York Times,* https:// www.nytimes.com/2021/10/13/crosswords/puzzle-constructor-mangesh -ghogre.html. Accessed 8 Jan. 2024.

Anslow, Louis. "A Time Before Wordle: Newspapers Used to *Hate* Word Puzzles." Nieman Lab, https://www.niemanlab.org/2022/02/a-time -before-wordle-newspapers-used-to-hate-word-puzzles/. Accessed 8 Jan. 2024.

Arnot, Michelle. *Four-Letter Words: And Other Secrets of a Crossword Insider.* First edition, Tarcher/Perigee, 2008.

Auden, W. H. "I'll Be Seeing You Again, I Hope: 'Whoever Invented the Myth That America Is a Melting Pot?'" *New York Times,* 18 Mar. 1972, https://www .nytimes.com/1972/03/18/archives/ill-be-seeing-you-again-i-hope-whoever -invented-the-myth-that.html.

Bailey, Steve. "The Last Days of Professor Donovan." *Boston* magazine, 29 June 2022, https://www.bostonmagazine.com/news/2022/06/29/john-donovan/.

Barron, Hal. "A Scholarly Sort of Fun." *The Chronicle of Higher Education,* 7 May 1999, https://www.chronicle.com/article/a-scholarly-sort-of-fun/.

Barron, James. "Eugene T. Maleska, Crossword Editor, Dies at 77." *New York Times,* 5 Aug. 1993, https://www.nytimes.com/1993/08/05/obituaries/eugene -t-maleska-crossword-editor-dies-at-77.html.

Barry, Rebecca. *Unpublished Memoir of Simon & Schuster Co-Founder Turns Up | Fine Books & Collections*, https://www.finebooksmagazine.com/fine -books-news/unpublished-memoir-simon-schuster-co-founder-turns. Accessed 7 Jan. 2024.

Basheda, Lori. "Teen Crossword Whiz Helps New York Times." *Orange County Register,* 15 Oct. 2012, https://www.ocregister.com/2012/10/15/teen-crossword -whiz-helps-new-york-times/.

Beard, Deanna Toten. "A Doughgirl with the Doughboys: Elsie Janis, 'The Regular Girl,' and the Performance of Gender in World War I Entertainment." *Theatre History Studies,* vol. 33, no. 1, 2014, pp. 56–70.

Berkeley, Edmund Callis. *Giant Brains; or, Machines That Think.* First edition, Wiley, 1949.

Berray, Mohamed. "A Critical Literary Review of the Melting Pot and Salad Bowl Assimilation and Integration Theories." *Journal of Ethnic and Cultural Studies,* vol. 6, no. 1, 2019, pp. 142–51.

Bilger, Burkhard. "Meet the Marquis de Sade of the Puzzle World." *The New Yorker,* 24 Feb. 2002, https://www.newyorker.com/magazine/2002/03/04 /the-riddler.

Biswas, Saptaparna, and Dharitri Ganguly. "Pandemic Puzzle: What's the Craze About?" *The Times of India,* 24 Jan. 2022, https://timesofindia.indiatimes .com/life-style/health-fitness/de-stress/pandemic-puzzle-whats-the-craze -about/articleshow/89090490.cms?from=mdr.

Bizzarri, Cosimo. "Bringing Order to Chaos." *New York Times,* 6 Apr. 2020,

https://www.nytimes.com/2020/04/06/crosswords/crosswords-coronavirus
-bizzarri-essay.html.

Bogost, Ian, Simon Ferrari, and Bobby Schweitzer. *Newsgames: Journalism at
Play*. MIT Press, 2010.

Bongartz, Roy, et al. "The Woman Behind the Crossword-Puzzle Craze." *The
New Yorker*, 13 June 1959, https://www.newyorker.com/magazine/1959/06/13
/few-gnus.

Bono, Andrea De. *Franklin Pierce Adams*. 18 Jan. 2022, https://www.leadersedge
.com/lifestyle/franklin-pierce-adams.

Borgmann, Dmitri. "More Quality Word Squares." *Word Ways*, vol. 21, no. 1,
Apr. 2012, https://digitalcommons.butler.edu/wordways/vol21/iss1/4.

"Both Cooking and Games Reach 1 Million Subscriptions." New York Times
Company, 14 Dec. 2021, https://www.nytco.com/press/both-cooking-and
-games-reach-1-million-subscriptions/.

Boyd, Brian. *Vladimir Nabokov: The Russian Years*. 1993, press.princeton.edu,
https://press.princeton.edu/books/paperback/9780691024707/vladimir
-nabokov.

Brinnin, John Malcolm. "Gertrude Stein in Paris." *The Atlantic*, 1 Sept. 1959,
https://www.theatlantic.com/magazine/archive/1959/09/gertrude-stein-in
-paris/640448/.

Brodeur, Michael. "Multimedia Artist Laurie Anderson Comes Full Circle at the
Hirshhorn," https://www.washingtonpost.com/arts-entertainment/2021/10/07
/laurie-anderson-hirshhorn/. Accessed 8 Jan. 2024.

Bruner, Raisa. "Jeopardy Player Wins Laughs by Answering with a Meme."
Time, 23 Oct. 2018, https://time.com/5431961/jeopardy-meme-answer/.

Burrows, Edwin G., and Mike Wallace. *Gotham: A History of New York City to
1898*. First paperback edition, Oxford University Press, 2000.

Carroll, Nicole. "The Backstory: How This Jeopardy-Winning 'Word Nerd' Is
Revolutionizing the Crossword Industry." *USA Today*, https://www.usatoday
.com/story/opinion/2021/10/08/usa-today-crossword-editor-erik-agard
-jeopardy-winner-strives-to-be-inclusive/6030158001/. Accessed 8 Jan. 2024.

Cascone, Sarah. "This Day in History: MoMA Hangs Matisse Upside Down."
Artnet News, 18 Oct. 2016, https://news.artnet.com/art-world/moma-hangs
-matisse-upside-down-683900.

"Censor Crossword Puzzles in Hungary to Curb Royalists." *New York Times*,
21 Oct. 1925, https://www.nytimes.com/1925/10/21/archives/censor
-crossword-puzzles-in-hungary-to-curb-royalists.html.

Changizi, Mark A., et al. "The Structures of Letters and Symbols Throughout
Human History Are Selected to Match Those Found in Objects in Natural
Scenes." *The American Naturalist*, vol. 167, no. 5, May 2006, pp. E117–39,
PubMed, https://doi.org/10.1086/502806.

Chrisafis, Angelique. "He Loves Me Not." *The Guardian*, 15 June 2007, https://
www.theguardian.com/world/2007/jun/16/artnews.art.

Clarke, Ted. "The Ten-Square: A Tribute." *Word Ways*, vol. 27, no. 1, Feb. 1994,
https://digitalcommons.butler.edu/wordways/vol27/iss1/5.

Clavurier, Vincent. "Les mots cachés de la psychanalyse." *Essaim,* vol. 16, no. 1, 2006, pp. 191–94, Cairn.info, https://doi.org/10.3917/ess.016.0191.

Coates, Ta-Nehisi. "The Mask of Doom." *The New Yorker,* 14 Sept. 2009, https://www.newyorker.com/magazine/2009/09/21/the-mask-of-doom.

Cohen, Ted. *Jokes: Philosophical Thoughts on Joking Matters.* First edition, University of Chicago Press, 2001.

Cole, Samantha. "New York Times Crossword Constructors Are Fighting Against Its Systemic Bias." *Vice,* 22 Apr. 2020, https://www.vice.com/en/article/qjd7kx/new-york-times-crossword-constructors-are-fighting-against-its-systemic-bias.

Conan Doyle, Sir Arthur. *Sherlock Holmes: The Redheaded League.* Library of Alexandria, 2020.

Connolly, Julian W., editor. *The Cambridge Companion to Nabokov.* Cambridge University Press, 2005. Cambridge University Press, https://doi.org/10.1017/CCOL0521829577.

Connor, Alan. *The Crossword Century: 100 Years of Witty Wordplay, Ingenious Puzzles, and Linguistic Mischief.* Reprint edition, Avery, 2015.

———. "Crosswords: The Meow Meow of the 1920s." *The Guardian,* 15 Dec. 2011, https://www.theguardian.com/crosswords/crossword-blog/2011/dec/15/crosswords-meow-meow-1920s.

"Corrections: Jan. 12, 2022." *New York Times,* 12 Jan. 2022, https://www.nytimes.com/2022/01/11/pageoneplus/corrections-jan-12-2021.html.

"Corrections: June 8, 2015." *New York Times,* 8 June 2015, https://www.nytimes.com/2015/06/08/pageoneplus/corrections-june-8-2015.html.

Couch, Cullen. "Will. Shortz '77. Writes. One. Word. At. A. Time." University of Virginia School of Law, https://www.law.virginia.edu/static/uvalawyer/html/alumni/uvalawyer/f05/shortz.htm. Accessed 8 Jan. 2024.

Counsell, Carl, et al. "Primary Intracerebral Haemorrhage in the Oxfordshire Community Stroke Project: 2. Prognosis." *Cerebrovascular Diseases,* vol. 5, no. 1, Feb. 1995, pp. 26–34, *Silverchair,* https://doi.org/10.1159/000107814.

"Cross-Word Headache Booms Optical Trade: New Strain on Eyes Reveals Defects in Vision, as Did the Early Motion Pictures." *New York Times,* 22 Dec. 1924, https://www.nytimes.com/1924/12/22/archives/crossword-headache-booms-optical-trade-new-strain-on-eyes-reveals.html.

Culler, Jonathan. *On Puns: The Foundation of Letters.* Blackwell, 1988.

Cytowic, Richard E., et al. *Wednesday Is Indigo Blue: Discovering the Brain of Synesthesia.* MIT Press, 2011.

Dauber, Jeremy. *American Comics: A History.* Standard edition, W. W. Norton, 2021.

Dehaene, Stanislas. *Reading in the Brain: The New Science of How We Read.* Reprint edition, Penguin, 2010.

Deming, William. *Work at Home: Data from the CPS: Monthly Labor Review: U.S. Bureau of Labor Statistics,* https://www.bls.gov/opub/mlr/1994/article/work-at-home-data-from-the-cps.htm. Accessed 7 Jan. 2024.

Division, Columbia University Libraries Digital Program. Columbia University

Libraries: Oral Histories Portal: Collection Overview, 2010, https:// oralhistoryportal.library.columbia.edu/document.php?id=ldpd_4074338.

Domosh, Mona. "A Method for Interpreting Landscape: A Case Study of the New York World Building." *Area*, vol. 21, no. 4, 1989, pp. 347–55.

Dunlap, David W. "Birth of the Crossword." *New York Times*, 17 Dec. 2022, https://www.nytimes.com/2022/12/17/insider/first-crossword.html.

Eckler, Faith. "Pop Culture in NY Times Crosswords." *Word Ways*, vol. 29, no. 4, Nov. 1996, https://digitalcommons.butler.edu/wordways/vol29/iss4/18.

Employment-Based Immigration: First Preference EB-1. USCIS, 1 Mar. 2022, https://www.uscis.gov/working-in-the-united-states/permanent-workers /employment-based-immigration-first-preference-eb-1.

Emre, Merve. "The Seductions of 'Ulysses.'" *The New Yorker*, 7 Feb. 2022, https:// www.newyorker.com/magazine/2022/02/14/the-seductions-of-ulysses.

Feigenbaum, Lynn. "Crosswords at a Crossroad: The Puzzle Turns 100. What Is the Clue to Its Survival?" *Institute for the Humanities Theses*, Apr. 2013, https://doi.org/10.25777/54gc-7d11.

Felski, Rita. *Doing Time: Feminist Theory and Postmodern Culture.* NYU Press, 2000.

Fleming, Vic. "Spare Moments of Litzing." *Memphis Daily News*, https://www .memphisdailynews.com/news/2012/aug/2/spare-moments-of-litzing/print. Accessed 8 Jan. 2024.

Forster, E. M. *A Passage to India.* Norton Critical Edition, edited by Paul B. Armstrong, W. W. Norton, 2020.

Foster, John Burt. "Nabokov and Modernism." *The Cambridge Companion to Nabokov,* edited by Julian W. Connolly, Cambridge University Press, 2005, pp. 85–100, https://doi.org/10.1017/CCOL0521829577.006.

Fox, Margalit. "Bernice Gordon, Crossword Creator for The Times, Dies at 101." *New York Times*, 31 Jan. 2015, https://www.nytimes.com/2015/01/31/arts /bernice-gordon-who-toyed-with-words-dies-at-101.html.

———. "Martin Friedman, Whose Vision Shaped Walker Art Center, Dies at 90." *New York Times,* 14 May 2016, https://www.nytimes.com/2016/05/14/arts /design/martin-friedman-whose-vision-shaped-walker-art-center-dies-at-90 .html.

Francisco, Eric. "The Dudes Behind 'Epic Rap Battles of History' Eye an Uncertain Future." *Inverse,* 29 Nov. 2017, https://www.inverse.com/article /38430-epic-rap-battles-season-6-youtube-trump-nazis.

Frank, Alan. "Logology by Computer." *Word Ways*, vol. 16, no. 4, Nov. 1983, https://digitalcommons.butler.edu/wordways/vol16/iss4/2.

Frank, Thomas. "Inside The New York Times' Crossword Correction on Coal." *E&E News by Politico,* 13 Jan. 2022, https://www.eenews.net/articles/inside -the-new-york-times-crossword-correction-on-coal/.

Freud, Sigmund. *Jokes and Their Relation to the Unconscious.* Read Books Ltd, 2014.

Funk, Joel. "Beyond Quinquennially." *Word Ways*, vol. 22, no. 2, May 1989, https://digitalcommons.butler.edu/wordways/vol22/iss2/13.

Gardner, Martin. *The Scientific American Book of Mathematical Puzzles & Diversions*. Simon & Schuster, 1959.

————. *The Universe in a Handkerchief: Lewis Carroll's Mathematical Recreations, Games, Puzzles, and Word Plays*. 1996 reprint of the original first edition, Copernicus, 2005.

Garner, Dwight. "Yours Ever, Sam." *New York Times*, 5 Mar. 2009, https://www.nytimes.com/2009/03/06/books/06Book.html.

Genzlinger, Neil. "Maura Jacobson, Creator of Witty Crosswords, Dies at 91." *New York Times*, 1 Jan. 2018, https://www.nytimes.com/2018/01/01/crosswords/maura-jacobson-crosswords-dies.html.

Ginsberg, Matthew L. "Dr.Fill: Crosswords and an Implemented Solver for Singly Weighted CSPs." *Journal of Artificial Intelligence Research*, 2011, arxiv.org, https://doi.org/10.1613/jair.3437.

————, et al. "Search Lessons Learned from Crossword Puzzles." *AAAI*, vol. 90, 1990, pp. 210–15.

Gloudeman, Nikki. "Elizabeth Gorski: New York Times Crossword Creator." 24 Dec. 2014, https://www.ravishly.com/ladies-we-love/elizabeth-gorski-new-york-times-crossword-creator.

Goldman, David. "10 Big Dot.Com Flops." *CNNMoney*, 2 Mar. 2015, https://money.cnn.com/gallery/technology/2015/03/02/dot-com-flops/.

Gordon, Ian. *Comic Strips and Consumer Culture, 1890–1945*. Smithsonian, 1998.

Greenemeier, Larry. "20 Years After Deep Blue: How AI Has Advanced Since Conquering Chess." *Scientific American*, https://www.scientificamerican.com/article/20-years-after-deep-blue-how-ai-has-advanced-since-conquering-chess/. Accessed 7 Jan. 2024.

Heller, Emily Palmer. "Introducing the Vulture 10x10 Daily Crossword." *Vulture*, 24 Jan. 2022, https://www.vulture.com/2022/01/introducing-the-vulture-10x10-daily-crossword-puzzle.html.

Herbert, A. P. *Uncommon Law: Being 66 Misleading Cases Revised and Collected in One Volume*. International Polygonics Ltd., 2001.

Herbko Intern., Inc. v. Gemmy Industries, 916 F. Supp. 322, Casetext Search + Citator, https://casetext.com/case/herbko-intern-inc-v-gemmy-industries. Accessed 7 Jan. 2024.

A History of "Adventure." https://rickadams.org/adventure/a_history.html. Accessed 7 Jan. 2024.

Ho, Rodney. "Social Media Savvy Shows: 'Scandal,' 'Love & Hip Hop Atlanta,' 'Pretty Little Liars,' 'The Walking Dead.'" *Radio & TV Talk Blog, Atlanta Journal-Constitution*.

Hoberman, J. "When the Yellow Press Got Color." *New York Review of Books*, 31 Dec. 2013, https://www.nybooks.com/online/2013/12/31/early-comics-society-is-nix/.

Hodgman, Lucy. "Students Preview 'Word Nerd' Musical at American National Crossword Puzzle Tournament." *Yale Daily News*, 5 Apr. 2022, https://

yaledailynews.com/blog/2022/04/04/students-preview-word-nerd-musical
-at-american-national-crossword-puzzle-tournament/.

"Homer and Lisa Exchange Cross Words." *The Simpsons,* directed by Mike B.
Anderson and Nancy Kruse, 16 Nov. 2008.

Hook, Henry. "Dialing 900-NYTIMES. . . ." *CROSSW_RD,* Feb. 1991.

Horne, Jim. "Explanatory Information Is Revealed." *Wordplay Blog,* 1238810440,
https://archive.nytimes.com/wordplay.blogs.nytimes.com/2009/04/03
/revealed/.

———. "Monday: Brown Week." *Wordplay Blog,* 1284328842, https://archive
.nytimes.com/wordplay.blogs.nytimes.com/2010/09/12/brown-week/.

———. "Web Master." *Wordplay Blog,* 1225576814, https://archive.nytimes.com
/wordplay.blogs.nytimes.com/2008/11/01/web-master/.

Hovanec, Helene. "A Crossword Hall-of-Famer: Margaret Farrar." *CROSSW_RD,*
Dec. 1992.

———. "A Man, a Plan, a Computer: Eric Albert." *CROSSW_RD,* Oct. 1992.

"How Did WWI Reshape the Modern World?" *USC Today,* 9 Nov. 2018, https://
today.usc.edu/impact-of-world-war-i-shaping-the-modern-world/.

"An Interview with French Artist Camille Henrot," *Crash* magazine, https://
www.crash.fr/an-interview-with-french-artist-camille-henrot/. Accessed
7 Jan. 2024.

Jackson, Roddy Howland. "Beastly Clues: T. S. Eliot, Torquemada, and
the Modernist Crossword." *The Public Domain Review,* https://
publicdomainreview.org/essay/beastly-clues/. Accessed 7 Jan. 2024.

Janis, Elsie. *If I Know What I Mean.* Literary Licensing, LLC, 2013.

Jaworski, Adam. "Metrolingual Art: Multilingualism and Heteroglossia."
International Journal of Bilingualism, vol. 18, no. 2, Apr. 2014, pp. 134–58,
SAGE Journals, https://doi.org/10.1177/1367006912458391.

Jelly-Schapiro, Joshua. *Names of New York: Discovering the City's Past, Present,
and Future Through Its Place-Names.* Pantheon, 2021.

Jennings, Ken. "How Merv Griffin Came Up with That Weird Question/Answer
Format for Jeopardy!" *Smithsonian Magazine,* https://www.smithsonianmag
.com/arts-culture/How-Merv-Griffin-Came-Up-With-That-Weird-Question
-Answer-Format-for-Jeopardy-180949815/. Accessed 8 Jan. 2024.

"John Lennon's Deportation Fight Paved Way for Obama's Deferred Action
Policy." *All Things Considered,* directed by Hansi Lo Wang, NPR, 23 Aug.
2016, https://www.npr.org/2016/08/23/490957803/john-lennons-deportation
-fight-paved-way-to-obamas-deferred-action-policy.

Johnson, D. Barton. "Nabokov as a Man of Letters: The Alphabetic Motif in His
Work." *Modern Fiction Studies,* vol. 25, no. 3, 1979, pp. 397–412.

Joyce, James. *Finnegans Wake.* Penguin Classics, 1999.

———. *Ulysses.* Vintage, 1990.

Karasik, Paul, and Mark Newgarden. *How to Read Nancy: The Elements of
Comics in Three Easy Panels.* Illustrated edition, Fantagraphics, 2017.

"The Keith Law Show: The Quest for 'Queen Bee' w/Sam Ezersky on Apple

Podcasts," https://podcasts.apple.com/sc/podcast/the-quest-for-queen-bee -w-sam-ezersky/id1499877854?i=1000541286581. Accessed 7 Jan. 2024.

Kelly, Jack. "The Rise of the Stay-at-Home Dad." *Forbes,* https://www.forbes .com/sites/jackkelly/2022/12/07/the-rise-of-the-stay-at-home-dad/. Accessed 7 Jan. 2024.

Killelea, Eric. "In South Texas SpaceX Country, Big Starship Impacts Come with Big Questions About the Future." *San Antonio Express-News,* 21 Apr. 2023, https://www.expressnews.com/business/article/spacex-south-texas-starship -elon-musk-17905158.php.

Klein, Allison. "Americans Are Stocking Up on Dry Goods, Toilet Paper . . . and Puzzles." *Washington Post,* 24 Mar. 2020, www.washingtonpost.com, https:// www.washingtonpost.com/lifestyle/2020/03/24/americans-are-stocking-up -dry-goods-toilet-paper-puzzles/.

Klein, Charlotte. "Inside The New York Times' Big Bet on Games." *Vanity Fair,* 19 Dec. 2023, https://www.vanityfair.com/news/inside-the-new-york-times -big-bet-on-games.

Kornbluh, Anna. *The Order of Forms: Realism, Formalism, and Social Space.* First edition, University of Chicago Press, 2019.

Krauss, Rosalind E. *The Originality of the Avant-Garde and Other Modernist Myths.* Reprint edition, MIT Press, 1986.

Kubala, Robbie. "The Aesthetics of Crossword Puzzles." *The British Journal of Aesthetics,* vol. 63, no. 3, July 2023, pp. 381–94, *Silverchair,* https://doi.org/10 .1093/aesthj/ayac049.

Kurzman, Charles, and Josh Katz. "What 74 Years of Crossword History Says About the Language We Use." *New York Times,* 6 Feb. 2016, https://www .nytimes.com/interactive/2016/02/07/opinion/what-74-years-of-times -crosswords-say-about-the-words-we-use.html.

Kustanowitz, Esther D. "Zach Sherwin's Live Jew-Ish Crossword/Rap Shows." *Jewish Journal,* 31 July 2019, https://jewishjournal.com/culture/302402/zach -sherwins-live-jew-ish-crossword-rap-shows/.

Kwong, David. *Spellbound: Seven Principles of Illusion to Captivate Audiences and Unlock the Secrets of Success.* Harper Business, 2017.

Last, Natan. "The Hidden Bigotry of Crosswords." *The Atlantic,* 18 Mar. 2020, https://www.theatlantic.com/culture/archive/2020/03/fight-to-make -crosswords-more-inclusive/608212/.

Lazarus, David. "Video Games Are Thriving amid COVID-19—and Experts Say That's a Good Thing." *Los Angeles Times,* 16 June 2020, https://www.latimes .com/business/story/2020-06-16/column-coronavirus-video-games.

Liu, Jonathan H. "Sam Loyd: Classic Puzzles and Riddles." *Wired,* www.wired .com, https://www.wired.com/2009/05/sam-loyd-classic-puzzles-and -riddles/. Accessed 7 Jan. 2024.

Lohr, Steve. "The Computer's Next Conquest: Crosswords." *New York Times,* 16 Mar. 2012, https://www.nytimes.com/2012/03/17/technology/computer -matching-wits-with-humans-in-crossword-tournament.html.

Lovecraft, Raven. "Computer Program Places 141st in National Tournament."

TGDaily, 19 Mar. 2012, https://tgdaily.com/science/62166-computer-program
-places-141st-in-national-tournament/.

Ludolph, Emily. *Want to Know What the Future Holds? Look No Further Than
the Nearest Crossword Puzzle,* https://www.behance.net/blog/want-to-know
-what-the-future-holds-look-no-further-than-the-nearest-crossword-puzzle.
Accessed 8 Jan. 2024.

Majid, Aisha. "Mail Joins 100k Club: Exclusive Ranking of World's Top
Paywalled News Publishers." *Press Gazette,* 6 Apr. 2023, https://pressgazette
.co.uk/paywalls/digital-news-subscriptions-ranking-2023/.

Maleska, Eugene T. *Across and Down.* Simon & Schuster, 1987.

Martin, Nick. "Tear Gas Doesn't Deploy Itself." *The New Republic,* 1 June 2020,
https://newrepublic.com/article/157942/tear-gas-doesnt-deploy.

Maynes-Aminzade, Liz. "Will Shortz's Life in Crosswords." *The New Yorker,*
15 Feb. 2023, https://www.newyorker.com/culture/the-new-yorker-interview
/will-shortzs-life-in-crosswords.

"Mending Wall by Robert Frost." Poetry Foundation, 7 Jan. 2024, https://www
.poetryfoundation.org/poems/44266/mending-wall.

The Mentor. https://www.brownalumnimagazine.com/articles/2015-09-01/the
-mentor. Accessed 7 Jan. 2024.

Merrell, Patrick. "'Ahead of the Curve' Reaction." *Wordplay Blog,* 1257181218,
https://archive.nytimes.com/wordplay.blogs.nytimes.com/2009/11/02/ahead
-reaction/.

Mills, Joseph Clayton. *Nabokrossvords.* First edition, Lulu.com, 2012.

Morgan, Timothy Prickett. *Humans Best Crossword-Puzzling Computer.*
https://www.theregister.com/2012/03/19/dr_fill_crossword_puzzler_solver/.
Accessed 7 Jan. 2024.

Nabokov, Vladimir. *Pale Fire.* Vintage, 1989.

Natarajan, C. S. *National Words: A Solution to the National Language Problem of
India.* Notion Press, 2018.

Nayak, B. B. "Navi Mumbai: Investment Banker's Crossword Features in Los
Angeles Times." *The Times of India,* 7 Sept. 2022, https://timesofindia
.indiatimes.com/city/navi-mumbai/navi-mumbai-investment-bankers
-crossword-features-in-los-angeles-times/articleshow/94055111.cms.

"New General Manager for Games." New York Times Company, 9 Sept. 2020,
https://www.nytco.com/press/new-general-manager-for-games/.

"News Paper Spires Walkthrough." The Skyscraper Museum, https://old.
skyscraper.org/EXHIBITIONS/PAPER_SPIRES/nw09_world.php. Accessed
7 Jan. 2024.

———. https://old.skyscraper.org/EXHIBITIONS/PAPER_SPIRES/metal02
.php. Accessed 8 Jan. 2024.

"The New York Times Buys Wordle for a Price in the 'Low Seven Figures.'"
Nieman Lab, https://www.niemanlab.org/2022/01/the-new-york-times-buys
-wordle-for-a-price-in-the-low-seven-figures/. Accessed 7 Jan. 2024.

Ngai, Sianne. *Our Aesthetic Categories: Zany, Cute, Interesting.* Reprint edition,
Harvard University Press, 2015.

Nguyen, C. Thi. *Games: Agency as Art*. Oxford University Press, 2020.

———. "Op-Ed: The Word on Wordle: It Is Bringing People Together by Letting Us See into Each Other's Minds." *Los Angeles Times,* 21 Jan. 2022, https://www.latimes.com/opinion/story/2022-01-21/op-ed-wordle-game-minds-play.

———. "Twitter, the Intimacy Machine." *The Raven,* 8 Dec. 2021, https://ravenmagazine.org/magazine/twitter-the-intimacy-machine/.

"November: Ben Lerner." *November: Ben Lerner,* https://novembermag.com/content/ben-lerner. Accessed 8 Jan. 2024.

Odell, Jenny. *How to Do Nothing: Resisting the Attention Economy*. Melville House, 2019.

O'Gieblyn, Meghan. *God, Human, Animal, Machine: Technology, Metaphor, and the Search for Meaning*. First edition, Doubleday, 2021.

O'Neill, Molly. "Old-Fashioned Beef Stew Recipe." *NYT Cooking,* https://cooking.nytimes.com/recipes/4735-old-fashioned-beef-stew. Accessed 7 Jan. 2024.

"Operation 'Barbarossa' and Germany's Failure in the Soviet Union." Imperial War Museums, https://www.iwm.org.uk/history/operation-barbarossa-and-germanys-failure-in-the-soviet-union. Accessed 8 Jan. 2024.

Palmer, Emily. "More Puzzles to Pass the Time." *New York Times,* 20 Apr. 2020, https://www.nytimes.com/2020/04/20/reader-center/more-puzzles-coronavirus.html.

Perec, Georges. *Les mots croisés*. P.O.L., 2003.

Perloff, Marjorie. "Gertrude Stein's Differential Syntax: Sarah Tryphena Phillips Lecture." *Proceedings of the British Academy, Volume 117: 2001 Lectures,* edited by F.M.L. Thompson, British Academy, 2003. *Silverchair,* https://doi.org/10.5871/bacad/9780197262795.003.0012.

Petherbridge, Margaret, Prosper Buranelli, and Frederic Gregory Hartswick. "The Cross Word Puzzle Book: First Series," https://www.Gutenberg.org/Files/68267/68267-h/68267-h.Htm, https://www.gutenberg.org/ebooks/68267/pg68267-images.html. Accessed 7 Jan. 2024.

Phillips, Adam. *Houdini's Box: The Art of Escape*. Vintage, 2002.

———. *Missing Out: In Praise of the Unlived Life*. Farrar, Straus & Giroux, 2013.

Pre-Shortzian Constructor Interviews. http://www.preshortzianpuzzleproject.com/p/pre-shortzian-constructor-interviews.html. Accessed 7 Jan. 2024.

"The Press: Barometer." *Time,* 5 Jan. 1925, content.time.com, https://content.time.com/time/subscriber/article/0,33009,719730,00.html.

"The Press: Turn to the Mirror." *Time,* 17 June 1929, content.time.com, https://content.time.com/time/subscriber/article/0,33009,723704,00.html.

"Prospering in the Pandemic: The Top 100 Companies." *Financial Times,* 19 June 2020, https://www.ft.com/content/844ed28c-8074-4856-bde0-20f3bf4cd8f0.

"Puzzle-Making Students Search for the Right Words." *Weekend Edition Sunday,* NPR, 19 Sept. 2010, https://www.npr.org/templates/story/story.php?storyId=129970015.

Pynchon, Thomas. *The Crying of Lot 49*. Harper Perennial Modern Classics, 2006.

Quenqua, Douglas. "No Puzzle in the Paper? I'm Blank!" *New York Times,* 11 July 2009, https://www.nytimes.com/2009/07/12/fashion/12puzzle.html.

Rangarajan, Sinduja. "Melania Trump Got an 'Einstein Visa.' Why Was It So Hard for This Nobel Prize Winner?" *Mother Jones,* https://www.motherjones .com/politics/2020/02/genius-green-card-visa-nobel-prize-trump/. Accessed 8 Jan. 2024.

Raphel, Adrienne. "The Crossword Mentality in Modern Literature and Culture." PhD diss., Harvard University, Graduate School of Arts & Sciences, 2018.

———. "How Crosswords Put Your Brain into Hyperdrive." *The New Yorker,* 16 Sept. 2019, https://www.newyorker.com/culture/video-dept/how -crosswords-put-your-brain-into-hyperdrive.

———. *Thinking Inside the Box: Adventures with Crosswords and the Puzzling People Who Can't Live Without Them.* First edition, Penguin, 2020.

Ratner-Rosenhagen, Jennifer. "The Vicious Fun of America's Most Famous Literary Circle." *New York Times,* 20 July 2019, https://www.nytimes.com /2019/07/20/opinion/the-vicious-fun-of-americas-most-famous-literary -circle.html.

Remnick, David. "Introducing The New Yorker Crossword Puzzle." *The New Yorker,* 30 Apr. 2018, https://www.newyorker.com/puzzles-and-games-dept /crossword/introducing-the-new-yorker-crossword-puzzle.

"Richard Leo Simon Dies at 61; Co-Founder of Publishing Firm; He and Max Schuster Began Business in 1924 with a Crossword Puzzle Book." *New York Times,* 30 July 1960, https://www.nytimes.com/1960/07/30/archives/richard -leo-simon-dies-at-61-cofounder-of-publishing-firm-he-and.html.

Roeder, Oliver. "An A.I. Finally Won an Elite Crossword Tournament." *Slate,* 27 Apr. 2021, https://slate.com/technology/2021/04/american-crossword -puzzle-tournament-dr-fill-artificial-intelligence.html.

———. *Seven Games: A Human History.* W. W. Norton, 2022.

Rothenberg, Randall. "The Media Business: Newspapers and Magazines Dial 900 for New Revenues," *New York Times,* https://www.nytimes.com/1991 /04/22/business/the-media-business-newspapers-and-magazines-dial-900 -for-new-revenues.html. Accessed 7 Jan. 2024.

Ruby, Ryan. "Dig It Up Again." Poetry Foundation, 7 Jan. 2024, https://www .poetryfoundation.org/articles/159319/dig-it-up-again.

Said, Edward W. *Culture and Imperialism.* Reprint edition, Vintage, 1994.

"Sandra Bullock Wins Both Best and Worst Actress." ABC News, https:// abcnews.go.com/Entertainment/Oscars/sandra-bullock-wins-awards-worst -best-actress-weekend/story?id=10038093. Accessed 8 Jan. 2024.

Scheffler, Samuel. *Equality and Tradition: Questions of Value in Moral and Political Theory.* Oxford University Press, 2010.

Semotiuk, Andy J. "Seven Ways to Get Your Green Card in the United States." *Forbes,* https://www.forbes.com/sites/andyjsemotiuk/2021/07/30/seven -ways-to-get-your-green-card-in-the-united-states/. Accessed 8 Jan. 2024.

Shaikh, Alfea. "I Want People to Think of Crosswords as Works of Art: Mangesh

Ghogre." *Hindustan Times,* 6 Feb. 2014, https://www.hindustantimes.com /books/i-want-people-to-think-of-crosswords-as-works-of-art-mangesh -ghogre/story-SI9m6x5DEk3RnKcuDhNBiI.html.

Share, Don. "Poetry Makes Nothing Happen . . . or Does It?" Poetry Foundation, 8 Jan. 2024, https://www.poetryfoundation.org/harriet-books /2009/11/poetry-makes-nothing-happen-or-does-it.

Shechtman, Anna. "Escaping into the Crossword Puzzle." *The New Yorker,* 20 Dec. 2021, https://www.newyorker.com/magazine/2021/12/27/escaping -into-the-crossword-puzzle.

———. "Puzzle Trouble: Women and Crosswords in the Age of Autofill." *The American Reader,* http://theamericanreader.com/puzzle-trouble-women-and -crosswords-in-the-age-of-autofill/. Accessed 7 Jan. 2024.

———. *The Riddles of the Sphinx: Inheriting the Feminist History of the Crossword Puzzle.* HarperOne, 2024.

Shelley, Mary. *Frankenstein; or, The Modern Prometheus.* Third edition, Dover, 1994.

Sher, Barbara, with Annie Gottlieb. *Wishcraft: How to Get What You Really Want.* Second edition, Ballantine, 2004.

Shortz, Will. "My Top 10: Unusual Crossword Ephemera." *The Ephemera Journal,* vol. 21, no. 1, Sept. 2018.

Silva, Christianna. "My One Consistent Source of Joy Is the Jingle at the End of the New York Times Crossword." *Mashable,* 1 Apr. 2022, https://mashable .com/article/victory-song-jingle-new-york-times-crossword.

Skrainka, Philip. "A Serum for a New Disease." *New York Times,* 11 Jan. 1925, p. 178.

Slaughter, Joseph R. "World Literature as Property." *Alif: Journal of Comparative Poetics,* no. 34, 2014, pp. 39–73.

Smith, Paul Jordan. *A Key to the* Ulysses *of James Joyce.* Ardent Media, 1969.

Soave, Robby. "Introducing the Reason Crossword, a Weekly Puzzle for Libertarians." Reason.com, 4 Aug. 2023, https://reason.com/2023/08/04 /reason-crossword-puzzle-introduction-libertarian-puzzle/.

Solomon, Charles. "Crosstalk: Letters to America's Foremost Crossword Puzzle Authority." *Los Angeles Times,* 17 Oct. 1993, https://www.latimes.com /archives/la-xpm-1993-10-17-bk-46569-story.html.

Sondheim, Stephen. "How to Do a *Real* Crossword Puzzle." 1968, https://nymag .com/arts/all/features/46798/.

Sosin, Deborah. "A Collaboration Across Time." *New York Times,* 28 Apr. 2021, https://www.nytimes.com/2021/04/28/crosswords/crosswords-puzzles -solverstories-sosin.html.

SPIN. SPIN Media LLC, 1995.

Stein, Gertrude. *Tender Buttons.* Unknown edition, Dover, 1997.

Steinmetz, Katy. "The Crossword Revolution Is upon Us." *Time,* 3 Aug. 2020, https://time.com/5871704/erik-agard-usatoday-crossword-diversity/.

Szymborska, Wisława. *Poems New and Collected.* First edition, Ecco, 2000.

Tausig, Ben. "The Crossword Puzzle: Where'd the Women Go?" *The Hairpin,* 2 June 2016, https://medium.com/the-hairpin/the-crossword-puzzle-whered -the-women-go-c25dee229b3f.

———. *The Curious History of the Crossword: 100 Puzzles from Then and Now.* CSM edition, Race Point Publishing, 2013.

Thompson, Clive. "The Puzzlemaster's Dilemma." https://nymag.com/arts/all /features/17244/. Accessed 7 Jan. 2024.

"Topics of the Times." *New York Times,* 17 Nov. 1924, https://www.nytimes .com/1924/11/17/archives/topics-of-the-times.html.

Totilo, Stephen. "Hearst Launches Puzzmo, an Alternative to the New York Times' Gaming Dominance." *Axios,* 20 Oct. 2023, https://www.axios.com /2023/10/20/puzzmo-hearst-zach-gage-new-york-times.

Troop, Don. "A Happily Puzzling Week for Students at Brown." *The Chronicle of Higher Education,* 19 Sept. 2010, https://www.chronicle.com/article/a-happily -puzzling-week-for-students-at-brown/.

Uitti, Jacob. "Pete Muller Discusses, Premieres His Latest Track 'God and Democracy.'" *American Songwriter,* 11 Sept. 2020, https:// americansongwriter.com/god-and-democracy-pete-muller-song-interview/.

Vardi, Nathan. "The Highest-Earning Hedge Fund Managers and Traders." *Forbes,* https://www.forbes.com/sites/nathanvardi/2019/03/20/the-highest -earning-hedge-fund-managers-and-traders/. Accessed 7 Jan. 2024.

Walters, Greg. "NYT Crossword Puzzle Called Coal a Greener Energy Source and People Hated It." *Vice,* 18 Jan. 2022, https://www.vice.com/en/article /3abv5n/nyt-crossword-coal-greener-energy-source.

Ware, Susan. *Notable American Women: A Biographical Dictionary Completing the Twentieth Century.* Harvard University Press, 2004.

Watson, Bruce. "The Strange Man Who Changed Fitness Forever." *Esquire,* 9 Sept. 2013, https://www.esquire.com/news-politics/news/a23610/strange -tale-historic-fitness-guru-bernarr-macfadden/.

Weintraub, Pam. "Are We All Born with a Talent for Synaesthesia? | Aeon Essays." *Aeon,* https://aeon.co/essays/are-we-all-born-with-a-talent-for -synaesthesia. Accessed 8 Jan. 2024.

Weprin, Alex. "Apple Beefs Up Podcast and News Offerings with Third-Party Subscriptions and Crossword Puzzles." *Yahoo Entertainment,* 27 Sept. 2023, https://www.yahoo.com/entertainment/apple-beefs-podcast-news-offerings -185037216.html.

"The Wild Men of Paris." *Architectural Record,* https://www.architecturalrecord .com/articles/11445-the-wild-men-of-paris. Accessed 8 Jan. 2024.

Wiles, Tim. "Baseball's Sad Lexicon Immortalized a Historic Infield." Baseball Hall of Fame, https://baseballhall.org/discover/baseballs-sad-lexicon -immortalized-a-historic-infield. Accessed 7 Jan. 2024.

Wilkinson, Alissa. "The Ancient Palindrome That Explains Christopher Nolan's Tenet." *Vox,* 4 Sept. 2020, https://www.vox.com/culture/21419050/tenet -explained-sator-square-nolan.

Wilkinson, Joseph. "Look at Me." *Smithsonian Magazine,* https://www

.smithsonianmag.com/arts-culture/look-at-me-54426200/. Accessed 8 Jan. 2024.

Willig, John M. "15 Letters: Most Popular Game; It's 'Crossword Puzzle.'" *New York Times,* 15 Dec. 1963, https://www.nytimes.com/1963/12/15/archives/15 -letters-most-popular-game-its-crossword-puzzle-a-form-of-almost.html.

"Will Shortz: Aging Gopher Maracas." NPR, 19 July 2012, https://www.npr.org /2013/03/08/156814226/will-shortz-aging-gopher-maracas.

Wodehouse, P. G. *The Butler Did It.* Amereon Ltd., 1996.

Wojcik, Erica Hsiung. "My Journey to Making a Crossword Puzzle That Looks Like Me." *New York Times,* 15 Mar. 2022, https://www.nytimes.com/2022/03 /15/crosswords/wojcik-diverse-crossword-puzzles.html.

Woolf, Virginia. *To the Lighthouse.* Harcourt Brace Jovanovich, 1989.

"Wordle Is Joining The New York Times Games." New York Times Company, 31 Jan. 2022, https://www.nytco.com/press/wordle-new-york-times-games/.

Wordplay. Directed by Patrick Creadon, Grinder Productions, O'Malley Creadon Productions, The Weinstein Company, 2006.

"The World Building." *NYC Urbanism,* 3 Aug. 2019, https://www.nycurbanism .com/blog/2019/8/3/the-world-building.

"World Building, 1890." World's Tallest Towers, https://skyscraper.org/tallest -towers/world-building/. Accessed 8 Jan. 2024.

"X-Word Fans Huge, Loyal." Newspapers.com, 17 July 1966, https://www .newspapers.com/newspage/1581274/.

XWord Info: NYT Crossword Answers and Insights. https://www.xwordinfo.com. Accessed 7 Jan. 2024.

Zalman, Jonathan. "How Teenage Crossword Puzzle Maven David Steinberg Is Changing the Game." *Tablet Magazine,* 7 Mar. 2014, https://www.tabletmag .com/sections/news/articles/teenage-crossword-puzzle-maven-goes-digital.

Zimmer, Ben. "'Mad Men'-ese." *New York Times,* 21 July 2010, https://www .nytimes.com/2010/07/25/magazine/25FOB-onlanguage-t.html.

Index

Page numbers in *italics* refer to illustrations.

ILLUSTRATION CREDITS

Page 6: Images of a lattice and American-style grid, original image.
7: Sam Loyd's "Trick Donkeys" puzzle, public domain.
39: Southern Manhattan's Newspaper Row, public domain.
40: Arthur Wynne's inaugural "Word-Cross," public domain.
46: The first-ever color comic supplement, from the *New York World* on May 21, 1893, public domain.
72: Still of Dr.Fill solving a crossword, used with permission of Matt Ginsberg.
75: Solution to Patrick Merrill's "Boustrophedon" crossword, used with permission of Patrick Merrill.
76: Dr.Fill logo, used with permission of Patrick Merrill.
170: Nabokov's butterfly crossword, public domain.
186: David Hockney's *The Crossword Puzzle, Minneapolis*, used with permission of David Hockney.
188: XWord Info still, used with permission.
190–205: Various *New York Times* crossword grids, used with permission of *The New York Times*.
205: Cootie catcher crossword, used with permission of Malaika Handa.
206: Every possible 7-by-7 crossword grid, arranged from least to most open, used with permission of Malaika Handa.
210: Kazimir Malevich's studio, public domain.
210: F. Gregory Hartswick at work on crosswords, public domain.
211: Early *Cross Word Cal* comic strip by Ernie Bushmiller, public domain.
213: Crossword peplum dress, public domain.
213: Crossword hat, ca. 1925, public domain.
217: Laurie Anderson's *Crossed Crosswords (New York Times Horizontal/ New York Times Vertical)* (2020), used with permission of the artist.
218: Laurie Anderson's *New York Times, Horizontal/China Times, Vertical* (1971–1979), used with permission of the artist.
221: Comic Crossword Postcard, ca. 1925, public domain.
221: Postcard from the "Cross-word Craze" series, ca. 1925, public domain.
223: Man in Telephone Booth Postcard, public domain.
223: Early *Cross Word Cal* comic strip by Ernie Bushmiller, public domain.
225: Photograph of Elsie Janis's *Puzzles of 1925*, used with permission of The New York Public Library Digital Collections.